The
Origins of Federal Support
for Higher Education

THE
ORIGINS OF FEDERAL SUPPORT
FOR HIGHER EDUCATION

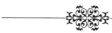

George W. Atherton
and the
Land-Grant
College Movement

Roger L. Williams

The Pennsylvania State University Press
University Park, Pennsylvania

Library of Congress Cataloging-in-Publication Data

Williams, Roger L. (Roger Lea)
    The origins of federal support for higher education : George W.
    Atherton and the land-grant college movement / Roger L. Williams.

        p.   cm.
    Includes bibliographical references and index.
    ISBN 0-271-00730-3
    1. Federal aid to higher education — United States — History.
    2. School lands — United States — History. 3. State universities and
    colleges — United States — History. 4. Atherton, George Washington,
    1837–1906. I. Title.
    LB2342.4.U6W55   1991
    379.1'214'0973 — dc20   90-44707
                                                                  CIP

It is the policy of The Pennsylvania State University Press to use acid-free
paper for the first printing of all clothbound books. Publications on uncoated
stock satisfy the minimum requirements of American National Standard for
Information Sciences — Permanence of Paper for Printed Library Materials,
ANSI Z39.48–1984.

PAGE ii: George W. Atherton in his later years. Courtesy of The Pennsylvania
State University Archives.

Contents

Illustrations and Credits

Preface

JUST OVER A CENTURY AGO, George W. Atherton and other land-grant college presidents pushed Congress hard to pass the 1887 Hatch Act and the 1890 Morrill Act for funding agricultural research and general educational programs at their fledgling schools. Though successful, they found their greatest obstacle to be the widespread conviction—often argued on constitutional grounds—that the federal government had no role to play in education, higher or otherwise.

Today these land-grant college leaders would be pleased with the extent of the federal government's commitment to higher education, especially during the forty-five years since World War II. So strong is that support that not even a force as formidable as the Reagan Revolution can shake it. Despite the Reagan administration's best efforts to cut federal student aid, Congress increased such spending in the 1980s by more than 107 percent in current dollars, or 33 percent in dollars adjusted for inflation. Just as dramatic was the increase in federal spending for research and development, much of which is conducted in university laboratories, by 110 percent in current dollars during the same decade. Within this broad category, spending for basic research grew by 94 percent between 1980 and 1988, although the defense-related share of federal R&D spending shifted from 50 percent in 1980 to an estimated 65 percent in 1990.

The precedents land-grant college leaders set in the late nineteenth century foreshadowed the modern covenant of federal support for higher education. That support may fluctuate somewhat with the vagaries of the economy, but growing appreciation of the importance of higher education for economic competitiveness makes it unlikely that it will diminish in the years ahead.

This study—a revisionist interpretation of land-grant college history—incorporates the contributions, insights, and support of many people. Foremost among them is Roger L. Geiger, professor of higher education at The Pennsylvania State University and formerly senior research scientist at the Institution for Social and Policy Studies and the Department of History at Yale University. A scholar's scholar, he helped shape this book from start to finish, and its strengths are due largely to his influence. His keen interest in this project will forever be appreciated.

Thanks are due as well to three other highly supportive Penn State faculty members: Robert M. Hendrickson, professor-in-charge of the higher education program; William E. Toombs, emeritus professor of education; and Gerald M. Phillips, professor of speech communication. Credit must also go to the late Hans Flexner of the higher education faculty, who awakened my interest in higher education history.

G. David Gearhart, senior vice president for development and university relations at Penn State, granted me a leave of absence to complete the project and was extremely supportive in many other ways. Bryce Jordan, Penn State president emeritus, approved the leave and showed continual interest in the work. Michael Bezilla, manager of development communications and special projects at Penn State and erstwhile university historian, read the manuscript and provided helpful comments. Arthur V. Ciervo, former director of public information and relations at Penn State, made it possible for me as a writer-editor on his staff to begin graduate study. Another mentor, Theodore L. Gross, former provost and dean at Penn State–Harrisburg, the Capital College, and now president of Roosevelt University in Chicago, strongly urged me to pursue graduate work.

University archivist Leon J. Stout and assistant archivist Jackie R. Esposito, both on the faculty at Penn State's Fred Lewis Pattee Library, provided invaluable help. Special thanks are also due to Lee Stout and to Ann M. Isenberg for organizing the Atherton Papers so effectively.

I am also especially grateful to Sanford G. Thatcher, director of Penn State Press, and to copyeditor Peggy Hoover, who were so helpful in bringing this project to completion.

Those who endure the writer's travail the longest and support him most fervently, however, are family. That circle begins with my always supportive parents, Grace F. and Herbert S. Williams, and my sister Melody and brother Keith, and ends with my loving and loyal wife, Nina, son Nathan, and daughter Andrea. It is to them that this book belongs.

Roger L. Williams
University Park, Pa.
February 1991

1

A New Interpretation

THE AMERICAN LAND-GRANT COLLEGE MOVEMENT, the context for this study, is not easily defined. In simple, concrete terms, the movement is the collective story of the emergence of seventy-one colleges and universities that were predicated on an exclusive relationship with the federal government and a shared set of obligations to their respective states. In more complex terms, the land-grant movement is the expression and diffusion of certain political, social, economic, and educational ideals. The motives typically attributed to the movement involve the democratization of higher education; the development of an educational system deliberately planned to meet utilitarian ends, through research and public service as well as instruction; and a desire to emphasize the emerging applied sciences, particularly agricultural science and engineering.

Of the original motives, the strongest was the urge to provide a "useful" form of higher education that would hold some appeal for the so-called "industrial classes." In 1862, when the enabling legislation was signed by Abraham Lincoln, that economic stratum included four of every five Americans—whether farmers, artisans, mechanics, or laborers. The vocation in which the majority of Americans were engaged—and with which the land-grant colleges were most strongly identified—was agriculture, which explains why the land-grant colleges were usually located in rural settings, far from the "corrupting" influences of cities. For some, including many land-grant college presidents, the agricultural orientation was overwrought. Even the father of the legislation, Senator Justin S. Morrill, was reputed to have disparaged the term "agricultural." He said the word "would never have been applied to the institution except that it happened to suit the casual convenience of an index clerk."[1]

The land-grant college movement must also be considered as a historical construct, an invention by scholars to give form and meaning to otherwise nebulous and uncertain developments. This becomes apparent when examining the literature on land-grant college history—when one can find it. The difficulty of defining the land-grant movement is compounded by the dearth of scholarship, especially recent scholarship, on the subject. While the history of American higher education has undergone substantial revision within the last fifteen years,[2] the history of the land-grant movement has remained largely untouched by the process. The corpus of land-grant history does contain a number of institutional histories, and an occasional biography of a land-grant college president or a prominent agricultural scientist, yet the quality of the works in both categories is uneven.[3]

There are only four major works on the history of the land-grant college movement proper: Joseph B. Edmond's *Magnificent Charter: The Origin and Role of the Morrill Land-Grant Colleges and Universities* (1978); Allan Nevins's *State Universities and Democracy* (1962); Edward D. Eddy's *Colleges for Our Land and Time: The Land-Grant Idea in American Education* (1957); and Earle D. Ross's seminal *Democracy's College: The Land-Grant College in the Formative Stage* (1942). Considered as a whole, the work of Ross, Eddy, Nevins, and Edmond tends toward a perspective of land-grant history that is evolutionary, impersonal, deterministic, and—especially—romantic. The overriding implication of their work is that the land-grant movement was inevitable, the colleges called into being by the educational demands of a rapidly expanding and democratizing nation. This growing nation, they averred, had been badly served by the antebellum college, which they depicted as unresponsive, inflexible, retrogressive, and — worst of all — undemocratic.

Those assumptions about the antebellum college have been challenged by such revisionists as Stanley Guralnik, Colin Burke, and David Potts.[4] This revisionism is yet to be applied to land-grant historiography, however, so the deterministic bias there reigns unchecked. Certain histories of U.S. agricultural science add valuable insights regarding the land-grant movement, but on balance they are contextually deficient, focusing on agricultural issues to the exclusion of all else.[5] In short, the complete land-grant movement history worthy of the canons of scholarship now prevailing in the field of higher education history has not been written.

Limited as the land-grant histories are, they do agree that the first quarter-century after the 1862 Morrill Act was a dismal period for the land-grant movement. The colleges did not fail in the sense of having to close their doors — indeed, by 1870 all thirty-seven states had founded or had laid the groundwork for establishing a land-grant college. But the colleges did not flourish. Enrollments — a high percentage of them college preparatory courses — grew slowly, and student attrition remained high. Professors were asked to endure low salaries, heavy workloads, and primitive facilities. State support was slim, if forthcoming at all. The land-grant colleges also attracted powerful enemies. Congress launched an investigation of the institutions in 1874. The Grange followed with a similar inquest, condemning the colleges for their inability to attract agricultural students and vowing to oppose the schools in every way.

Between 1887 and 1891, the colleges finally began to stabilize. Through two acts of Congress, the Hatch Act in 1887 and the second Morrill Act in 1890, continuous federal appropriations began to flow, and the example of the national government encouraged state governments to begin or renew their support. The Hatch Act, providing for establishment of agricultural experiment stations, presented the colleges with the means to serve their agricultural constituencies in practical ways and inadvertently provided some general financial underpinnings. The 1890 Morrill Act provided what the Hatch Act did not: annual federal appropriations for general academic programs, from English to engineering. With the increased funds came growing numbers of students; by 1900, some 19,268 baccalaureate students were enrolled in sixty-five land-grant colleges.[6]

Land-grant historiography notwithstanding, these acts, and the political climate that gave rise to their passage, did not simply evolve. The study that follows tries to correct errant or incomplete interpretations of the lengthy transition from the era of strain and struggle to that of growth and relative prosperity.

It does so by examining the contributions to the land-grant movement of George Washington Atherton, seventh president (1882–1906) of the Pennsylvania State College, now The Pennsylvania State University, and its so-called "second founder." Atherton's work at the Pennsylvania State College is well documented. Three Penn State historians have credited him with effecting a "complete transformation" of a foundering school during his twenty-four-year tenure.[7]

Yet Atherton is virtually a forgotten figure in the history of higher education in the United States, despite his role as the leading land-grant college advocate of his day. His most important contributions to the land-grant movement lay not in his "local" work at Penn State, but in his activity on the national stage. He played the pivotal role in instigating and promoting the legislation that started the flow of continuous federal financial support to higher education. In addition, his leadership within the fledgling national association of land-grant colleges and agricultural experiment stations was critical to the progress of those institutions during the period 1885–1905.

Atherton was the motive force behind the Hatch Act, which encouraged establishment of agricultural experiment stations at land-grant colleges and provided an annual appropriation of $15,000 for the stations' work. And although the Department of Agriculture historian Alfred C. True stated that a legislative committee headed by Atherton was largely responsible for the success of the legislation,[8] Atherton's role was actually that of prime mover. His role in the campaign for the 1890 Morrill Act was equally significant. A group of land-grant college presidents, led by Henry E. Alvord, president of Maryland Agricultural College, and Atherton, worked unremittingly through the spring and summer of 1890 to bring the legislation to fruition. After passage of the second Morrill Act, which guaranteed annual appropriations that ultimately reached $25,000 for a range of educational programs, Atherton received a glowing letter from a colleague at Ohio State:

> We are much elated over passage of the Morrill Bill with our own amendment. Too much praise cannot be given to Major Alvord and yourself for your wise and prudent direction of

Fig. 1. **George Washington Atherton, 1837–1906.**

the forces which have wrought so noble a result. Some day we
will build a monument to you.[9]

The successful passage of both acts was inextricably tied to the tight
network of land-grant college presidents and agricultural scientists that
became the Association of American Agricultural Colleges and Experiment Stations, the first organization of peer higher education institutions in the nation. In this collectivity, Atherton also played the leading
role, particularly in the 1885–90 period. At the Association's preliminary meeting in 1885, for example, he was named chairman of the
executive committee and appointed to chair a three-member committee
charged with securing experiment station legislation. During the
Association's founding convention in 1887, which was called to discuss
implementation of the Hatch Act, Atherton was elected the Association's
first president, and he served two terms through November 1889. Informally, Atherton was the Association's chief legislative architect and
emissary to Congress and the federal administrative agencies, and he
also involved himself in Association work on a variety of other fronts.

Aside from his work with Congress and the federal agencies, George
Atherton played the critical role in keeping the Association intact.
Early on, the organization gave rise to an internal power struggle
between the college presidents and the experiment station directors.
Atherton first articulated and later epitomized the presidents' position,
which sought to keep the stations in their place as subordinate
"departments" of the colleges—with the attendant responsibilities for
teaching, research, and service that such a relationship implies. The
station directors, most forcefully represented by Pennsylvania State
College's Henry P. Armsby, argued that the stations should focus
exclusively on research.

The Association itself is fertile ground for scholarly study, as it
sheds new light not only on the nature and value of higher education
associations, but on land-grant historiography as well. In the main,
higher education historians have overlooked the institutional associations.[10] Yet it would have been impossible to conduct this study without a careful examination of this seminal organization, as it provided
the matrix for Atherton's national advocacy on behalf of the land-
grant movement.

The Association of American Agricultural Colleges and Experiment Stations (hereafter, the Association) preceded the founding of
the National Association of State Universities by eight years and the

Association of American Universities (AAU) by thirteen. Whether the Association, by its own example, had an effect on the formation of the AAU in 1900 is difficult to determine, but it is significant that the Association was the first in a sequence of similar organizations. The final chapter in this book presents some evidence that the Association did influence the formation of the National Association of State Universities in 1895. Although the two organizations eventually merged in 1963 as the National Association of State Universities and Land-Grant Colleges, their initial relationship was competitive rather than cooperative. Indeed, the old-line state universities—those without benefit of the land-grant in their respective states—flared with envy over the land-grant colleges' success in winning annual federal appropriations from Congress and sought to do likewise.

The Association not only helped to build the stature of the land-grant colleges, but also contributed to standardized entrance requirements, balanced curricula, and rationalized methods. Through a variety of initiatives involving graduate education, military instruction, mining engineering, and curriculum reform, and through the evolving relationships with the federal departments of Agriculture, Interior, and War, Atherton and his presidential colleagues used the Association to forge their vision of the land-grant college as a comprehensive institution attending to the liberal, scientific, and even civic education of well-rounded men and women, not merely the technician or vocationalist.

In fact, Atherton's view of land-grant colleges did not differ dramatically from the perception of the mainstream developing universities of his day, most of which had already adopted science in their curricula.

From the early 1870s, Atherton contended that the term "agricultural college" was a misnomer and that "national schools of science" was the more accurate term. Indeed, Atherton and his close colleagues were fully aware of the extent to which the popular conception of land-grant colleges as mainly "agricultural colleges" had impeded the institutions' broader development, and they sought to use the Association to effect their vision of the land-grant colleges as mainstream institutions in the forefront of liberal and scientific education. This is not to imply that Atherton disdained agricultural science, for he worked tirelessly in its cause. He did, however, resent its powerful capacity for characterizing the land grant colleges as single-mission institutions.

While the efforts of the Association of American Agricultural Colleges and Experiment Stations offer a new lens for examining the land-grant college movement, and thus the beginnings of federal support for higher education, this study's main interest is a critical examination of George W. Atherton's nationally significant contributions on the colleges' behalf. Without the impetus provided by the Hatch Act and the 1890 Morrill Act, for which Atherton worked so hard, the development of land-grant colleges into consequential research universities would have been far more difficult. An investigation that focuses on the champion of the legislation not only provides insight into the motivations for such initiatives, but also makes the overtones of inevitability in the land-grant saga quickly fade away when the thoughts and actions of the movement's principals are brought to light.

The history of higher education has not been remiss in its valuation of outstanding leaders. The premier work on the nineteenth-century university movement, Laurence R. Veysey's *Emergence of the American University* (1965), examines the themes of the movement largely through the contributions of the leading institutional presidents: Charles Eliot of Harvard, Noah Porter of Yale, Nicholas Murray Butler of Columbia, James McCosh of Princeton, Daniel Coit Gilman of California and Johns Hopkins, Andrew White of Cornell, and others. Burdened by its deterministic historiography, land-grant history has been not nearly so concerned with identifying its "great men" (although this is not to argue for a "great man" theory of land-grant history). In fact, the most ambitious attempt to identify the "great men" of the land-grant movement was made by historian Earle D. Ross in a 1961 article. His "Great Triumvirate of Land-Grant Educators" included Daniel Coit Gilman, Andrew D. White, and Francis Walker.[11] Gilman is cited for his presidency of the land-grant institution that became the University of California at Berkeley; for his 1867 seminal article about land-grant colleges, in which he prescribed the means for their emergence as "national schools of science"; and for the first comprehensive survey of land-grant institutions, which he undertook in 1871 for the Bureau of Education. White's direct service to land-grant education was his role in the founding and shaping of Cornell, the "first visible spectacular fruit of the Morrill Act."[12] Walker's contributions to land-grant education lay in bringing the Massachusetts Institute of Technology (which received the engineering share of that state's divided land-grant endowment) to the apex of instruction and research in applied science and technology.

Drawing inspiration from Ross, this book searches for other leading lights. Indeed, it suggests a second and even more central "great triumvirate": George W. Atherton, of the Pennsylvania State College; Henry E. Alvord, president of Maryland Agricultural College; and Henry H. Goodell, president of Massachusetts Agricultural College. It also suggests a different criterion for determining "greatness," for none of this latter triumvirate built a leading university during his lifetime. Rather, this second triumvirate was responsible for securing important legislation and leading the Association of American Agricultural Colleges and Experiment Stations into the early twentieth century. Thus, their "greatness" stems from systemic contributions. They were key to transforming a stalled movement into a vigorous system of colleges with similar purposes, curricula, standards and constituencies—and a shared relationship with the federal government.

However justified Ross may have been in choosing his triumvirate, his selection is ultimately flawed. Gilman, White, and Walker reigned during the difficult first quarter-century of land-grant college struggle, but by 1885 Gilman and White, both of whom had a high regard for Atherton, had left the land-grant college scene. They played no role in the passage of the Hatch Act and the 1890 Morrill Act, which ushered in the new age. To ignore the principals, such as George Atherton, who brought this seminal "enabling" legislation to fruition is to leave a serious void in land-grant history.

The American land-grant saga was not so deterministic or romantic as it has been portrayed. It involved the rough-and-tumble of politics, including pressure tactics, aggressive lobbying, persuasion, agitation, and of course compromise. It resounded with the clash of competing ideas and interests—inside the movement as well as outside. And it is a story rife with paradox, inconsistency, and ambiguity. After twenty-five hard years of struggle and disappointment, the land-grant colleges turned the corner about 1890. This happened not because the institutions were destined to do so in response to some vague national demand, but because certain individuals were resolved to create the means—through federal legislation and through an organization of peer institutions—for the colleges' sustenance. And no one was more prominent in this work than George W. Atherton.

2

The Land-Grant Movement's
First Fifty Years

THE LAND–GRANT COLLEGE MOVEMENT, to which George W. Atherton devoted his professional life, coalesced in the half-century before the Civil War from a quickening confluence of forces: an expanding democracy; a utilitarian impulse that sought to create a "practical" education; the ascending influence of science and the beginnings of agricultural science; an emboldened agrarianism, active and agitational; an emerging industrial economy; and the influence of educational and political innovators whose perception of the inability of the antebellum college to accommodate these changes provided the impetus for new forms of higher education.

The movement's enabling legislation came in June 1862, the path cleared by the absence of opposition by southern states and the presence of a sympathetic U.S. President who would not oppose the measure in the manner of his predecessor. The Morrill Land-Grant College Act of 1862, along with kindred legislation that same year establishing the Homestead Act and the Department of Agriculture, constituted both an acknowledgment of the emerging patterns of American life and a mechanism for hastening their development. Using land to be taken from the vast public domain, the 1862 Morrill Act provided an indirect endowment to the states to maintain

> at least one college where the leading object shall be, without excluding other scientific and classical studies, and including military tactics, to teach such branches of learning as are related to agriculture and the mechanic arts . . . in order to promote the liberal and professional education of the industrial classes in the several pursuits and professions of life.[1]

Early land-grant college presidents interpreted the act as an expression of purposeful federal involvement in higher education. The first attempt at similar legislation had narrowly passed both houses of Congress before the Civil War but had been vetoed by President James Buchanan, largely on the grounds that a federal role in education was unconstitutional. The Morrill Act of 1862 without a doubt marked an important breakthrough.

Land-grant leaders inferred from the act a special relationship between their colleges and the federal government, and they used that nexus as the basis for arguing for even closer ties. In 1867, Daniel Coit Gilman, soon to lead the University of California and later Johns Hopkins University, proclaimed that the new land-grant colleges were

> in fact, if not in name, the "National Schools of Science," distinguished from all other schools and colleges by the reception of an endowment from the nation, obliged to conform to certain requirements of the national legislature. . . . The nation is to reap the benefits which they are designed to render.[2]

George W. Atherton, speaking to the National Education Association in 1873, went a step further. He called for proceeds from all remaining public lands to be placed in a federal endowment to support all public education: "The nation as a nation must educate," he said. "There is no argument to prove the duty of the state governments in this respect which does not apply with at least equal force to the national government."[3]

Eventually, land-grant leaders were successful in realizing what they saw as a federal obligation to support land-grant colleges. But this success did not come until a quarter-century after the original Morrill Act—not until the Hatch Act of 1887 and the Morrill Act of 1890. Although it is difficult to rank in importance the forces behind the 1862 Morrill Act, most historians agree that educational concerns were outweighed by sociopolitical factors, particularly agrarian discontent and the incipient industrial movement.[4]

A less visible but equally significant force was the emergence of science. And despite a handful of notable achievements on the American continent, the scientific advance was mainly a European contribution. Americans interested in obtaining the best scientific grounding were compelled to study in Europe. The subdiscipline of agricultural science also was a European contribution, beginning mainly with the organic chemistry of Justus von Liebig, a German scientist of international repute, in the 1840s; the establishment of James Johnston's agricultural experiment laboratory in Scotland in 1842; the founding in 1843 of the private Rothamsted Experiment Station in England, which provided perhaps the greatest inspiration to U.S. agricultural researchers; and the rise of the state-supported German agricultural experiment stations, from a single station in 1852 to more than seventy by 1875.[5]

Thus, the desire to link science with the development of agriculture, a central impulse of the land-grant movement, was not a uniquely American phenomenon. Though many of the ideas and developments of the movement took root in native soil, others emanated from Europe and were adapted to the American condition.

Higher Education in the Antebellum Period

In America, democracy's pervasive influence was to inspire a system of education reflecting the values of the republican form of government that had been invented after the Revolution. The new American education, observed Lawrence A. Cremin, was to be "purged of all vestiges of older monarchial forms and dedicated to the creation of a cohesive and independent citizenry." Educational initiatives were tied increasingly to the responsibilities of active citizenship, and by the

1820s the proposition that universal education was essential to the vitality of a self-governing people had become a staple of American politics. Against that ubiquitous rhetorical backdrop, "popularization and multitudinousness"—practical and useful education that appealed to the common people—became the dominant motifs of nineteenth-century American education.[6]

American democracy was, of course, an expanding proposition. By 1828, on the eve of Andrew Jackson's election as President, universal male suffrage had been achieved in all states north of Virginia save Rhode Island. Voting rights were in most cases secured merely by establishing residence in a community and showing some means of financial support. This development held ramifications for American education: the franchise had been extended to all adult white males before the agitation for educational facilities began in earnest, and, thus empowered, the electorate could have some influence on the course of public education. In France and England, by contrast, public education was developing as a means of protecting the elite from the perceived dangers of an extended franchise; the educational system was designed to inculcate the common people with the knowledge and responsibilities attendant to their lower station in life.[7]

The expansion of American democracy received further impetus with the election of Jackson, which ushered in the so-called "age of the common man." Jacksonian Democracy affected higher education in curious and somewhat paradoxical ways. It created pressure in certain educational and political circles to extend education to the "industrial" classes, yet it prompted the nation's intellectual elite to look even more longingly to Europe both for inspiration and for a respite from the encroaching crudities of an emboldened popular culture.[8] Jacksonian Democracy engendered a distrust of experts, of book-learning, and of higher education in general. The idea of using the public treasury for such an elitist enterprise was deemed inimical to the interests of the larger citizenry, and the development of the nascent state university movement was thus retarded. On the other hand, the age encouraged the emergence of smaller, "private" colleges. The protection from undue governmental influence afforded by the 1819 Dartmouth College case—which held that colleges were essentially private rather than public corporations—was coupled with the entrepreneurial spirit of the times resulting in a surge of college-founding,[9] although perhaps not as vigorously as some historians have assumed.

The Jacksonian Zeitgeist was felt more decidedly at the common or primary school level. Between 1830 and 1860 the American people came to accept the idea that the provision of common schools was a public obligation. This belief predominated in the East and West, where the populace was willing to tolerate modest taxation for that purpose, but it did not hold sway in the paternalistic South. The 1830s, in fact, gave rise to an educational awakening, led by such reformers as Horace Mann, James G. Carter, Henry Barnard, and William Russell, all of whom used Massachusetts and other New England states as their laboratory. Their crusading helped to generate public support for common schools. Mann, acknowledged as the father of the common school movement, argued that these institutions should be publicly controlled, publicly supported, and open to all. Just as important, he believed the common schools should emphasize moral education—civic and religious—to provide the basis for the exercise of responsible citizenship. Mann's philosophy took hold and influenced American public education for more than a century.

The effect of the common school movement was profound. Although school-going had reached impressive rates before Jackson, it increased dramatically in the decades to follow. By 1830, aggregate (primary, secondary, and higher) school attendance rates for whites between the ages of five and nineteen were about 35 percent. By 1860, the rates had risen to about 58 percent of the eligible population: in absolute numbers, 5.5 million of 9.5 million white children between five and nineteen years old were enrolled in school of some sort.[10]

The state of affairs for higher education during these years is less well understood. The older higher education historians, and land-grant historians in particular, place the antebellum or "old-time" college in a pejorative light: as bastions of pious yet petty denominationalism. The institutions are described variously as being anachronistic, backward-looking, and wedded to a static, conservative curriculum that centered on the classical languages. The colleges also are characterized as being socially restrictive and unreceptive to new ideas and new forms of knowledge. In Richard Hofstadter's influential interpretation, the opening of the nineteenth century introduced a "great retrogression" in American higher education: "a decline in freedom and the capacity for growth that universally afflicted the newer institutions and in all but a few cases severely damaged the older ones."[11]

The pathology of the antebellum college was reinforced by a picture of widespread institutional instability, of schools struggling to establish themselves by the hundreds and failing on a grand scale. In his oft-cited 1932 work, Donald Tewksbury claimed to have found records of 516 colleges that were established in sixteen states before the Civil War. Of these, he stated, only 104 (19 percent) survived.[12] Even as recently as 1980, Lawrence Cremin observed that colleges and seminaries were "founded in droves" during the nation's first century, but added that an accurate count was impossible because so many of them failed.[13] Other historians claimed that, in addition to rampant institutional instability, college enrollments actually declined and their prestige plummeted.[14] This, they averred, was stark evidence that the antebellum college was an untenable institution, that it did not fit the demands of a boisterous, growing democracy increasingly driven by the egalitarian spirit.

These reputed failings made a compelling case for a new form of higher education.

But this traditional interpretation of the antebellum college has been challenged by the recent scholarship of Stanley Guralnik, Colin B. Burke, David B. Potts, and other revisionists. Less elegantly said, they have turned the theory of antebellum college untenability on its head. Burke's work in particular has important implications for the idea of democracy in the saga of nineteenth-century higher education, because it refutes the historiographical consensus that the antebellum college served only an elite clientele.

In the main, Burke contended that the antebellum college—itself a historical construct—was a far more successful, flexible, progressive, and accommodating enterprise than has been previously recognized. He found Tewksbury's account of institutional founding and failure to be flawed. Tewksbury had built his count mainly on the issuance of college charters; he did not ascertain whether the institutions had, in fact, become operational, and, seeing no twentieth-century vestige, concluded that they had failed. Burke's more rigorous analysis revealed that 241 institutions were founded between 1800 and 1860, of which 40, or 17 percent, failed—a sharp contrast to Tewksbury's 81 percent failure rate. Moreover, enrollments in liberal arts colleges increased fourteen-fold between 1800 and 1860, from 1,156 students to 16,600. Just as significant, the percentage of young men between the ages of fifteen and twenty who chose to go to colleges increased between 200 and 250 percent.[15]

The idea of declining enrollments came from a faulty generalization based on a regional aberration. Toward the end of the 1840s, New England experienced a 5 percent decrease in enrollments, relative to 1839. But other regions—the South Atlantic region and the Midwest in particular—were surprisingly vigorous in the growth of both the number of institutions and the number of enrollments. Nevertheless, the New England experience wielded a disproportionate influence over the general perception of the national enrollment dynamic. The crisis produced, among other things, the Brown report of 1850, in which Brown President Francis Wayland argued for a flexible curriculum reconciled to the emerging sociopolitical sensibilities and designed to counter the supposed enrollment declines. In many ways, the report prefigured the concerns of the land-grant movement in its criticism of higher education aimed solely at the learned professions:

> Every man who is willing to pay for them, has a right to all the means which other men enjoy, for cultivating his mind by discipline, and enriching it with science. It is therefore unjust, either practically or theoretically, to restrict the means of this cultivation and discipline to one class, and that the smallest class in the community.... Any one who will observe the progress which, within the last thirty years, has been made by the productive [industrial] classes of society, in power, wealth, and influence, must be convinced that a system of education, practically restricted to a class vastly smaller, and rapidly decreasing in influence, cannot possibly continue.... Men who do not design to educate their sons for the professions, are capable of determining upon the kind of instruction they need. If the colleges will not furnish it, they are able to provide it themselves; and they will provide it. In New York and Massachusetts, incipient measures have been taken for establishing agricultural colleges.[16]

Wayland's proposed reforms were attempted, but were dismantled because the expensive new programs bred faculty dissatisfaction and were incompatible in many respects with the traditions of the antebellum colleges.

According to Burke, however, the antebellum colleges, with their constantly increasing enrollments, worked well as democratizing agents by accommodating a variety of students from nonelite backgrounds. Indeed, the newer colleges in the states west of the Appalachians could hardly expect to attract the sons of the well-to-do. In general, college enrollment patterns tended to be local and regional, and the social backgrounds of a college's students reflected local socioeconomic conditions.

The issue of student backgrounds is particularly important, because the land-grant movement proposed to extend higher education to previously unserved student constituencies. Burke suggested that, had the success of the antebellum college been better known at the time, federal policy might have taken a different course. Rather than creating the means for bringing the land-grant colleges into being, Congress might have been persuaded to encourage scientific and technical training by providing grants for those purposes to existing colleges.[17]

Indeed, Guralnik maintained that, in collegiate populations during the first half of the nineteenth century, "the sons of the poor always outnumbered the sons of the rich." He noted that 40 percent of all college students in New York State in 1859 received free tuition. These attendance patterns characterized even the presumably elite seaboard colleges. President Arthur T. Hadley of Yale, for example, recalled that before the Civil War "most of the students were poor."[18]

As historian David Potts observed, "even brief exploration of student statistics within their institutional contexts gives little support to the established interpretation of antebellum colleges."[19] Other historians, such as Roger L. Geiger, have observed that the dissatisfaction with the antebellum college stemmed mainly from the issue of curriculum, rather than enrollments, although the two are related. Critics of the curriculum argued for new kinds of knowledge, especially in the natural sciences; practical training to prepare students directly for careers; and advanced study, which at the time was available only in Europe.[20] Even so, Burke argued that the antebellum colleges were more accommodating of new knowledge than had been supposed, and that their putative religiosity had been interpreted out of context. He suggested that because the colleges' source of sustenance was the denomination, the presidents shaped their descriptions of the institutions accordingly. Guralnik, for his part, described the antebellum colleges as being entirely receptive to the inclusion of science in their curricula.

However proficient the antebellum colleges might have been, their collective "success" went unnoticed by their contemporary observers and was thus buried by history. In the main, these were small institutions, greatly differentiated one from the other, and they could hardly speak in a unified voice. Those that did speak—Yale conservatively in 1828, Brown liberally in 1850—received disproportionate credit for epitomizing the state of American higher education. The failure of the antebellum college may have lain not in its curriculum or in its accommodation of students from humble backgrounds, but in its inability to call attention to itself and to counter the rhetorical excess of an expanding democracy and its more aggressive proponents of educational and political reform.

In any event, the idea of democracy remained a powerful causal agent in the land-grant movement, and the consequent urge to create new institutions that proposed to reach beyond the traditional student constituency proved to be a powerful stimulus. The largest nontraditional constituency was that of agriculture. Before 1860, the nation remained overwhelmingly rural and agrarian. In 1820, only 5 percent of the population lived in cities over 8,000; by 1830, that figure had risen only slightly, to 6.75 percent. Even by the Civil War, 80 percent of the population fell into the so-called "industrial classes," composed mainly of farmers but including mechanics, artisans, laborers, and—to a degree—shopkeepers and businessmen.[21]

Yet the nation was beginning its industrial transition. Steam power, applied to transportation and manufacturing, and the growth of the factory system spurred by the New England textile industry prefigured a new age. In certain respects, the American industrial revolution began in the 1820s. One of the marker events was the founding of the Mechanics Union of Trade Associations in Philadelphia in 1827, enshrined as the true beginning of the American labor movement. The day of research technology had not yet arrived, but inventions, based mainly on empirical observations rather than scientific principle, began to multiply. The 1840s and 1850s introduced the reaper, the telegraph, and the sewing machine. Patents issued by the government grew in number from 436 in 1837 to 993 in 1850 and to 4,778 in 1860.[22]

Educational and political reformers continued to seek ways to make higher education more available and accommodating to the men of the field and of the machine—whether they desired it or not (and the evidence suggests that in the main they did not, at least not until very late in the nineteenth century). The impetus to the land-grant movement, Allan Nevins said, was that "liberty and equality could not survive unless all men had full opportunity to pursue all occupations at the highest practicable level."[23] The notion is romantic, to be sure, but it is rooted in the perception—warranted or not—that the antebellum colleges were in no position to respond to the growing needs and interests of the industrial classes. And Nevins's observation was but an echo of Morrill's, who late in life recalled that one of the motivations for his original act was

> that most of the existing collegiate institutions . . . were based upon the classic plan of teaching those only destined to pursue the so-called learned professions, leaving farmers and mechanics and all those who must win their bread by labor, to the haphazard of being self-taught or not scientifically taught at all, and restricting the number of those who might be supposed to be qualified to fill places of higher consideration in private or public employments to the limited number of the graduates of the literary institutions.[24]

The Utilitarian Impulse

The utilitarian impulse—to provide a "useful" and practical form of higher education yielding the greatest benefit to the greatest number— became a central tenet of the land-grant movement. Although the 1862 Morrill Act had proposed "to promote the liberal and practical education of the industrial classes," the irony is that its author seemed to have intended that liberal education predominate. The object of the 1862 act, Morrill told the House Education Committee in 1890,

> was to give a chance to the industrial classes of the country to obtain a liberal education, something more than what was bestowed by our universities and colleges in general, which seemed to be more based on the English plan of giving education only to what might be called the professional classes, in law, medicine, and theology.[25]

Nonetheless, the influence of utilitarianism was irrepressible, especially since it had found a sympathetic home in institutions outside the land-grant movement. The two principal champions of utility— President Charles Eliot of Harvard and President Andrew White of Cornell—were along with Gilman the most consequential figures in

American higher education of their day. By the 1890s, the utilitarian impulse had permeated the university movement. Speaking to the Association of American Agricultural Colleges and Experiment Stations in 1898, President Enoch A. Bryant of Washington State University said somewhat hyperbolically that education should not train "for a holiness class which is rendered unclean by contact with material concerns."[26] But David Starr Jordan of Stanford caught the full significance of the idea when he said, "The entire university movement is toward reality and practicality."[27]

The antecedents of "useful" education stretch back into the eighteenth century in America, to Benjamin Franklin's early experiments at the Philadelphia Academy and, by implication, to the Enlightenment and to one of its signal antecedent works, Francis Bacon's *Advancement of Learning* (1623). Aside from a few notable experiments to infuse the elements of a practical education at Pennsylvania and Columbia (then Samuel Johnson's King's College), the first instance of a curriculum's centering on anything other than classicism came with the founding of the U.S. Military Academy at West Point in 1802, where military engineering was emphasized. In 1824, the first distinct technical college was established at Troy, New York, by Stephen Van Rensselaer. A harbinger of the land grant college, the institution was founded primarily as an agricultural college, although agricultural instruction soon fell by the wayside, supplanted by civil engineering. The example of Rensselaer stirred a few other colleges to similar action.

Agricultural societies provided much of the impetus for a "practical" education in the United States. The first school devoted exclusively to agriculture, the Gardiner Lyceum in Maine, was founded in 1823 and lasted a decade. It too prompted other attempts at agricultural schools, primarily in the Northeast. Alexis de Tocqueville, in his visit to America in the 1830s, observed that the new nation needed an educational system that delivered more than antiquarian literary sensibilities. "The education of the greater number should be scientific, commercial, and industrial, rather than literary," he said.[28]

By the 1840s, the growing interest in useful education began to crystallize into the movement for vocational training. The movement was fueled by a rising class-consciousness of both farmers and labor groups, by educational reformers, and by a growing awareness of the relationship of science and technology to industry. The changes wrought by industrialization in the factory and on the farm, and the creation of an infrastructure of canals, railroads, telegraph lines, and roads, fueled a demand for individuals with new technical skills. The vocationalists eventually wielded a strong influence in the land-grant movement and in the broader university movement—not all of it entirely salubrious. The cruder strain of vocationalism spawned the manual labor school fad of the 1830s, and later urged the idea of manual labor for college students, but by 1890 the manual labor phenomenon had largely disappeared. Less ephemerally, the vocationalists—in their advocacy of training for a particular line of work and nothing more—engendered a mistrust of bookishness and academic study. As late as 1905, University of Illinois President Edmund J. James proclaimed that the state university must "stand simply, plainly, unequivocally and uncompromisingly for training for vocation, not training . . . even for scholarship per se."[29]

The popularity of such views—which more often than not emanated from the president's office—created tension with the "pure" scientists dedicated to the German university model and the humanists who espoused the eternal verities and sonorities of liberal culture. Nonetheless, utilitarianism by the end of the nineteenth century had suffused all of higher education, and nowhere more vigorously than in the land-grant colleges. It is fair to say, however, that a number of land-grant college presidents, George Atherton prominent among them, just as vigorously resisted a purely vocational approach to land-grant education.

The Rise of Science

The fundamental force underlying the reconstitution of education in the nineteenth century was science. Yet science was hardly new with the nineteenth century. It had, in fact, done its essential cosmological damage two centuries before. The work of Copernicus, Kepler, Galileo, and especially Newton had, for thinking people, written the epitaph for the medieval world-view, in which man occupied the center of the universe. Their mathematical and scientific contributions had established a physic that held nature to be more independent, more determinative, and more permanent than man.[30] The shock posed by evidence of man as the dependent variable in the cosmic equation was rationalized somewhat by the Enlightenment view of science as a method for revelation—for unlocking the mysteries of Nature's laws—

and thereby a tool for attaining perfection. This view persisted in the antebellum college, where religion and science were deemed to be entirely compatible.[31]

In addition to religion, technology served as a spur to science in America. Before 1850, however, most of the technological innovation that took place resulted more from the "empirical observations of practical men, most of them ignorant of contemporary science" than from those working deductively from scientific principles.[32] Whether the early scientific work of Benjamin Franklin, Benjamin Rush, David Rittenhouse, and Thomas Jefferson was approached deductively or in the method of Baconian induction, science assumed an eminently practical cast on the American continent. More than science driving technology, the need for useful knowledge in various fields spawned scientific investigation. Thus, most of the early chemical experiments in the United States were associated with plants, soils, minerals, and medicines.

Before 1820, the American scientific establishment, such as it was, existed not so much in the colleges as in the various learned societies formed for the promotion of knowledge. Aside from the two major learned societies of the day—the American Philosophical Society (1745) and the American Academy of Arts and Sciences (1780)—Philadelphia gave rise to the Philadelphia Society for Promoting Agriculture (1785), the Academy of Natural Sciences (1812), and the Franklin Institute (1824), emphasizing mechanical improvements. The other hub of learning, Boston, was home to the Massachusetts Society for Promoting Agriculture (1792), the Linnean Society of New England (1814), and the *New England Journal of Medicine and Surgery* (1812).[33] However, even the best of these were hardly great national institutions, relating mainly to their local constituents.[34]

Science in early nineteenth-century America still retained a decidedly deductive air, but the scientific spirit, or at least the enthusiasm for empirical investigation, enjoyed a remarkable popularity in the 1830s and 1840s. Not a little of the popular interest in science was sparked by Benjamin Silliman. Trained successively at Yale, in Philadelphia, and in Europe, he lectured extensively across the nation in the 1830s on a variety of scientific subjects. The unlimited potential of science and its cornucopia of practical benefits for a democratic society even caught the fancy of the literary and transcendentalist communities.[35] And during the 1840s more permanent mechanisms for disseminating scientific knowledge were established, notably the Smithsonian Institution and *Scientific American* magazine.

This scientific efflorescence was nowhere more glowing than in the established eastern colleges, particularly between 1825 and 1860. In those years, science was raised "to an unprecedentedly important, almost dominant, position in the structure of the liberal arts program," according to Guralnik. In 1800, all scientific subjects typically engaged one professor per college. By 1830, the average science faculty had grown to two, and by 1860 to four. In the aggregate, the numbers of science professors on college faculties grew from about 25 in 1800 to 60 in 1828 to more than 300 in 1850. Occasionally, the science professors constituted a majority of the faculty. By 1836, three of the six-man faculty at the University of Pennsylvania taught mathematics or science. At the time he issued his noted 1850 report, President Francis Wayland of Brown had four scientists on his faculty of seven.[36]

The same professors represented an important segment of the national scientific community, and their contributions went well beyond teaching. One study of the "most prolific" scientists during the Jacksonian era found that forty-one of fifty-six, or 73 percent, "were usually employed as professors of science in a college or university." Moreover, most of these scientists received their inspiration and training (to the extent possible) in the antebellum college. Another study of a group of selected scientists active in 1846 found that although 80 percent received no special scientific or technological course outside the regular college curriculum, college was "of primary influence in . . . choice of career" for more than half these scientists. The older historiography has argued that the antebellum colleges kept science out of the curriculum, but more recent research has demonstrated otherwise.[37]

By the late 1840s, the leading eastern seaboard colleges had begun to lay the groundwork for the establishment of scientific schools. In 1846, the Yale Corporation established two new professorships—one in agricultural chemistry and animal and vegetable physiology, and the other in practical chemistry. In 1847, Abbott Lawrence through a philanthropic gift laid the foundation for the Lawrence Scientific School at Harvard. The founding of the Lawrence School was closely associated with the 1846 arrival of Louis Agassiz in Boston to deliver a course of popular lectures at the Lowell Institute. The agriculture historian Alfred C. True describes Agassiz's visit as "an event of very great importance in the history of science teaching in this country." After his appointment to the new Lawrence School as a professor of zoology and geology, Agassiz wrote, traveled, and lectured widely in America, giving impetus to the movement to incorporate science in collegiate and secondary school curriculums.[38]

In the main, however, the locus of advanced science during this time was the German states. Thomas Clemson, the eventual founder of Clemson University, lamented in 1826 the lack of a single institution in America where "proper scientific education can be obtained." He continued, "Those who wish to cultivate science are compelled to resort to institutions maintained by the monarchial governments of Europe."[39] The great exodus of American students in pursuit of the German Ph.D. did not occur until after the Civil War. Despite a visit of Franklin to Goettingen in 1766 and the pilgrimage of the famous foursome of Edward Everett, George Ticknor, George Bancroft, and Joseph Green Cogswell in 1815, not more than two hundred Americans studied at German universities before 1850, and those who did were interested for the most part in subjects and methods other than those of the laboratory sciences.[40] As Laurence Veysey explained:

> Only in the 1850s did the concept of research begin to come to notice in connection with the German educational experience, and not until the mid-seventies did the ideal of research clearly dominate discussions of German education on the western side of the Atlantic. In the early seventies, knowledge of German universities in the United States was still often astonishingly vague.[41]

Although some scholars claim that chemistry was "the first real science of the age,"[42] the natural sciences, particularly geology, commanded the greatest attention in the United States. Most of the early learned societies were preoccupied with natural history—the distinctive plants, animals, fossils, and minerals of the North American continent—because it was one of the most feasible routes to international recognition.[43] And Jacksonian Democracy too spurred the rise of geology. Increasingly influential manufacturers, businessmen, and farmers pressed state legislatures to survey natural resources. As early as 1830, the states were providing such a volume of surveys that geologists became more professionally organized and self-conscious than any other scientific group.[44]

Despite the surge of interest in scientific affairs during the Jacksonian period, and the eager incorporation of science in the curriculum by the antebellum colleges, the land-grant college leadership of the late nineteenth century would forever view the 1862 Morrill Act as the seminal event in bringing science into academic respectability and in prompting other colleges and universities to incorporate science in their curricula as well. In his 1903 address to the Association of American Agricultural Colleges and Experiment Stations, President James K. Patterson of the University of Kentucky praised the land-grant colleges for their scientific leadership: "By their bold experiments and stupendous results they startled the old institutions out of their complacent lethargy and roused them to an activity hitherto unknown."[45]

But Patterson and his colleagues vastly overstated the case. In his 1867 article, Daniel Gilman had observed: "Independent of what the government might do, schools of science were not likely to be neglected by the people of this country," noting further that, by 1862, about twenty colleges could be classified as scientific institutions.[46] And in many of these colleges, science was studied not for its own sake but with an eye toward its practical applications. Yale's Sheffield Scientific School, Rensselaer, and Union College, to name three, were strongly oriented toward applied science, and civil engineering had long been a standard course.

The 1862 Morrill Act nevertheless provided impetus for the accelerated inclusion of science in the nation's colleges and emerging universities. At the very least, the legislation offered irrefutable evidence that Congress had deemed science in the collegiate curriculum to be in the nation's interest. With its sister legislation of 1862 establishing the Department of Agriculture, the first Morrill Act marked a definite turning point for the federal government's involvement with science.[47] The constitutionality of a federal role in education and science had been resolved, or at least gone unchallenged, and the era of scientific and educational "bureau-building" was under way. The role of the federal government in these areas would remain tentative and limited for years to come, but the Rubicon had been crossed.

The Beginnings of Agricultural Science

In the United States, the science of agriculture did not emerge until the last thirty years of the nineteenth century. Indeed, historian

Margaret Rossiter asserted that it did not come into being until after the Hatch Act of 1887 had brought a national system of agricultural experiment stations to life.[48] Europe was well ahead of the United States. In Great Britain, two influential agricultural research stations got their start in the early 1840s. In the German states, the first state-supported agricultural research station began in 1852, and more than seventy such stations were in operation by the mid-1870s. Not until the late 1890s was American agricultural science equal to that of the Europeans.

Two seminal books published in the first half of the nineteenth century were to form the theoretical underpinnings for agricultural science. Sir Humphrey Davy's lectures from 1802 to 1812 before Great Britain's Board of Agriculture were published as *Elements of Agricultural Chemistry* and opened up a new method of soil management. More influential, especially in America, was the *Organic Chemistry in Its Application of Agriculture and Physiology* of Justus von Liebig of Germany. Before its publication in 1840, most people accepted the Aristotelian theory that plants obtained nourishment from soil in the form of humus. Liebig showed that the roots do not absorb humus or any other compound, but rather the ions of simple inorganic substances, such as the nitrate ion, the phosphate ion, and the potassium and calcium ions.[49]

But Liebig's chemistry of soils revealed only so much. The conceptual framework for experimentation on the plethora of other variables bearing on agricultural productivity was yet to be devised. As Rossiter analyzed it:

One reason why the diffusion of agricultural innovations went through a boom and bust cycle in the nineteenth century was that there was available no adequate experimentation including statistical controls and cost-benefit analysis to determine what was or what was not a useful innovation. There were so many factors—climate, rainfall, and other moisture, soil porosity, previous use of soil, etc.—the effects of which were neither measurable nor subject to controls, that it was practically impossible to tell what constituted an improvement or really applicable "useful knowledge" and even harder to tell if it was economic or transferable to other soils and localities.[50]

Only one leg of the triad of fundamental biological processes for crop plants—photosynthesis—was known to scientists by 1845. The precise role of the other two processes related to the crop yield—respiration and water absorption-transpiration—awaited illumination.[51]

In the 1850s, those interested in the agricultural sciences began to leave for Europe to study and do research. Two such young Americans were Samuel Johnson and Evan Pugh, both of whom later played prominent roles in the land-grant movement. Pugh, after working as a blacksmith's apprentice, studying at the Whitesboro manual labor school, and tending a Pennsylvania academy, left in 1853 for Germany and graduate work in chemistry. In 1854, at Leipzig, he formed a friendship with a fellow American student, Samuel Johnson. Pugh went on to earn his Ph.D. at Goettingen and then traveled to the Rothamsted station in England, where under Sir Gilbert Lawes he initiated a research program on the assimilation and sources of nitrogen. Returning to America in 1859, Pugh was elected founding president of the Farmers' High School in Centre County, Pennsylvania, which in 1862 he renamed the Agricultural College of Pennsylvania and which eventually became the Pennsylvania State College and then the Pennsylvania State University. Johnson returned to New York State, where he failed in his effort to establish his own college. He secured an appointment in Yale's Sheffield Scientific School and from there, and later as the director of the Connecticut station at New Haven, played a leading role in the experiment station movement in the United States.[52]

Despite the absence of a mature agricultural science, the United States from its earliest days was never without a core of individuals interested in the improvement of farming through science. Though often scorned by tradition-bound farmers, innovative agriculturalists established experimental farms in the years after the Revolution. The various societies for the promotion of agriculture that sprang up in several states in the waning years of the eighteenth century awarded prizes for individual investigation and urged the establishment of experimental gardens.[53] Two early U.S. Presidents, George Washington and Thomas Jefferson, were noted agricultural experimenters in their own right. And in a 1796 address, Washington called for creation of a federally funded board of agriculture that would serve as a center for encouraging experimentation.

The state agricultural society movement, dominated by politically active farmers, culminated in 1852 with the creation of a national organization, the United States Agricultural Society. Among other things, this national society agitated successfully for a federal Department of Agriculture, established in 1862. When the national society was established—ten years before the 1862 Morrill Act—there were some 300 active farm organizations in thirty-one states and five territories; by 1860, that number had increased to nearly 1,000. In addition, an active agricultural press had come into being by 1840, providing the means for spreading agricultural information—and misinformation. Nearly twenty agricultural newspapers were in existence by this time, a figure that would increase to thirty-six by 1850.[54]

With the establishment of the agricultural press and publication of Liebig's *Organic Chemistry* in 1840, the essential ingredients for an early experiment in agricultural "extension" were in place. Liebig's work suggested that soil fertility could be maintained permanently by restoring the proper balance of nutrients. Many of the agricultural journal editors enthusiastically endorsed Liebig's theories, and the "soil analysis" fad began to run riot. The expected benefits seldom materialized, as chemists began to appreciate the complexities of soil analysis and left the field to quacks, who exploited the farmers' hopes for miraculous solutions. Unfortunately, the legacy of the soil analysis craze was solidification of farmers' distrust of innovations arising from agricultural chemistry.[55] The cycle was repeated for agricultural innovations beyond the sphere of soil analysis. Agricultural editors and local suppliers were never without the latest "wonder drug" for their clientele—be it electroculture, silkworms, or sorghum. By the 1850s, however, agricultural scientists shrewdly began using this faddism as a rationale for systematic research programs funded by the state.[56]

Except for some important advances in chemistry, agricultural science before the 1870s remained inchoate. The absence of a mature science had distressing implications for classroom instruction, which typically consisted of whatever the teacher of agriculture wanted it to be. The experiment stations—the first being established in 1875—helped to provide the infrastructure and method for the science, which in turn improved the content and quality of classroom instruction. In the meantime, however, the deficit of knowledge remained large:

> By 1862 animal scientists knew that free oxygen is absorbed and that carbon dioxide is given off in respiration, but they had very little knowledge of the effect of various kinds of feed on the rate of the process and on the production of beef and pork, the production of milk, and the production of eggs.

Moreover, many basic sciences underlying agriculture were either in the embryonic stage or had not been initiated. For example, sciences in the embryonic stages were those pertaining to anatomy and physiology of crop-plants and crop-animals, and sciences that had not been started were those pertaining to genetics and plant and animal breeding, the biochemistry of crop-plants and crop-animals, design and statistics for experimental work in agriculture, and the processing and marketing of plant and animal products.[57]

The acts of 1862, providing for land-grant colleges and a federal department of agriculture, marked the beginning of the federal commitment to the science of agriculture. They laid the foundation on which the national framework for research and experimentation could later be built. And although fourteen state-supported experiment stations were in existence by the late 1880s, the movement did not take off until the passage of the Hatch Act of 1887. This landmark legislation offered a dependable flow of federal dollars for the stations' work, thus launching an era of station-founding.

The Emergence of Agricultural Colleges

The first half of the nineteenth century was a time of far-reaching economic change. New transportation systems—canals and, later, railroads—facilitated the movement of produce to market, and new markets were continually appearing. The West—at this point the lands of the old Northwest Territory just beyond the Alleghenies as well as the larger Mississippi Valley—was open to settlement and cultivation. Pioneers attracted to its rich virgin soil soon became a competitive threat to their brethren in the East, where soil exhaustion was a fact of life. Eastern farmers now faced the agonizing questions of whether to move West and, if not, how to adopt new farming practices that would make their operations profitable. These considerations made them increasingly receptive to innovation in their quest for new crops and new procedures.[58]

In addition, farmers began to complain about their plight. The details of their economic distress, and the complaints about their perceived sense of social inferiority and political impotence, began to work their way into letters, the agricultural press, and speeches. The catalyst for this dissension was the crop failure of 1838, prompting agricultural productivity to become a pressing issue not only for farmers but also for the nation as a whole.

It was at this time, roughly 1840, that the urban industrial movement reached the takeoff stage. In the cities, mechanics, tradesmen, and laborers formed associations to advance their interests. A similar class-consciousness began to burn among the nation's farmers, fanned by a new breed of agricultural reformer: the editors of the agricultural newspapers and journals.[59] Politicians too began to appeal to the farmers' discontent, bewailing the disparities and discrimination that had been thrust upon the nation's largest political constituency.

At about the same time, the agricultural college movement took its first tentative steps. These steps were directed by educational reformers, not the industrial classes, which for the most part considered education beyond the three R's unnecessary. The first noticeable articulation of the idea of agricultural colleges in America came in 1819 from Simeon De Witt, surveyor-general of the state of New York, in his pamphlet *Consideration on the Necessity of Establishing an Agricultural College, and Having More of the Children of Wealthy Citizens Educated for the Profession of Farming.* Rensselaer, founded as the Troy Polytechnic Institute in 1824, was a viable precursor of the agricultural colleges that would emerge in the 1850s, although engineering soon superseded agriculture in the Rensselaer curriculum. Other "farm schools" came into being on a less ambitious scale. In 1823, the Gardiner Lyceum, along Maine's Kennebec River, became the first institution to offer "scientific" agriculture. The Boston Asylum and Farm School was founded in 1832 for poor children. The Cream Hill Agricultural School in rural Connecticut was founded in 1845 and continued successfully until 1869. The Farmers' College, founded near Cincinnati, Ohio, in 1846, was more a center of agitation than teaching and research.

Other agricultural colleges had been promoted, but not established. In 1825, a four-year Massachusetts Agricultural College was proposed. In 1837, a committee of the Pennsylvania state legislature reported that agriculture "must in some way be interwoven with our system of education" and broached the idea of establishing an agricultural school with an experiment farm.[60] Of all the false starts, however, the best known was the People's College in the upstate New York town of Havana. Planning for the school began in 1848, but the cornerstone was not laid until a decade later. Founded by a group of progressive thinkers, the college embarked on a broad, ambitious, and egalitarian mission. Agricultural and industrial arts were to be interwoven with the curriculum, manual labor was required of all students, and women were to be admitted.[61] The People's College finally opened in 1860, but was foreclosed by the start of the Civil War. Despite its failure, the college fired the imagination of progressive educators. From 1848 onward, the plans for the People's College attracted considerable attention and inspired kindred efforts elsewhere.

The two attempts to establish agricultural colleges that were finally successful occurred almost simultaneously in Michigan and Pennsylvania, with the acts of incorporation for each being signed in February 1855. In Michigan, the state agricultural society, founded in 1849, began to lobby for the establishment of a state agricultural college. A committee of the society visited the University of Michigan in 1854 to determine whether the agricultural college should be appended to it. Committee members talked with President Henry P. Tappan and listened to three scientific lectures, but found them insufficient for the making of a practical farmer. "An agricultural college should be separate from any other institution," the committee declared, and it successfully lobbied for a new institution. The governor signed the act of incorporation on February 12, 1855, placing the new agricultural college on a farm near Lansing and under the jurisdiction of the state board of education. In May 1857, the college was dedicated, entrance examinations were held, and an entering class of seventy-three students was admitted.[62]

Pennsylvania's Farmers' High School also grew out of the state agricultural society, formed in 1851. The society sponsored a special convention in 1853 to discuss a course of action in regard to the proposed agricultural school:

> It was to have convenient access to agricultural markets but should not be near a large town. Students should be required to perform manual labor, and their classroom studies should include not only agricultural subjects but a sampling of classical subjects as well. To demonstrate that this institution was truly different from its classical counterparts, the committee suggested that it be given the title of "The Farmers' High School." The name would allay the suspicions of farmers who might be distrustful of traditional colleges. But the academic

work was to be of collegiate grade, and baccalaureate degrees
were to be awarded.[63]

The legislature authorized a charter for the school, which the governor signed in April 1854. The charter specified nearly sixty trustees,
one from each county agricultural society. Because this unwieldy
number made it impossible to schedule an inaugural meeting, the
legislature repealed the act of incorporation and passed a new one
stipulating only thirteen trustees. This new act of incorporation, from
which the Pennsylvania State University dates its birth, was signed by
the governor on February 22, 1855.[64]

The Farmers' High School was able to attract the thirty-one-year-
old Evan Pugh—the Goettingen Ph.D. and friend of Samuel Johnson
who had just returned from research at Rothamsted in 1859—when
instruction actually began at the institution. Regarded as one of the
"conspicuous" examples of early presidents in the land-grant college
movement,[65] Pugh had a grandiose scheme for the aborning school. It
was to include a central campus with branch schools in each county,
experiment stations in each township, and observers on every farm.
The college would train not only farmers and their wives, but also
research specialists and teachers for rural schools. Pugh opposed
manual labor and wanted an institution that would be professionally
scientific in the best sense of the term. He also wanted to combine
agriculture and the mechanic arts in a single college.[66]

Pugh's interests were national as well as local, and he is cited as
being one of four college presidents who worked vigorously for the
passage of the 1862 Morrill Act. In the words of Earle D. Ross, Pugh
"led the Pennsylvania group with characteristic zeal and with effective
if not determining influence on the final result."[67] Unfortunately, in
1864 Pugh died at just thirty-six years of age from complications of
injuries received in an accident. It is interesting to speculate how
Pugh, "one of the ablest and most versatile applied science scholars
and administrators of the time,"[68] might have influenced the land-
grant movement had he lived to a ripe old age. Might Ross's "Great
Triumvirate of Land-Grant Educators"—Gilman, White, and Walker—
have become a quartet?

Other notable agricultural colleges were established in Maryland
and Iowa. The Maryland Agricultural College, chartered in 1856,
opened for instruction in 1859. In Iowa, the state in 1858 appropriated
$10,000 and created a board of trustees for the Iowa State Agricultural

Fig. 2. **Evan Pugh.** Photograph taken shortly before his untimely death in 1864 at age 36.

College and Farm, but this institution was not able to begin full operation until the Morrill Act was passed.

On the eve of the Morrill bill's enactment, in early July 1862, there were three self-described agricultural institutions in operation at the collegiate level. These were the struggling schools that in time would become Michigan State University, the Pennsylvania State University, and the University of Maryland.

The Politics of the 1862 Morrill Act

For Allan Nevins, the significance of the 1862 Morrill Act lay in its acceleration of a process that had been under way for seventy-five years: the creation, via land grants, of state universities. The act, however, substantially altered that process. Rather than leaving the fate of the new institutions entirely in the hands of the respective states, Congress attached certain conditions to the educational enterprises that were expected to emerge. In introducing newer areas of study—science, agriculture, and engineering—the act broadened the scope of the institutions beyond what might have existed otherwise. It also introduced the notion of accountability and cooperation. The colleges were required to produce an annual report not only for the governors and for their sister land-grant institutions, but for the secretary of the interior as well.

Thus the new colleges, as they came to interpret the act, considered themselves to be as much the instrument of the federal government as of their respective states, and that interpretation would be key to generating additional federal support. Although Nevins's "acceleration thesis" bears further scrutiny, an analysis of the struggle to produce the legislation suggests that the perceived need was to create a class of colleges required to perform certain functions and to account for their performance to the federal government, not merely to speed the emergence of additional state universities.

Land grants for educational institutions at all levels were common before the Civil War. By 1857, more than six million acres had been set aside for such purposes. The federal government made land grants not only for education but also for road construction, railroads, and other kinds of internal improvements.[69] For educational purposes, the first land grants were authorized by the Land Ordinance of 1785. These were the so-called "section grants" to establish grade or "common" schools (first through eighth grades). At first, the sixteenth section of each township was reserved for these schools. Later, the grant was increased to two sections and eventually four sections. A township was, ideally, a perfect square with six miles on each side, for a total of 36 square miles. Each section was one square mile. Ultimately, under this program, one-ninth of most established townships was set aside for maintaining a common school.

The Northwest Territory Ordinance of 1787 established a similar scheme for institutions of higher learning, called township grants. Two townships near the center of the state were to be reserved for the support of a "literary institution." In 1836, Congress altered this system slightly, authorizing one township for establishment of a "seminary of learning" within a given territory, and one other for the establishment of a first state university within any given state. The result was that the location of the seminary of learning often became the site of the first state university. Louisiana State University, the University of

Michigan, and the University of Wisconsin are prominent examples. Over time, 46,080 acres in all were allotted to the endowments of the state universities, and for this reason these first state universities may be considered land-grant institutions.[70]

A new type of land grant was introduced by the 1862 Morrill Act: the proportional or quantity grants, expressly for establishment of colleges in which agriculture and the mechanic arts were to be the "leading objects." These grants were distributed on the basis of a state's congressional representation. For every member of Congress, the state received 30,000 acres in land or land scrip. Thus some states, New York and Pennsylvania in particular, received large land grants, while others received smaller allocations.

If the Morrill Act of 1862 can be viewed as accelerating a long-standing policy of providing land grants for education, it might also be looked at as a response to an era of increased "privatization" in higher education stemming from the Dartmouth College case of 1819. Before that time, colleges tended to be viewed more ambiguously, as public agencies of the community or state rather than as unfettered private corporations:

> Colonial leaders used the English tradition of the corporation as a mechanism for conducting certain public services, such as the colleges (and toll roads and bridges, public wharves, canals, parish organizations, towns, etc.), separate from agencies of government. As corporations, the early colleges owed organizational existence to the sovereignty of the state but functioned as relatively autonomous social agencies. . . . The point here is not that the establishment of the nine colonial colleges as chartered corporations provided them with the same kind of institutional autonomy we have known in the present century. Quite the contrary, until the Dartmouth College Case decision of 1819, they were viewed as public institutions subject to the direction and even control as appeared necessary from the colonial and state governments.[71]

In addition, it is worth noting that the U.S. Constitution says nothing on the subject of education. Perhaps the framers did not believe that federal authority in the realm of education was either feasible or desirable. Thus, by default, education fell into the purview of the states with the ratification of the Tenth Amendment to the Constitution in 1791, which gave to the states all other powers not specifically granted to the federal government.

With most colleges having been adjudged to be essentially private corporations, with the nascent state university movement providing few inspirational examples beyond Michigan and Virginia, and in the absence of a clear federal educational mandate from the Constitution, the 1862 Morrill Act served to restore a measure of public interest and direction to higher education. That is not to imply that the pendulum had swung dramatically in favor of public control, because it had not. It is to say only that Congress quietly had laid the foundation on which public-interest higher education could emerge.

The passage of the 1862 Morrill Act, capping an eight-year political struggle, received great impetus from agrarian agitation. Nowhere was this agitation more vigorous than in the state of Illinois in the early 1850s and in the person of Jonathan B. Turner, an inveterate reformer who was then a professor at Illinois College. Turner formulated a plan for an industrial university which, in 1851, he modified into a populist scheme for an agricultural university. Turner and a group of educational and agricultural leaders formed an "industrial league," a group devoted to enlisting the aid of the federal government in educational reform designed to benefit farmers, mechanics, and laborers.

The main significance of the Illinois industrial movement lay in its influence on the development of federal land-grant policy. In 1854, in fact, resolutions adopted by the Illinois legislature at the insistence of the industrial league were presented in Congress. The resolutions, precursors of the original Morrill Act, called for Congress to donate

> to each state in the Union an amount of public lands not less in value than five hundred thousand dollars, for the liberal endowment of a system of Industrial Universities, one in each State in the Union, to cooperate with each other, and with the Smithsonian Institution in Washington, for the more liberal and practical education of our industrial classes.[72]

The resolutions bore no fruit. In October 1857, Turner was advised of a growing opposition in Congress to making further land grants to states.

The nation's sectional tensions were played out viciously in Congress during the 1850s, and legislation typically was viewed from a sectional perspective, not a national one. In fact, the United States at this time has been described as "three countries living under the same flag," the Northeast, the South, and the West.[73] In the case of the 1862 Morrill Act, congressional opposition materialized from the South and the West, but not in sufficient strength to outvote proponents of the measure.

The first Morrill bill, written solely by Vermont Representative Justin S. Morrill, was introduced in Congress in December 1857. It differed in some important ways from the proposal of Turner's Illinois industrial league:

> In contrast to equality of grant favored by the West there was the compensatory proportional distribution sought by eastern interests [a flat grant of 60,000 acres to each state, plus 20,000 additional acres for each senator and representative]; the Illinois plan guaranteed a certain minimum endowment; the bill left the states to realize what they could from the grant. Turner was doubtful of the inclusion of classical studies in his university, and the league's memorial called only for "liberal and varied" studies, but the easterner's bill gave the old "disciplinary" subjects an express safeguard.[74]

The old South–West sectional alliance mounted its opposition to the bill. Chief among the objections was the "unconstitutionality" of the proposed federal incursion into state prerogatives. Nevertheless, the measure passed, by margins of five votes in the House and three in the Senate. In February 1859, President James Buchanan vetoed the bill, finding it potentially unconstitutional. He also deemed the bill to be a dangerous financial drain on the national treasury; a burden to the new states in the West because of the land speculation that would work against their interests; an exercise in futility because the federal government could not compel the states to carry out the mandate of the act; and a threat to existing colleges.

After the secession of the southern states in early 1861, Morrill introduced a revised bill, with four major differences from the earlier bill: the territories were omitted; the land grant for each member of Congress was increased from 20,000 to 30,000 acres; benefits to states in rebellion were excluded; and military tactics was included in the curriculum, a need made obvious by the rout of General Irvin McDowell's Union army at the first Battle of Bull Run in the summer of 1861.

This new measure encountered opposition from the western states, where congressmen viewed it as a ruse for placing valuable lands in the hands of eastern speculators. They also believed the bill was fundamentally inequitable, designed to benefit the more populous eastern states at the West's expense.[75] Opponents argued further that the Morrill bill would obviate the beneficial intent of the Homestead bill, which was also making its way through Congress. The Homestead Act provided 160 acres of land free to any citizen who would settle on the tract for five years and farm a portion of it. The fear, however, was that the eastern land-scrip speculator—having bought land procurement certificates from eastern states to purchase federal domain wherever it was available (almost exclusively in the western states)—would buy the best land and wait for its value to rise. In the meantime, the growth of farms and communities would be retarded, if not precluded outright.[76]

Nonetheless, the Morrill bill introduced in the House on December 16, 1861, passed the Senate by a vote of 32 to 7 on June 11, 1862, and the House on June 19 by a vote of 90 to 25. President Abraham Lincoln, who had no strong feelings about the bill yet whose concurrence was never in doubt, signed the measure on July 2, 1862.

Morrill's motives in introducing the bill covered a complex web of concerns. Certainly the urge to provide a practical and, especially, a liberal education for the industrial classes was salient, as this constituency comprised 80 percent of the population. The perceived reluctance of existing colleges to tend to new subjects and new kinds of students was another concern. But other factors entered the picture: the inability of the newer states to provide such colleges without federal help (twenty new states were formed in the years between 1820 and 1860); concern over the rapid dissipation of public lands to private interests, such as the railroads; concern over soil deterioration and wastage; the competition from Europe's agricultural and industrial movements, and the fear that the United States should not fall behind; and the political desire to bring the industrial movement, particularly the agrarian interests, into the fold of the Republican party.[77]

The Land-Grant Colleges in Their First Decade

By 1865, the North and South had been reunited, but a new and different nation had begun to emerge. The Civil War had, as Mark Twain put it, "uprooted institutions that were centuries old, changed the politics of a people, and wrought so profoundly upon the entire native character that the influence cannot be measured short of two or three generations."[78]

Amid such a turbulent state of affairs the land-grant colleges would be born. The 1862 Morrill Act itself had passed unheralded, inconsistent with the difficulties that were to beset the colleges in the decade ahead. In some states, bitter political fights over the land-grant designation broke out between institutions, for private colleges too sought the potential bonanza of the act. There also would be little uniformity to the new "class" of land-grant institutions that began to emerge. In some states, the land-grant status would go to the agricultural colleges founded before the war; in others, to the existing state universities; and in other states, brand-new institutions were built on the promise of the land-grant designation. State funding would be irregular, if forthcoming at all. Faculty would be difficult to find. Facilities generally were limited to a single, all-purpose building. In many cases, the students enrolled would be unprepared for college work. Yet despite these difficult beginnings, twenty-four land-grant institutions were by 1873 enrolling more than 2,600 students—about 13 percent of the total U.S. collegiate population of 20,000 students at the 217 institutions reporting their enrollments to the commissioner of education.[79] The federal sponsorship of these institutions—and their desire for even more federal aid—aroused the ire of such opponents of public higher education as James McCosh of Princeton and Charles Eliot of Harvard. After only a decade, the land-grant colleges had become a presence to be reckoned with.

This is not to suggest that land-grant colleges had "arrived" ten years after the Morrill Act. From 1862 to 1890 and the passage of the second Morrill Act, the land-grant colleges continuously faced hard times. Aside from the difficulties presented by the varying interpretations of what these colleges were expected to do, money was scarce. The North had accumulated a huge debt from the Civil War, and the South was broke. State legislators from both sections were reluctant to make appropriations for the land-grant colleges. The Panic of 1873 threw business and commerce into the first postwar recession and sparked an unrelenting agricultural discontent that gave rise to the Populist party and William Jennings Bryan more than two decades later.

Yet the underlying trend of the period was growth — in population, in industry, and in world prestige. Toward the end of the century, many Americans believed the nation was on an ascending spiral of progress destined to create a perfectible society. The growth in the nation's manufacturing capacity was particularly impressive. In 1860, the total value of manufacturing products was about $1.9 billion; by 1894, it had risen five-fold, to $9.5 billion. Products made from iron and steel amounted to $36.5 million in 1860 and $479.0 million in 1890.[80] This manufacturing explosion was to benefit the land-grant colleges immensely, as they could not educate engineers quickly enough to satisfy the new machine-operated society.

The emergence of the various land-grant colleges in the 1860s and early 1870s is best described case by case, for each college's founding or designation was uniquely determined by a complex set of conditions and circumstances within its respective state. Nevertheless, despite the difficulty of generalizing, certain patterns did emerge, prompting several scholars to devise their own taxonomies. According to Edward D. Eddy, the land-grant designation went to seventeen institutions (in three categories) extant in 1862:[81]

- Five private colleges: Rutgers (New Jersey), Vermont, Sheffield at Yale (Connecticut), Brown (Rhode Island), and MIT (Massachusetts, mechanic arts only)
- Eight state universities or colleges: Georgia, Tennessee, Delaware, Missouri, Wisconsin, Minnesota, Florida, and Louisiana
- Four agricultural colleges founded by the state: Michigan, Pennsylvania, Maryland and Iowa

The same pattern continued between 1862 and 1879:

- One private university: Cornell (New York)
- Eleven state universities or colleges: Massachusetts, Kentucky, Maine, New Hampshire (affiliated with Dartmouth until 1893), Illinois, California, West Virginia, Nebraska, Arkansas, Ohio, Nevada
- Eight separate A&M colleges: Colorado, Mississippi, Kansas, Oregon, Purdue, Texas, Alabama, Virginia

- Six separate black colleges: Alcorn in Mississippi, Lincoln in Missouri, Arkansas, Alabama, Prairie View in Texas, and Kentucky

One problem with Eddy's taxonomy is the implication that the land-grant designation went to eleven state universities founded after the 1862 Morrill Act. In most cases, these institutions were founded as land-grant colleges and eventually grew into state universities. Thus, the taxonomy devised by J. B. Edmond presents a more accurate picture:

- As an integral part of the first state university: Arizona, California, Georgia, Idaho, Louisiana, Minnesota, Missouri, New Jersey, Nevada, New York, Puerto Rico, Tennessee, Wisconsin, Wyoming
- As a separate institution: Alabama, Colorado, Indiana, Iowa, Kansas, Michigan, Montana, North Dakota, New Mexico, Oklahoma, Oregon, Pennsylvania, South Dakota, Texas, Utah, Virginia, Washington
- As an A&M college that developed into the first state university: Alaska, Connecticut, Delaware, Florida, Hawaii, Kentucky, Maine, Maryland, Massachusetts, Nebraska, New Hampshire, New Mexico, Ohio, Rhode Island
- As industrial universities: Illinois and Arkansas
- As an integral part of the first state university but later established as a separate institution: Mississippi, North Carolina, South Carolina[82]

In the first decade after the land-grant act, there were no foregone conclusions as to which institution, or institutions, would receive the funds. Pennsylvania provides a case in point. In the spring of 1862, as the Morrill bill was gathering steam, the Farmers' High School changed its name to the Agricultural College of Pennsylvania. The school's trustees approved the change of name on May 6, 1862, about two months before Lincoln would sign the act, so that the school could stake a stronger claim on the land-grant designation.[83] The Agricultural College and another school—the Polytechnic College of the State of Pennsylvania, a privately endowed engineering school in Philadelphia—each pleaded its case for land-grant designation before the Pennsylvania General Assembly. On April 1, 1863, Governor Andrew Curtin signed a bill naming the Agricultural College as sole recipient of the land-grant funds.

When the General Assembly reconvened in early 1864, however, it had before it petitions from a half-dozen colleges asking for a share in the land-grant endowment.[84] Evan Pugh inveighed thus:

> That literary institutions should, with such undignified haste, grasp at resources (secured for the endowment of Industrial Colleges to which they had not the slightest legitimate claim), is a melancholy illustration of the terrible extremities to which they are driven in the struggle for existence.[85]

Pugh believed that a land-grant college could not survive as an appendage to a literary college. He failed to convince Pennsylvania state senate, but his arguments carried the day in the lower house, which voted to postpone indefinitely consideration of any amendments. The other competitors—including the University of Lewisburg (Bucknell), Pennsylvania College at Gettysburg (Gettysburg College), Western University at Pittsburgh (University of Pittsburgh), and the Polytechnic College at Philadelphia—were forever locked out of the land-grant bounty.

In Massachusetts, a college to provide "economical and sufficient instruction in the practical arts and sciences to that class of persons who do not desire or are unable to obtain a collegiate education" had been studied by the state legislature as early as 1826. By 1856, the legislature issued a charter to establish the Massachusetts Agricultural College to a group in eastern Massachusetts, but in 1860 shifted the site of that charter to Springfield, although the school did not get started. In January 1863, the governor introduced a plan that differed radically from anything the supporters of the agricultural college expected. He proposed adding more schools, including a college of agriculture, to Harvard University.

At the same time, however, William Rogers applied to the legislature for aid for his recently chartered (1861) Massachusetts Institute of Technology. Amherst and Williams colleges also sought the grant on the basis of their lecture courses in agricultural science. A committee, after listening to the arguments of industrialists and farm interests from the western part of the state, recommended a separate and independent agricultural school, as well as a separate school for the mechanic arts. The committee further recommended that one-tenth of the land-grant endowment be used to purchase an experimental farm, two-thirds of the endowment go to the agricultural college, and one-third go to the engineering school. In April 1863, the legislature approved the plan. The school would not open until the land scrip had been sold and an endowment realized. Meanwhile, five towns began vying for selection as its site: Lexington, Springfield, Chicopee, Northampton, and Amherst (the last four in the Connecticut Valley). Amherst won the competition, and the Massachusetts Agricultural College, now the University of Massachusetts at Amherst, opened for instruction in October 1867.[86]

In Illinois, according to historian Winton U. Solberg, "rival groups gathered like sharks around the carcass of the land grant, and Illinois Industrial University received its baptism in bloody political waters." At the opening session of the Illinois General Assembly in 1863, Knox and Shurtleff colleges, two old-time schools, introduced a bill to set up agricultural schools in northern and southern Illinois. Rudely awakened by this sectarian sortie, the Illinois Industrial League called a convention in Springfield in June 1863 to discuss the matter. Jonathan Turner persuaded the convention, dominated by agriculturalists, to ask the legislature to postpone its decision. He also set up a committee to collect facts relative to the proposed single institution the league desired, with a mandate to report its findings to the General Assembly in 1865.

In the interim, Chicago industrialists made a bid to establish an industrial university in that city, while the agriculturalists, meanwhile, deliberated over two sites: Centralia and Champaign–Urbana, although they were willing to locate it as far north as Chicago or as far south as Cairo. A bill to "provide for the organization, endowment and maintenance of the Illinois Industrial University" was introduced in the Illinois General Assembly in January 1865. Because the proposed legislation provided for establishment of a commission, with one member from each congressional district, to recommend a site, Chicago and Champaign interests united to obstruct the provision for location. In February, an amendment was introduced charging the university board of trustees with locating the institution at Urbana "as soon as Champaign County conveyed to the board in fee simple and free of encumbrances certain properties with a stated value of $160,000." As things turned out, the General Assembly failed to enact any bill establishing a Morrill Act institution in 1865.

Turner renewed his agitation for the Illinois industrial university in 1866. Denominational educators from Augustana, Chicago, Eureka, Knox, Lombard, Monmouth, Northwestern, and Wheaton broached a plan in 1867 to form a central board of higher education under the guise of a single college. This college, to be called the Illinois Agricultural and Mechanical College, would in reality exist at all of the aforesaid colleges—provided each would establish a model farm and appoint a professor of agriculture. The heads of the church-related colleges did not, however, push their plan with the state legislature.

When the Illinois General Assembly convened in 1867, location of the new college was the object of contention. A committee of the legislature made site visits, ranking Champaign–Urbana fourth. In February 1867, after a vigorous objection and lobbying effort from the Champaign interests, the legislature voted to locate the university there. John Gregory was appointed first regent (president) on April 1, 1867, and the university opened for instruction in March 1868. The first two faculty members appointed were George W. Atherton, to teach history, and William M. Baker, to teach English.[87]

In Wisconsin, where the University of Wisconsin had opened for instruction in 1849, the process took an entirely different route. There, the legislative "organic act" of 1866 reorganized the university—the obvious recipient of the grant—in response to the necessity of implementing the Morrill Act. After defeating the bids of Ripon College and Lawrence Institute for the land grant, the legislature, in designating the university as the recipient, required the regents to establish a college of arts and a college of letters and to purchase an experimental farm.[88]

Thus went the politics of land-grant designation in the ten-year "shakeout" period of 1862–72. Iowa, Vermont, and Connecticut took action immediately, followed by fourteen other states in 1863. Arkansas, Maryland, and Ohio followed in 1864. By 1870, all thirty-seven states in the union had followed suit, though not all the institutions were open and operating by that time. Under the terms of the 1862 Morrill Act, each state had to accept the grant within two years, and establish a college within five. But the acceptance period was extended in 1864 and again in 1866.[89]

As complicated as the politics of designation might have been, the matter of realizing an endowment for the colleges from the land grants proved even more problematic. By and large, land-grant colleges did not generate endowments large enough to sustain their operations. The colleges' plight was confounded by the reluctance of state legislatures to appropriate funds for anything other than a building, and even those appropriations were difficult to procure. The lack of capital for educational operations—theoretically available from the land-grant endowment—severely retarded the development of the institutions. Not until the 1890 Morrill Act would they again receive financial support from the federal government for educational programs.

The 1862 Morrill Act distributed a total of 17,430,000 acres of land to the various states, with each state's total based on the formula of 30,000 acres for each member of Congress. The total ultimately realized was $7,545,405 for purposes of endowment. By 1953, this original sum had grown to provide interest totaling about $1.8 million to the land-grant colleges—by that time a paltry percentage of their total operating budgets.[90] Although there is no denying the largesse of the federal government in providing 17.4 million acres, the sum pales in comparison with the eventual distribution of land under the Homestead Act, also passed in 1862—about 234 million acres.

With the exception of Illinois, Michigan, and Wisconsin, no state east of the Mississippi had any public land remaining by 1862. For these states, Congress authorized the use of land scrip, or land procurement certificates. In general, after a state had received its scrip, the governor appointed a commission to advertise and receive bids for the sale of the scrip. In most cases, the bidders were private citizens or land companies that dealt in large blocks of scrip. Ohio, for example, received land scrip for 630,000 acres. The entire amount was bought by thirty-six people, with three of them accounting for a total of 576,000 acres.[91] A state could not own or hold title to land in another state, but the individuals who bought scrip entitling them to the purchase of federal lands could buy it wherever it was available, be it Nevada, Wyoming, or California.

A number of states fared poorly with the sale of their land scrip. According to Nevins, the states that "did worst in betraying their children" were Rhode Island, Connecticut, Pennsylvania, and New Jersey:

> Pennsylvania, which enjoyed one of the greatest opportunities of all, let all her golden chances slip away. The state obtained scrip for 780,000 acres, the second largest grant in the nation. It was assigned to the Agricultural College of Pennsylvania, then a struggling, primitive, isolated school. A few farsighted friends wished to locate the land and conserve

it for the future. Against their protests, however, the legislature just after the war decreed the sale of the scrip. Heavy pressure had come from an unholy partnership of land speculators, anxious to obtain a bargain, and officers of the state college, anxious to get funds for a new start. "Together," writes the historian of Pennsylvania education, "they brought to bear an influence which proved irresistible." The speculators obtained nearly all of this immense domain for $439,000, or an average of less than sixty cents an acre.[92]

At that time, the standard government price for an acre of land was $1.25. Rhode Island, where 120,000 acres in scrip were assigned to Brown University, fared even worse. The president and a professional fund-raiser went west in the summer of 1863 to inspect and select the lands. When they returned, they reported that the chore was quite complex, involving not only selecting the lands but also negotiating sales, defending titles, and paying taxes. Brown opted to sell the entire 120,000 acres to the fund-raiser for $50,000—about 40 cents an acre.[93]

The most adroit use of land scrip took place in conjunction with the founding of the "first spectacular visible fruit of the Morrill Act"—Cornell University in New York State.[94] After evolving his idea for a major university and having served notably as a professor of history at the University of Michigan, Andrew D. White won election to the New York state senate in 1864. There he befriended fellow senator Ezra Cornell, a man of wealth and philanthropic impulse. After convincing Cornell of the merits of concentrating his fortune on funding a single university, rather than splitting it between two struggling schools as Cornell had intended, White engineered a series of remarkable maneuvers that provided Cornell University—operational by 1868 with the largest freshman class the nation had yet seen—with an ample site, liberal operating funds, and the prospect of a rich endowment.[95]

New York had received the largest grant—980,000 acres, 76,000 of which had been sold off quickly for 85 cents an acre. Had this price held, the state would have had an endowment of $800,000. But Ezra Cornell agreed to pay the university about $300,000 for the unsold scrip, 813,920 acres. Ultimately, he arranged to double the $300,000 as the land-grant endowment. In addition, he held the lands until they became profitable, intending to have the proceeds go into the endowment as well. By 1905, Cornell University had received from its land

Fig. 3.   **Andrew Dickson White.**

grant nearly $5.8 million, or $5.82 an acre. With one-tenth of Morrill Act acreage, the university was able to generate more than one-third of the money the act provided in its entirety.[96]

While questions of means consumed many land-grant educators in the 1860s, questions of ends weighed on others—in particular, Daniel Coit Gilman. One of Ross's "Great Triumvirate of Land-Grant Educators," Gilman was a professor at Yale's Sheffield School at the time, teaching physical and political geography as well as history and, later, political economy. He was one of three Yale men who lobbied successfully in the Connecticut statehouse in May 1863 to have the land-grant fund assigned to the "scientific school."[97]

As secretary of the Sheffield School in 1866, and soon to decline the presidency of the University in Wisconsin (in 1867), Gilman published an article in the *North American Review* in which he lamented the lack of dialogue regarding the educational scope of such institutions.[98] He argued that the colleges

> are in fact, if not in name, the "National Schools of Science," distinguished from all other schools and colleges by the reception of an endowment from the nation, obliged to conform to certain requirements of the national legislature, and bound to print and publish annually a report of their progress. . . . The nation gave birth to them; the nation provided their dowry; the nation is to reap the benefits which they are designed to render.

Yet Gilman feared that, without discussions about their fundamental educational purpose, the land-grant colleges would never achieve the status he desired for them. The basic problem before them—the question that was being ignored—was: "How can the methods and results of modern science be made most conducive to the education of young American men?" He stated his concern:

> We cannot but regret that an educational problem so important as that which is involved in the establishment of these National Schools of Science is to be settled, at any rate, for a time, with so little comparison of views among the educators of the country. . . . There is no public conference of scholars or statements respecting the legitimate scope of the institutions. . . . As usual, this country cannot wait for the slow gathering of wisdom. "Something must be done."

Gilman railed against the misnomer "agricultural college," stating in his article that "it is the comprehensiveness of the Morrill Bill which constitutes its highest excellence." He noted: "Two critical epochs have been passed—the congressional and the legislative. Now comes the third, the period of development, more critical and embarrassing perhaps than either of the others." Forthwith, he offered "a few suggestions" to ensure that the land-grant institutions would emerge as comprehensive institutions of strong academic reputation, in accordance with the design of the 1862 Morrill Act. His suggestions included studying the "scientific schools" of Europe to gain an understanding of how they influenced "the efficiency of industrial institutions"; encouraging each of the state institutions to develop "its special and peculiar characteristics, its individuality . . . in California, Nevada, Pennsylvania, the mining interest should receive particular attention"; emphasizing the importance of educating "men of science, able to investigate, competent to teach, proficient in specialities"; watching "that the study of language is not undervalued"; and ensuring the military instruction "be taught in a scientific method by a scientific man." Finally, he advocated a "broad-gauge," sublime approach for land-grant colleges:

> We trust that the managers of the National Schools of Science will feel that a great responsibility rests upon them to maintain these institutions on as elevated a plane as the means at their command will permit. We do not think it likely or desirable that they should train young men to go back and labor with the hoe or the anvil. They are rather to train men by scientific courses of study for the higher avocations of life, and especially to take charge of mines, manufactories, the construction of public works, the conduct of topographical and other scientific surveys—to be leading scientific men.

Four years later, in the fall of 1871, Gilman completed the first comprehensive national study of land-grant institutions for the commissioner of education, whose office was in the U.S. Department of the Interior.[99] To gather information, Gilman visited the colleges in eight states and had "prolonged conversations" with the presidents of eight others. He reported that "every state in the Union has accepted and taken measures to secure the grant," but noted, "It is still very difficult

Fig. 4.   **Daniel Coit Gilman.**

in many states to give an absolute statement of the result of the grant."
He criticized the disparity of names attached to these institutions and
suggested again that the qualifying terms "national" and "science" be
incorporated in a generic name to give the schools a stronger identity.

He then included, somewhat perfunctorily, paragraph descriptions of each institution proper, as well as descriptions of the agricultural facilities owned by each college. Gilman concluded by describing three distinct tendencies evident at the land-grant colleges — toward science, toward technology, and toward industry (manual–vocational), noting that the technical aspect predominated. He also pointed out that the land-grant colleges were already influencing other colleges and universities, prompting them to introduce scientific departments and courses of study.

As the first decade for the land-grant colleges came to a close, the meeting of minds Gilman had called for in his 1867 *North American Review* article finally took place: in August 1871, on the heels of a convention of the Society for the Advancement of Science. The thirty land-grant college delegates failed to address Gilman's central question of how best to provide a scientific education, but they did discuss cooperation in agricultural research and experimentation and explored the issue of forging a permanent organization, perhaps as an appendage to the National Education Association.[100]

The same issues — strategies for moving a bill to establish federally funded agricultural research stations, and the desirability of forming a permanent organization — would persist into the mid-1880s, finding resolution at the preliminary convention of the Association of American Agricultural Colleges and Experiment Stations in Washington, D.C., in July 1885.

Other problems too were foreshadowed during this first decade. Already, agricultural interests were voicing displeasure over the manner in which the colleges had been evolving. Perhaps more significant, the colleges already manifested strong internal tensions — a push and pull between the disciplines of classical culture and the newer scientific and technological fields. These tensions would become one of the hallmarks of Clark Kerr's multiversity: an "inconsistent institution" formed not from one community but from several — the humanist, the social scientist, and the scientist.[101] Nowhere was this new form more strongly suggested than in the academic oxymora that were the land-grant universities of the 1860s and 1870s, where the classical tradition, opposed to specialization, was sharply juxtapositional with scientific and technical education and their multiplicity of arcane subjects. Already, the institutions were sparring internally. And at land-grant institutions a third strain — the vocational element — introduced additional tension, as Gilman suggested in his 1871 report. Land-grant educators who called for a mastery of science above all and concentrated on little else infuriated those concerned mainly with inculcating the manual arts of the farm, mill, and workshop.

Internal tension quickly became a leitmotif of the land-grant movement. Beginning in the late 1880s, the experiment station directors and college presidents began to draw themselves into opposing camps over the stations' purpose, scope, and operation. In the meantime, the colleges would endure a difficult birth and face lean times. As difficult and complex as their first decade had been, the fifteen years to follow would prove no easier. The enemies of land-grant education were gathering, and their criticism would prompt national-scale investigations of the colleges. Coupled with this would be the difficult and typically unrewarded struggle for state funds. Soon came the realization that the new colleges could never flourish without a stronger federal subsidy. The 1870s—the decade in which Atherton emerged as a forceful land-grant college advocate—would suggest that such aid could be procured only by extraordinary effort.

3

A New Advocate Emerges

IN HIS DAY, GEORGE W. ATHERTON came to be regarded as one of the foremost proponents of the "new education" propounded by the 1862 Morrill Act. His reputation extended beyond educational circles. "Dr. Atherton has had a more active part in the recent legislation favorable to the 'land-grant' colleges than any other man outside of Congress," declared the Philadelphia *Farm Journal* in 1891. "He was consulted often and freely ... by Senator Morrill, congressman Hatch and others ... and no man in the country, outside of National official life, had more of the confidence, or is oftener consulted by the Department of Agriculture."[1] The *Arizona Daily Star,* taking note of his visit to Tucson in 1906, informed its readers: "Dr. Atherton is one of the great educators of the United States."[2]

Yet for all his work in the service of a new educational philosophy, Atherton was a man steeped in the classical tradition. One of the ironies of the land-grant movement is that its framers were graduates, by and large, of the antebellum classical college. For example, Jonathan B.

Turner, Andrew D. White, Daniel C. Gilman, and George W. Atherton were Yale men, and they were hardly disposed to dissociating themselves from the best Yale's curriculum had to offer. Gilman, White, Atherton, and others came to be known as "broad-gauge" land-grant leaders, favoring a liberal and comprehensive interpretation of the 1862 Morrill Act. Their interpretation gave sanctuary to classical studies as well as to scientific and technical courses. In his 1867 article, "Our National Schools of Science," Gilman cautioned that the study of language and languages not be "undervalued" in the new institutions.[3] In his inaugural address at the Pennsylvania State College in 1883, Atherton said,

> To the opinion that the Old Classical Course furnishes a very high order of intellectual discipline, I have already expressed my full and unqualified assent, and I may add the conviction that for the end sought no other instrument of equal effectiveness has ever been devised. But that an effective and valuable discipline may be acquired by the Study of the Sciences is equally beyond question.[4]

To Atherton, merely equipping his students with the skills to earn a living was a disservice:

> We mean that this College shall be a place to which the parents can safely send their sons and daughters, with the assurance that they will receive a sound and thorough intellectual training in directions that will furnish them an effective equipment for life. But while the College will keep this practical aim constantly in view, it will also endeavor to secure that harmonious and symmetrical development of all the faculties which distinguishes the thoroughly educated from the half-educated. Not simply the artisan, but the scholar; not simply the scholar, but the man.[5]

But Atherton had formed his educational and political philosophy, and established his reputation as a land-grant college advocate, long before he arrived at the Pennsylvania State College in 1882. As a professor at Rutgers, he played a central role in the land-grant saga of the 1870s and was well positioned for national leadership in the movement's behalf by the time of his appointment, at age forty-five, as Penn State's seventh president.

Formative Years

Atherton was born in Boxford, Massachusetts, on June 20, 1837. His ancestors had emigrated from a town near Manchester, England, to the Massachusetts Bay Colony between 1620 and 1630. One of those immigrants, Major-General Humphrey Atherton, was "to the Massachusetts Colony what Miles Standish was to the Plymouth Colony."[6] In 1849, Atherton's father died, and the twelve-year-old boy was left to earn his own living and contribute to the support of his mother and two sisters. This he did by working in a cotton mill and on a farm. He also managed to secure an education sufficient for teaching and tutoring. In November 1855, at eighteen years of age, he left Boxford for his first teaching post, the location of which is unknown. His first day left him nonplussed:

> I found myself almost entirely deprived of the use of my tongue. I was startled at my own voice—I could not realize, that I was the teacher, the centre, around which all these [indecipherable] are to move, and whose future life will bear the impress of my teachings—I could not trust myself to reprove, to encourage, or to chide. I never saw my own weakness so completely as now—I never felt so much need of God's grace and assistance. I trust He will grant it.[7]

In February 1856 he left for Phillips Exeter Academy in Exeter, New Hampshire, where he was to remain for three academic years less a term, graduating with the Class of 1858. A eulogy by a classmate recalled Atherton as "a champion in the recitation room" and "a tower of strength on the football field."[8]

Through the recommendation of Professor J. E. Hoyt, Atherton left Exeter for a post teaching Latin and Greek at the Albany (New York) Boys' Academy. There he remained until mid-summer 1860, when at age twenty-three he left to enter the sophomore class at Yale. Atherton by this time had emerged as a young man much in the mold of his Puritan forebears—straightforward, honest, hard-working, sober, pious, with a mind well furnished and highly disciplined yet receptive to new ideas. Excerpts from his diary for the year 1860—the first half spent at Albany, the second half at Yale—reveal his cast of mind:

> Friday, Feb. 3: Attended a "Woman's Rights" convention. There is much work to be done in this sphere. What is it? We must see.

> Friday, Feb. 24: Spent a pleasant evening at the . . . Mission School. God give me more of the Mission spirit when I see so many hungering for bodily and spiritual food.

> Wednesday, June 6: A beautiful day—Everything in nature has a most delightful appearance. Had a delightful prayer meeting this evening.

> Tuesday, Sept. 11: Presented myself for admission to the Sophomore Class at Yale—Passed without the slightest deficiency in Latin and Greek—failed in mathematics—Am to make up in next branch.

> Thursday, Sept. 20: Presented myself for examination in mathematics—passed without difficulty. Attended first recitation—a lecture. Am resolved to be present at every exercise during my course—and in season—unless it is absolutely impossible.

> Saturday, Sept. 22: Joined I.N. this eve—count it a good step. College men, I find, run in strata. I think I have fallen upon a good layer.

> Monday, Sept. 24: Am revelling in the delight of study—I trust I am not wholly ungrateful for the privileges I enjoy.

> Saturday, Oct. 6: A new system of composition writing was adopted today. We all—the class—assembled at Alumni Hall, where subjects were given us, and we were allowed two hours to write in—good practice.

> Thursday, Nov. 8: My good message of yesterday is confirmed [i.e., "Honest Abe" appears to be elected]. Thank God for the triumph of free and righteous principles.[9]

In his junior year, Atherton left Yale for the Union army. On the recommendation of Professor Woolsey and others, he secured a first lieutenancy in the Tenth Connecticut Volunteers, which formed a part of General Ambrose Burnside's expedition against North Carolina. He took part in the relatively minor clashes at Roanoke and New Bern, after which he was promoted to captain. The next several months of camp life took their toll on his health, and he suffered a near fatal illness of the swamp-fever type. He therefore resigned his commission in late spring 1863.[10]

Atherton returned to New Haven in June 1863, in time to see his class graduate. There he spent the summer recuperating, and in September resumed his teaching career at the Albany Boys' Academy, this time as professor of Latin. In December, he left for New Haven to marry Frances W. D. Washburn on Christmas Day, the ceremony being performed by the Reverend Professor Timothy Dwight. He and his wife returned to Albany, where in addition to his work at the academy he studied for his final examinations at Yale. The faculty had told him that by passing the examinations for the terms he had missed he might graduate to rank with his own class (of 1863). In July 1864, he took his examination, running this intellectual gauntlet:

> The first examination being with Professor Dwight, in Butler's Analogy; the second with Professor Porter, in Stewart's and Hopkins' moral science; the third with Professor Woolsey, in Lieber's civil liberty, Whyland's [sic] Political Economy, and his own book of international law; the fourth with Prof. David in his "Manual of Geology"; and the fifth and last with Prof. [indecipherable], in Spalding's English Literature. The result of all was far more favorable than I had dared to anticipate.[11]

Having passed his examinations and received his bachelor's degree, Atherton returned to the Albany Academy, where he taught for two years. For 1866–67, he accepted a professorship at St. John's College in Annapolis, Maryland, where he also acted as principal almost the entire year, in the absence of Dr. Henry Barnard.[12]

His next step was to accept Regent John M. Gregory's offer to join the faculty of the new Illinois Industrial University, scheduled to open on March 2, 1868. Atherton and William M. Baker were the first faculty members hired, at $2,000 per year. The University of Illinois historian Winton Solberg has noted: "Gregory unquestionably intended Baker for English and Atherton for history, but slyly secured their appointments without naming their duties." Atherton would stay only

a year, resigning on January 1, 1869.[13] He did, however, solidify a
lifelong friendship with John Gregory—who at Atherton's invitation
came to the Pennsylvania State College during the 1895–96 academic
year "as a regular preacher and as a lecturer to the Senior Class on
branches of political and sociological science."[14] Atherton later recounted
the circumstances of his resignation in a 1905 letter to the new Illinois
president, Edmund J. James, who had implored Atherton as a founding
faculty member to attend his installation as president:

> You are probably not aware of the fact that I was the first
> member of the Faculty appointed and on the ground after Dr.
> Gregory assumed his office—that was the latter part of 1867 or
> the early part of 1868, several weeks before the opening for
> students. I spent many days and nights with Dr. Gregory
> going over the whole scheme of classification, and became
> thoroughly informed of his standards and methods. I left at
> Christmas 1868, not on account of any dissatisfaction on either
> side, but with real regret on both sides; but I was only just
> getting started in my professional career, and received a very
> unexpected offer of a professorship in Rutgers College.[15]

Rutgers had offered the thirty-two-year-old Atherton the Vorhees
Professorship of history, political economy, and constitutional law,
endowed with a $25,000 gift from Abraham Vorhees in 1867 which was
later increased to $54,000.[16] The initiative to secure Atherton for
Rutgers evidently came from the former principal of the Albany
Academy, David Murray, who had since taken a post at Rutgers.[17]

Rutgers and National Service

Atherton held the Vorhees Professorship at Rutgers College for thirteen and a half years, from 1869 to 1882, until accepting the presidency
of the Pennsylvania State College. His immediate challenge at Rutgers
was to "secure recognized standing for a new department in an old and
conservative . . . institution." That goal evidently was met within a
matter of months.[18] Nothing relative to Atherton's academic career at
Rutgers exists in his own hand, but the Rutgers historian William
Demarest offered this profile:

In addition to serving as professor he was military superin-
tendent at Rutgers from 1871 to 1880. . . . Professor Atherton
remained only until 1882 but the thirteen years were years of
very great efficiency, of very strong classroom work. He was a
master in the subject he taught; he was a rigid disciplinarian;
he required that work be done with fullness and with exactness.
He did not abound, perhaps, in personal sympathy and he
wrought more by fear than by love, no doubt; but he wrought
well, and many a student looks back to him in gratitude for
the mental discipline and the sound principles of civic and
economic life received in his room. He was naturally interested in public affairs, in politics, and he was at one time
candidate for election to Congress.[19]

Atherton's interests in matters beyond the campus began at an early
date. In 1873, he was a member of the Board of Visitors to the U.S.
Naval Academy. In 1875, he was appointed by a proxy of President
Ulysses S. Grant to be a member of the commission to investigate
charges levied by Professor O. C. Marsh, a Yale geologist, of mismanagement and fraud at the Red Cloud Indian Agency; he helped prepare
the final report and wrote the cover letter submitting it to President
Grant.[20] In 1876 Atherton reluctantly accepted the Republican nomination for Congress, in a heavily Democratic district, and lost; he did,
however, manage to run ahead of the national ticket. In the spring of
1879, he was named chairman of a commission to study the New Jersey
tax system, completing this task in February 1880.[21] He also found
time to study law during this period and was admitted to the New Jersey
Bar. In short, Atherton at Rutgers was a man enmeshed in public affairs.

He also was recognized as an attractive candidate for a college
presidency. Only four years after arriving at Rutgers, at thirty-six
years of age, Atherton was recruited to become the first president
of Arkansas Industrial University, the land-grant school in that state;
for reasons unknown, he declined the offer.[22] In late 1874, he was
offered the presidency of Howard University in Washington, D.C., at a
salary of $2,500.[23] Despite a vigorous recruitment effort by Howard
officials, Atherton finally declined that offer too. In 1876, after Howard's
second choice had died in office, Howard again offered Atherton
the presidency, which he again declined.[24] In the meantime, Atherton had received a letter from the University of Missouri asking
whether he would be interested in either a presidential vacancy or a

professorial vacancy.[25] And Daniel Gilman, in the waning months of his presidency at the University of California, offered Atherton a professorship at the handsome salary of $3,600.[26]

In 1878, Atherton apparently sought a position at the University of Iowa in Iowa City, although it is uncertain whether the position was a presidency or a professorship. In any event, Atherton secured the recommendation of Senator Morrill, with whom he had enjoyed a working relationship of five years. Said Morrill in his letter to Iowa President C. W. Slagh: "I esteem him as one of the most efficient and painstaking educators of the country."[27]

By the mid-1870s, Atherton had established a national reputation in collegiate circles, having been sought for the presidency at two and possibly three universities, as well as for a professorship under Gilman at California. His reputation stemmed mainly from an address he

Fig. 5.   **George W. Atherton in 1875.**

gave to the National Education Association (NEA) in August 1873 at a controversial convention in Elmira, New York. There, Atherton made a strong case for the success of the land-grant movement and issued a ringing call for federal funding of public education.

That positions came his way after the Elmira address is not surprising. What is surprising is why the Arkansas presidency came his way when he was relatively unknown. There is little evidence of publication before his 1873 address to the NEA titled "The Relation of the General Government to Education," which brought him into the spotlight. One eulogist states: "He was not a voluminous writer, although his published titles aggregate some thirty or more in number."[28] It is certain, however, that early on his interests in higher education and in the broader stream of life ran far beyond the walls of his classroom.

Atherton's interest in land-grant advocacy stemmed, he recalled, from his connection with the "scientific" department at Rutgers, New Jersey's land-grant college. The relationship led him to examine the legislation in some detail: "I had become convinced that it was not only a measure of far-reaching wisdom as a means of promoting Higher public education, but that it was peculiarly in keeping with the genius of our system of institutions."[29] Others have speculated that his interest in land-grant education began much earlier, during his year at the University of Illinois. The Penn State historian Michael Bezilla suggests that, at Illinois, "Atherton first became intrigued with the idea of combining technical and traditional subjects in a college curriculum."[30] In his eulogy on Atherton, Henry P. Armsby observed that his interest in land-grant institutions was a natural outgrowth of his academic and civic activity, adding, "We may suspect . . . that his early connection with the movement in Illinois had much to do in turning his thoughts in that direction."[31] If, as Atherton himself had stated, he and Illinois president John Gregory had "spent many days and nights . . . going over the whole scheme of classification" for the aborning land-grant college, it is likely that Atherton became intimately acquainted with the terms of the 1862 Morrill Act at Illinois.

An Ambitious Land-Grant Agenda

There is no evidence that Atherton attended the first formal meeting of land-grant college and state agriculture representatives at Washington,

D.C., in February 1872. The call for convention was issued by Frederick Watts, longtime president of the Pennsylvania State College board of trustees who the year previous had been appointed U.S. commissioner of agriculture.

Watts's agenda included four items: the expediency of asking Congress for additional land grants for the struggling colleges; the establishment of experimental farms and stations for the promotion of agricultural knowledge; the modification of military instruction at the colleges; and the best methods of cooperating with one another and with the Department of Agriculture.[32] These were issues that would preoccupy the land-grant colleges for years to come. The first would culminate in the Morrill Act of 1890, the second in the Hatch Act of 1887. Military instruction, in particular, and the colleges' relationship with the Department of War would, thirty years hence, still be commanding Atherton's attention, in his capacity as chairman of the Association's committee on that subject. Similarly, the issue of cooperation, particularly with the Department of Agriculture, would be a constant during Atherton's lifetime.

At the Washington convention, a committee on experiment stations issued a report calling for prompt establishment of such institutions with the help of individuals, agricultural societies, the states, and the federal government under the aegis of the Department of Agriculture. On the subject of additional federal aid for the colleges, another committee called for an additional land grant of not less than one million acres to each state "for the institutions receiving the benefits of the act of 1862."[33] Senator Morrill, who attended the convention, would soon incorporate that request in a bill.

At the same time, momentum was building for a different kind of educational movement that would have implications for the land-grant colleges. The week prior to the Washington convention, U.S. Representative George F. Hoar had introduced a bill to generate federal aid for common or primary schools, an especially urgent need in the southern states. The common school movement held great allure for land-grant leaders—particularly Morrill and Atherton, who would yoke the two interests in a steady stream of unsuccessful "educational fund" bills over the next eighteen years. This joint approach to additional federal aid became an albatross around the neck of the colleges, however. Not until they divorced their appeal from that of the common schools would such aid be forthcoming, in the 1890 Morrill Act.

The Hoar "common school" bill of 1872 purported to establish an endowment fed by the proceeds of public land sales. Half the proceeds were to be distributed to the states on the basis of need, as determined by their illiteracy rates; later, funds were to be disbursed on the basis of population. In addition, a small portion of the fund was to be used for "normal schools," or teacher training institutes, which were at the time undergoing phenomenal growth. The Hoar bill passed the House but not the Senate.[34]

Meanwhile, in the aftermath of the 1872 Washington convention, Morrill introduced a bill (S. 693), drafted by the convention committee, to appropriate one million acres of public land to each state for the further endowment of land-grant colleges. In May 1872, Morrill substituted an amendment reducing the grant to 500,000 acres. The bill was brought before the Senate in December, and in mid-January 1873 passed by a vote of 39 to 14. In the House, however, a substitute bill—designed to placate the common school supporters—had passed by a wide margin. The House bill stipulated that one-fourth of the annual proceeds of public lands should be invested in U.S. bonds, with the interest going to support land-grant colleges; an additional one-fourth of the proceeds would go directly to the colleges. Half the proceeds could then be used by the government however it deemed fit—presumably in support of common schools. The bill died with the closing of the congressional session. Especially stern opposition was mounted by Senator John Sherman of Ohio, who considered permanent appropriations to be in violation of long-standing government policy. Sherman also found the proposed distribution of funds to be unequal and unconstitutional because it disregarded the relative wealth and population of states. Most telling, perhaps, he found the legislation to be "a palpable discrimination against existing colleges supported by State and private funds."[35]

The first plausible evidence of Atherton's involvement in land-grant advocacy was a circular dated January 13, 1873—seven months before the Elmira NEA convention—from Rutgers College and New Jersey agricultural interests urging support for Morrill's Senate bill. The circular maintained that the bill would compensate for the inadequate and inequitable endowments, weighted in favor of populous states, that resulted from the 1862 act. It also contained a basic argument that Atherton would employ at every opportunity in his campaigns for federal support: The government "by the very act of encouraging the establishment of institutions inadequately supported, has placed itself under obligation . . . to render such additional aid as will make the first effective."[36]

Meanwhile, private higher education was beginning to mount its opposition to the land-grant colleges. The attack was foreshadowed in an 1870 volume by President Noah Porter of Yale (partly in response to Gilman's 1867 article, "Our National Schools of Science"):

> The claim that the Scientific School proposes a better educa-
> tion for most men or even a more desirable or useful educa-
> tion for any man than the colleges, would seem to be premature
> to one who reflects how very short has been the experience of
> the oldest of these schools and how very discordant with one
> another are the theory and practice of those schools which
> have been organized the longest. The New Education, if it
> had been in operation long enough for its advocates to define
> or describe what it is, has not yet been proved by its fruits,
> and it would be the height of presumption and folly to pro-
> nounce it so far a success as to justify the abandonment of the
> old system which has at least a definite character and has
> produced some good results.[37]

Atherton's Debut as Advocate for Land-Grant Colleges

The battle lines were drawn for all to see at the August 1873 convention of the National Education Association in Elmira, New York. Presidents James McCosh of Princeton and Charles Eliot of Harvard led the attack. In an otherwise innocuous address, McCosh suddenly expressed indignation over Morrill's recent bill to endow each land-grant college with an additional half-million acres. "Some of us, when we learned that such a measure was quietly passing the House and Senate, courageously set ourselves against the allocation of so large a sum of money to so narrow and so sectional a purpose," McCosh said. "We argued that, so far as these schools were simply agricultural ones, they were not accomplishing so great a good as to entitle them to so large an endowment."

For his part, Eliot recalled the "humiliating spectacle" in the halls of Congress of "a half-dozen men, representing a few institutions of education, many of them half-born, vieing [*sic*] for a share in the public gifts. I was thankful to President McCosh when he ventured to go before Congress and protest against this demoralizing use of public money." McCosh, who called for a special investigation of the new institutions, voiced particular opposition to the "principle of partiality" introduced by the federal government in supporting the land-grant colleges. If such grants were to be made, he argued, they should go to the strongest institutions, not the weakest. Furthermore, McCosh added, federal funds should be used to support secondary schools, where the need for aid was even more pronounced, rather than colleges. Eliot went a step further, voicing visceral opposition to all federal grants to education on any level. He characterized federal support as inimical to the democratic underpinnings of independence and self-reliance.

The land-grant college proponents made vigorous rejoinders to the arguments of McCosh and Eliot. President Daniel Read of Missouri cited the beneficent government policy of making section and township grants for educational institutions, a practice that began with the federal ordinances of 1785 and 1787. "Was a nobler ... policy ever adopted by this or any government?" he asked. "Look at the universities founded by these grants, beginning with the Ohio and Miami universities, at the Michigan, the Indiana, the Illinois Normal University, Minnesota and Iowa, Kansas and California universities. ... These are the fruits—here is my argument: Who would reverse this policy?" Joseph White of Massachusetts Agricultural College objected to the narrow manner in which the land-grant colleges had been defined, and then criticized, as purely agricultural schools deficient in the production of farmers: "Education should teach not only skill of how," he said, "but intellect to guide the skill."

Atherton also took exception to the "very mistaken attack on the 'Agricultural Colleges' so-called." He noted that, in preparing material for his address, he was surprised by the extent of their accomplishments:

> I wish to call attention to the fallacy implied in speaking of these institutions as "agricultural" simply, and then proposing to test their results by asking how many "farmers" they turn out. ... These institutions do not profess to teach the process of manual labor on the farm or in the workshop, nor are they by any means exclusively schools for the teaching of agricultural science. They are, on the contrary, colleges

> founded . . . for the purpose of bringing a good scientific and
> liberal education within reach of the graduates of the public
> schools.[38]

Whether inadvertently or by design, the most effective response to
McCosh and Eliot had been prepared. It was Atherton's carefully
wrought 1873 NEA address, "The Relation of the General Government to Education." A political economist as well as a historian,
Atherton sought to show that the new colleges had already justified
the cost of the original federal "investment," and his analysis surprised friend and foe alike.

Atherton reviewed what the states and the national government
had done prior to 1862 in support of education. He found that each of
the thirty-seven states had recognized in its constitution its responsibility to maintain the work of education and that "all except Delaware
have systems . . . of free common schools." The "general" (federal)
government, he observed, had "followed uniformly a single line of
policy—that of donating to the states certain portions of the public
lands for educational purposes." In terms of higher education, Atherton
was not so impressed with the result as his colleague President Reed of
Missouri. Before 1862, the lands donated to colleges amounted to 1.1
million acres, "and the benefit derived from them has been exceedingly small." The 1862 Morrill Act set a precedent, he averred, in
attaching conditions to the grants of land. He then proceeded to show
what the government had received for its investment. The "cost" to the
government for the 9.6 million acres ceded by the act amounted to
$6.72 million—about 70 cents an acre across all states. The average
endowment was $179,645—the largest was $630,000, the smallest, $50,000.

For the twenty-six institutions reporting on their property, Atherton
found the average physical plant value (buildings, apparatus, and
farms) to be $129,743, for a total value of nearly $3.5 million. Extrapo-
lating to the day when forty-one land-grant colleges would grace the
nation, he observed, "These items alone would amount to $5,319,463—or
nearly 73 percent of the value of the original grant." Even more
important, he said, the act had prompted financial support for the
colleges from a variety of other sources. At the fifteen institutions
reporting data in this regard, contributions from states, counties,
towns, and individuals amounted to nearly $5 million.

And in the numbers of students and faculty, the colleges, ten years
after the enabling legislation, were competitive with any. The twenty-

four institutions responding on those items showed an aggregate enrollment of 2,604 students, with 321 faculty members and assistants—an
average of 109 students in the agricultural and mechanical departments,
and 13.3 instructors. The average land-grant college enrollment was
already about 10 percent higher than that of 217 colleges reporting to
the Commissioner of Education the previous year. These other institutions enrolled 20,866 undergraduate and graduate students, with 3,018
faculty members—an average of 96 students and 13.8 instructors per
institution. While lauding the government for the isolated example of
success the land-grant colleges represented, Atherton also chastised it
for failing to devise a comprehensive policy of educational assistance.
The result of this "inconstant and inadequate" federal response, he
said, resulted in a national illiteracy rate of 20 percent—one in every
five people over the age of ten being illiterate. Atherton's implication
was clear, and it called for an aggressive federalism:

> The nation as a nation must educate. There is no argument
> to prove the duty of the state governments in this respect
> which does not apply with at least equal force to the na-
> tional government. If the welfare of the individual citizen is
> the welfare of the particular commonwealth, in which he
> happens to reside, much more is it the welfare of the entire
> nation. . . . The nation [ought] to see that all are educated—
> not primarily . . . because it will make him a wiser and hap-
> pier man, but because it will enable him better to discharge
> the duties of citizenship. . . . Education alone may not make a
> free country; but there can be no such thing as a free country
> without education. The question whether a free country has a
> right to educate its citizens is no other than the question
> whether it has a right to live, as a free country.

With a philosophical as well as statistical response to the criticism
of McCosh and Eliot, Atherton called on the federal government
to take four steps to improve public education: (1) The proceeds
from the sales of unappropriated public lands should be permanently
invested and set apart as a perpetual endowment for the support
of public education; (2) in order to ensure this result, all grants
to corporations must cease. Since 1859, he added, when the policy
of giving land to railroads was begun, Congress had donated to these
corporations more than 186 million acres (compared with 17.4 million

acres dispensed by the 1862 Morrill Act); (3) a portion of the educational fund should be dedicated to the further endowment of the land-grant colleges, these institutions being "the logical and fit completion of the common-school system of the country"; and (4) "The government must hold the states to an account for the right of its donations." Atherton summarized by exhorting the federal government to "take a more direct and active interest than it has hitherto done in the promotion of public education."[39]

Atherton's address has been cited erroneously by some sources as the first attempt to make "so systematic an inquiry" of the land-grant colleges.[40] The address benefited from the visibility of a public forum, but Gilman's report to the commissioner of education in 1871 constituted the first systematic inquiry. Indeed, evidence suggests that the first survey was a five-question exercise conducted in 1868 by President James K. Patterson of the University of Kentucky. His effort drew eighteen responses, including those of the Pennsylvania State College, Cornell University, and Yale's Sheffield School, but the results were not made public in the manner of Gilman's or Atherton's studies.[41]

The Gilman and Atherton studies were different in their design and intent. Gilman's work, which took him to eight states and engaged him in "prolonged conversations" with the presidents of eight other institutions, was essentially a status report resembling a census more than anything else. In only two areas was Gilman interpretive rather than expository: in suggesting that a generic name for the institutions containing the qualifiers "national" and "science" would provide a stronger identity, and in observing that of the three tendencies he discerned at the institutions—toward science, toward technology, and toward industry—the tendency toward technology predominated.

Atherton's study was far more ambitious and analytical. He provided a statistical update, but as the basis for a quantitative exercise designed to show that the colleges' "return" already had exceeded the original investment. Of the approximately $7 million in "cost" to the federal government from the endowments created by the sale of land, the "return" had already exceeded $10 million—approximately $5.3 million (an extrapolated figure for the forty-one institutions that would be in place eventually) for aggregate physical plant value, plus an additional $5 million realized from grants and gifts from sources other than the federal government. And this data was, in turn, offered to buttress Atherton's philosophical argument for a greatly expanded role for the national government in all realms of public education.

Though Eliot of Harvard disdained public aid for any educational enterprise save on the elementary level, and though McCosh of Princeton disallowed it for weak agricultural colleges (though not for high schools or for stronger colleges), Atherton had implicitly criticized their reasoning: the principle that permitted state assistance on the common school level—to produce a citizenry capable of executing their responsibilities in a democratic system—should obtain as well for the federal government in the realm of higher education and, more logically, education at all levels.

Atherton's address before the NEA drew a positive response from at least part of his audience. John Hancock of Ohio proposed that the National Education Association endorse the idea of a federal endowment for public education. Professor W. P. Atkinson of Boston said: "It has given me a new idea of the value and usefulness of that grant in establishing scientific education where it would have waited long before it had an existence in many regions, in promoting and assisting it where it was already established."[42] Nevertheless, McCosh remained skeptical. He wanted to know how Atherton derived his enrollment figures and how many of the students at Cornell and Sheffield had been included in the count.

Atherton had mailed a questionnaire dated July 10, 1873, under his signature to the land-grant colleges. It asked for financial and enrollment data along the lines of what he provided at Elmira.[43] Whether he received these completed forms in sufficient supply for his August 6 address is unknown. He told McCosh that he had derived his figures from advance sheets of a report pending publication by the U.S. commissioner of agriculture. Among these tables was a list of students in "agricultural and mechanical colleges" and a second list of students in schools associated with them, but the latter were not included in the 2,604-enrollment statistic Atherton cited. McCosh replied that the answer was unsatisfactory.

Atherton did respond to McCosh's question in a letter published in the *New York Tribune* on August 22, 1873. He found that the Department of Agriculture had made intelligent judgments in accounting for the structural differences among the land-grant colleges. Cornell was listed as having 207 students in the agricultural and mechanical departments; the additional 318 students in other departments were not included in the count. Likewise, in the case of Yale's Sheffield School, 157 were listed in Atherton's count—not the 809 students belonging to the entire university. In the case of Illinois, however, an institution founded on the land-grant act, all 318 students were listed, regardless of their academic departments. Atherton ended his letter by striking out at McCosh's insistence on judging the land-grant colleges by their performance in only one dimension, agricultural instruction:

> It is a distinct fallacy ... to convey the implication that the usefulness of these institutions is to be tested by the questions, how many of their students are studying "agriculture," or how many "farmers" have they turned out? The true test is indicated by the terms of the act of Congress of 1862 ... to provide a "liberal and practical education for the industrial classes" ... and to this end the institutions were to teach, not necessarily manual farming, but "subjects related to agriculture and the mechanic arts." It is the more important to note this, because the fallacy mentioned is partly suggested by the misleading name "Agricultural College," and lies at the bottom of the popular misapprehension as to what any institution of learning aims to do. ... The enemies of the colleges perfectly understand this, and are likely to repeat the fallacy until the good sense of the public makes them ashamed to do so.[44]

The National Education Association convention at Elmira caught the fascination of the eastern press. The *New York Independent* published a synopsis of the conclave, calling it "one of the most interesting in the history of the organization." The *Independent*'s coverage focused on three addresses: those of Eliot, McCosh, and Atherton. Of Atherton's study the *Independent* noted that the land-grant colleges, "so far from being in any sense a failure, are doing a work in every way remarkable considering the short time that they have been established—less than five years, on average."[45]

The Nation of August 28, 1873, published an inflammatory reference to the proceedings in an article titled "American Colleges and Legislators":

> The addresses of Dr. McCosh and Prof. Atherton at Elmira not only demonstrate the stupendous ignorance of Congress in matters of education, but show that in the last reckless attempt to fling 90,000,000 acres to a few agricultural colleges,

"so-called and miscalled," the members really could not have known what they were themselves doing. Agricultural colleges are a failure in other countries; a failure, so far as students go, in our own; Cornell receiving $900,000 under the grant of 1862, and giving as a dividend upon it two agricultural graduates a year . . . and, finally, a ring in Congress trying to give the last of the public lands to the same 41 institutions that received the avails of the last endowment, without the slightest enquiry or consideration, and with the whole educated intelligence of the country opposed to the reckless act — these are facts which suggest some enquiry as to the amount of educated material which is to be found in Congress.[46]

Atherton wrote an extended rebuttal, attempting to correct the errors and misinterpretations in the article, but *The Nation* refused to publish it. With a prefacing note, Atherton then sent copies of his rebuttal to several other newspapers, including the *New Brunswick Daily Times*. In his response, he corrected six points: (1) that the 90 million acres the Morrill bill of 1872 was reputed to have allocated was in reality 18.5 million acres; (2) that the colleges were not a failure, because their educational mandate extended to all realms — not only agriculture; (3) that Cornell did not receive $900,000 under the act of 1862, but 990,000 acres of land; (4) that the accusation of Cornell's "two agricultural graduates a year" was negated by the 207 students currently enrolled in that university's "Agricultural and Mechanical Colleges"; (5) that the congressional "ring" wanting to dispose of the "last of the public lands" to the colleges was erroneous, and that in fact, according to government estimates, more than 1.1 billion acres of land remained to be sold; and (6) that Congress did not act "without the slightest inquiry or consideration" in relation to Morrill's 1872 bill. Atherton pointed out that the Department of Agriculture had for several years published a brief annual statement on the condition of the colleges and that the Bureau of Education had done likewise. He also referred to Gilman's 1871 report to that bureau and added that each land-grant college was required to submit an annual report to its state legislature.[47]

Atherton's work at Elmira also inspired the admiration of colleagues within the land-grant movement and helped establish his reputation as an advocate. Wrote Andrew White on August 25: "I thank you most heartily for your good service at Elmira. You stood in the breach nobly. . . . We cannot labor too much pain to show the fact that Congress did not intend to endow 'Agricultural Colleges' unevenly or to provide unevenly for Agricultural Departments in Colleges."[48]

The Elmira convention had placed Atherton at the center of the storm over land-grant colleges. More significant, it was the point of demarcation for his new and highly visible land-grant advocacy — carried out from the pulpit of a professorship rather than a college presidency — during the balance of the 1870s. Atherton would now commence a working relationship with Senator Justin Morrill, as he would with other land-grant leaders, such as Gilman and White. With Elmira behind him, Atherton stood at the threshold of a thirty-three-year career to advance the status, quality, and effectiveness of land-grant colleges. The key to that process, he was convinced, lay in the nation's capital.

First Efforts in Drafting Land-Grant Legislation

Atherton's "active association" with Justin Morrill had begun with an inquiry to the senator in preparation for the Elmira address.[49] Thus, Atherton's ensuing efforts in support of the land-grant colleges were pursued in accordance with Morrill on two fronts: to draft and generate support for Morrill's new bill, S. 167, introduced in the first session of the Forty-third Congress on December 15, 1873; and to help the colleges navigate the precarious waters of the congressional investigation about to be launched in their direction.

Morrill's previous bill (S. 693), intended to authorize land grants of 500,000 acres to each state to endow further its agricultural and mechanical college, had died with the closing session of the Forty-second Congress, with McCosh in no small way responsible for the bill's demise. The new bill (S. 167) purported to further endow "the national colleges for the advancement of general scientific and industrial education" by establishing an educational fund supported by proceeds from public-land sales and earmarked for the support of public education.[50] Atherton later asserted that the bill was his and that Morrill had "accepted as his own a bill which I drafted and which, with modifications, was kept alive in Congress after Congress until the final passage of the act of 1890."[51] The circumstantial evidence strongly suggests Atherton's involvement, if not his full authorship. The bill was predicated on the recommendations of Atherton's Elmira address and represented a sharp departure from Morrill's previous legislation. In addition, a letter from Morrill acknowledged Atherton's suggestions but stopped short of suggesting his full authorship: "The bill has been and will be put into a somewhat improved form and many of your suggestions will be pertinent, and will be readily accepted. The title I hesitate to adopt. We can make more out of the nickname than our enemies will gain by it."[52]

Despite its yoking of common school and land-grant college interests, and the introduction of a method of financing other than outright grants of land, the bill was doomed to fail. It was introduced in a troubled time, in the wake of the Panic of 1873. Although the measure took the economic turmoil into account in offering to delay appropriations for a year, Congress was in no mood to place new strains on the national treasury. In addition, its introduction came at the worst possible time, sandwiched between the Elmira controversy and an impending congressional investigation of the very institutions the bill was designed to benefit. Ultimately, S. 167 was referred to the appropriate committee, from which it never emerged.

Congressional Investigation of 1874

Atherton's defense of the land-grant colleges at Elmira was not enough to stay the momentum toward the investigation McCosh had demanded. In February 1874, the House on the motion of James Monroe, an Oberlin College professor, passed a resolution authorizing the Committee on Education and Labor to investigate the colleges. The intent was to ascertain whether the colleges were fulfilling the law in terms of their organization, their programs, and their finances. Morrill immediately asked Atherton and his Rutgers colleague, scientist George H. Cook, for their help in advising the colleges how best to respond to the inquiry:

> The investigation foreshadowed by Dr. McCosh in the House has been set in foot for mischief. Interrogations will be sent to each National college to convict them of inutility and of a

non-compliance with the conditions of the land grant. Now let all questions be fully considered and more too. Show what you are doing. Let it be an advertisement of your health and of the great merits of your performance of your duties thus far, according to the meager outlay, and the bright promise of the future.

If you and Prof. Cook could find time to write to each of the other colleges and put them in a state of preparation to respond to this attachment, you will do an excellent service. I wish I could also have copies of their reports. This movement is intended to delay and preferably kill it [a reference to S. 167].[53]

Atherton and Cook lost no time issuing a printed circular under their signature on February 25, 1874. They noted that House Committee on Education and Labor was sending a series of questions reputed to be "of the most searching nature" and that the chairman of the House committee launching the inquiry was "one of the most uncompromising opponents of the bill relating to this subject that was before Congress last winter" (Morrill's bill of 1872, S. 693). Atherton and Cook concluded: "It is, therefore, fairly supposable that the present investigation is unfriendly in motive and in aim." They offered a five-point strategy for answering the questions. Those points are worth examining because they influenced the quality of response, which in turn helped to shape the final judgment of the congressional committee:

1. Since one object of the inquiry is to promote delay, the answers to the questions should be prepared as promptly as is possible. . . .
2. It may be well to indicate to the Committee that, as the institution . . . is under the control of a body appointed under the laws of the state, it did not feel authorized to reply without the sanction of that body. But in any case it will be well to have the Trustees . . . endorse any communication that may be sent to the committee.
3. Let the answers be as full and comprehensive as possible. It may be necessary to answer specific questions categorically; but additional statements should be made whenever they are needed to bring out the whole case.
4. The intimations given by Washington correspondents make

it appear likely that the questions will assume the old and exploded fallacy that these institutions are solely "agricultural," and that their results are to be computed by counting the number of "farmers" they have turned out. The replies should show that the law of Congress did not permit their work to be so restricted, but required them to provide a "liberal" as well as a "practical" education for all "the industrial classes." It should be shown, however, that while this larger work has been kept steadily in view, agriculture, and especially "the branches of learning related to agriculture," have not been neglected or subordinated. In fact, these institutions are coming to fill the place of the Agricultural Experiment Stations of Europe which are supported by the various Governments.

5. It should be shown that the institutions provide many free scholarships; that the students are, in fact, drawn almost exclusively from the industrial classes, that they comprise very many promising young men who . . . would never have received an education; that these young men . . . go with their trained and disciplined intelligence directly back to industrial pursuits; and that the institutions doing this work and occupying this peculiar field are in no proper sense hostile rivals to the established classical colleges.[54]

Atherton's advice did not go unappreciated. Said Andrew White: "I have just received your circular which seems to me timely. . . . I shall be glad to pass forward the report to the Committee that it may be in their hands at the earliest day possible."[55] Said Benjamin L. Arnold, president of Corvallis State Agricultural College, later the Oregon State University: "The leaders of the movement against us pretend that they do not see the fallacy of the reasoning by which they conclude, because the students in our Colleges do not all devote themselves . . . to agriculture exclusively that ergo the colleges are not in reality Agricultural colleges at all. . . . Not a whit more absurd would be to infer, because all the graduates from Literary Colleges do not pursue a literary life; that, therefore, their Alma Mater is not literary at all."[56] And from Daniel C. Gilman, president of California: "I don't remember that I ever thanked you for the various printed missives which I received from you early last winter . . . often did I wish that you were at hand for counsel and support. . . . What is to be the next phase of the Ag. College discussion?"[57]

The House investigation, designed to probe "the condition and management of the agricultural and other colleges" that received Morrill Act funds, declared that the colleges were in a "state of formation" and absolved them, as a class, of any glaring deficiencies. Upon closer examination, the House report reflects the extent to which the colleges heeded the suggestions of Atherton and Cook: "The committee take pleasure in stating that a majority of the colleges replied with commendable promptness," the report declared, reflecting the schools' compliance with Atherton's first recommendation. The report also mentioned that committee members "have no reason to suspect the present officers of the institutions . . . of a disposition to withhold any information," reflecting Atherton's second injunction. Finally, the committee observed "a certain fresh interest, a spirit of youth, a new enthusiasm, which, when intelligent and enduring, is one of the best prophecies of success."

On the financial side, the House Committee on Education and Labor found the colleges' responses to be "very satisfactory," and added: "There is no reason to believe . . . that there has been any serious mismanagement of the fund received from the United States." The committee also found the colleges, in the main, to be free from debt, but this finding may have led some legislators to conclude that the "agricultural colleges" were in relatively strong financial shape, making further federal aid unnecessary. In terms of educational results, the committee concluded, "There is nothing in the results thus far attained that can be called discouraging." Indeed, "a few of those earliest organized have already found time to take high rank among the institutions of the land."

Finally, the committee accepted a more comprehensive view of the colleges, finding evidence of an "honest purpose to make the studies pursued such in variety, in extent, and in value as shall meet the requirements of the law to which they are indebted for their endowment."[58] Atherton's plan to disabuse the committee of the idea that the colleges were exclusively agricultural had met with some modest success.

Return to the Legislative Arena

With the House investigation successfully negotiated, supporters of the land-grant colleges could again focus on promoting a bill to endow the institutions further. The next strategic step was to align the interests of the land-grant colleges more explicitly with those of the common schools in a single piece of legislation, despite the failure of Morrill's 1873 bill in that regard.

Andrew White, pessimistic because of the fate of Morrill's 1873 bill, urged a bill jointly sponsored by Senator Morrill and Representative Hoar, the champion of the common schools. White wrote to Atherton in March 1874: "The course I proposed a year ago to the Joint Committee of Senate and house in Washington—that is, of amalgamating the Morrill Bill and Mr. Hoar's Bill—is the only one that presents a chance of early success."[59] But such a combination was easier to suggest than to accomplish. In December 1874, John B. Bowman, founding regent (i.e., president) of the University of Kentucky, was in Washington, D.C., trying to influence the course of the legislation combining federal aid for common schools and land-grant colleges. He wrote to Atherton that efforts to get Hoar and Morrill together had failed miserably.[60]

In January 1875, Morrill tried again, introducing S. 1187, which combined the intent of the earlier Hoar bill to aid common schools and his own previous bills to endow the land-grant colleges further.[61] Again, there is evidence that Atherton was involved in drafting this bill as well.[62] In addition, upon its introduction Bowman wrote to Atherton, asking him to testify before the appropriate House committee.

Although Morrill had introduced his bill in the Senate, a House member had introduced a bill providing for the common schools but omitting the land-grant colleges. Bowman also intimated that Representative Hoar had "gone back on his compromise [to combine the two interests] agreed upon last winter."[63] Hoar's apparent disenchantment with the measure also was reported by Morrill five months later.[64] The lack of support in the House for a compromise may have stemmed from Hoar's resentment over what he viewed as Morrill's derailment of his original common school bill in the Senate. In his autobiography, Hoar recalled that his bill "passed the House, but was lost in the Senate mainly because Senator Morrill ... insisted that the money should go to the agricultural colleges, and not to common schools."[65] Hoar had also served on the same House Education and Labor

Committee that investigated the land-grant colleges. Whatever his reasons, he seemed opposed to legislation designed to benefit land-grant colleges, even if it benefited his common schools in the process.

In January 1876, both Morrill and Bowman informed Atherton that House Representative Gilbert C. Faulkner had introduced a bill (H.R. 748) to establish an endowment from the sale of public lands for common schools only—a reprise of the Hoar bill.[66] "I am satisfied Eaters and Hoar are at the bottom of it, and are unfriendly to the Colleges," said Bowman. In the meantime, Bowman was drafting another bill to be introduced by Faulkner; this bill would benefit both the common schools and the land-grant colleges, but it ultimately failed too. A steady stream of similar bills, including at least five more from Morrill's hand, would be introduced through 1890. There is no record of Atherton's involvement in these latter efforts, but there is no reason to suspect that he and Morrill would not have remained conversant on such matters. Indeed, the passage of the second Morrill Act would depend heavily on Atherton's involvement.

Land-grant college leaders decided to meet again in late 1877—the first such meeting since the Watts-sponsored Washington convention of 1872—and this time Atherton was among their number. Gathering in Columbus, Ohio, on December 27–28, 1877, the attendees discussed reports of degrees, courses of study, military training, the scope and aim of university education, and the omnipresent topic of an increased congressional appropriation. Atherton was appointed to a committee charged with visiting Washington, D.C., to "secure a proper recognition of these institutions in any measures that Congress might adopt for the promotion of public education." The committee also included John M. Gregory, of Illinois; C. L. C. Minor, of Virginia Polytechnic Institute; William W. Folwell, of Minnesota; and John B. Bowman, of Kentucky.[67]

In the wake of that conference, Atherton issued a printed circular calling for support of a new House bill (of unspecified number). The bill stated that one-fourth of the funds appropriated by the act would be given to land-grant colleges. Atherton advised:

> The time has now come for a united and vigorous effort to impress upon members of the House . . . the importance of this measure. . . . Personal visits to Washington are probably not necessary, though they may be very useful; but letters addressed to members by gentlemen connected with the

Colleges, or by influential citizens, will be of great service, and are in fact indispensable if the passage of the Bill is to be assured. It is especially desirable that members be fully informed of the results already accomplished by the Colleges . . . and the directions in which additional aid is needed or can be wisely used.[68]

But this bill, like others to follow, would fail.

The Land-Grant Colleges
After Nearly Two Decades

By the late 1870s, the status of the land-grant colleges remained uncertain and tentative. They had, as a group, parried the assault by McCosh and Eliot and received unexpected vindication in the House investigation of 1874. Yet they had failed to produce the federal legislation that would provide the sorely needed financial under-pinning. Bill after bill—whether garnished with Morrill's prestige or not—failed to clear the two houses of Congress. Not until the 1880s would a more aggressive Department of Agriculture and a new cause—the agricultural experiment station—arrive to change the nature of the colleges' quest for supportive legislation.

Meanwhile, state support remained limited and in most cases sporadic. The Pennsylvania State College, for example, received a special appropriation from the legislature in 1878 for $80,000—the first direct allocation it had received from the commonwealth since 1861, and the last until 1887. The money was requested to pay the debt from an $80,000 bond issue from 1866, an emergency measure under-taken to keep the college afloat until all of its land scrip was sold.[69]

During the 1870s, the colleges also endured a crescendo of com-plaints from American agriculture. The disgruntlement came not so much from individual farmers, who were generally apathetic about the very idea of agricultural colleges, but from the leadership of increasingly powerful agricultural organizations, particularly the Grange and the National Farmers' Alliance. The Grange, organized by Oliver H. Kelley, came into being in the late 1860s and early 1870s and was galvanized by the Panic of 1873.[70] Agriculture had now entered an era in which the depression of prices for farm commodities, coupled with years of drought in the Midwest, would pose enormous hardships for farmers.

The land-grant colleges became a lightning rod for agrarian discontent; complaints over the perceived lack of agricultural instruction and the consequent failure to educate agriculture students were sounded loudly and often. "Not a single land-grant institution has escaped an ugly quarrel over agricultural instruction," one observer wrote in the mid-1870s.[71] The agricultural organizations agitated for exclusively agricultural colleges that would in effect function as finishing schools for farmers, taking awkward boys and girls and sending them back as polished agriculturalists. But though the colleges soon began making contributions in agricultural research, they failed to attract appreciable enrollments of agricultural students until after the turn of the century. The colleges fared much better in finding engineering students. Most young men, and their families, failed to see how "book farming" could ever prove more valuable than practical farm experience, and not many farm families could afford to lose a young laborer in the prime of manhood. Thus, Cornell enrolled only three seniors in agriculture in 1874, and only one agriculture graduate emerged from the University of Wisconsin before 1880.

The historical judgment of the land-grant colleges' first twenty years is dismal, and that is a judgment rendered by their most enthusiastic historical advocates: Nevins, Ross, and Eddy. To Nevins, the period illustrated all the shortcomings of American democracy—its impatience, its eagerness for quick results. Ross saw the period, at best, as indeterminate and unstable. And Eddy, who saw some of the obstacles in the colleges' way, characterized the era as one of "controversy, criticism, and disappointment." Before the colleges could find their place in the national scheme, Eddy observed, "the colleges would have to find themselves."[72]

But the 1870s were valuable in laying the groundwork for future accomplishment. For one thing, a group of land-grant advocates emerged in the 1870s. Justin Morrill proved himself to be the tireless legislative champion of the land-grant movement. His efforts would prove fruitless for nearly two decades, from 1872 to 1890, but the eventual success would breathe real life into the land-grant colleges. In addition to Morrill, a cadre of land-grant leaders emerged—intent on working to benefit not only their particular institutions but also the entire class of land-grant colleges, primarily through the federal legislative process. These leaders held certain things in common: the aforementioned "systemic" perspective of land-grant colleges; a "broad-gauge, liberal interpretation" (or, as Atherton might argue, a literal interpretation) of the 1862 Morrill Act and a consequent vision of the colleges as comprehensive, scientifically based universities; a familiarity with legislative process and tactics; and a belief that their eventual success lay in the institutions' willingness to work in concert. These leaders included Andrew D. White, of Cornell; Daniel C. Gilman, of the University of California; John B. Bowman, of the University of Kentucky; and George Atherton, of Rutgers.

Atherton was not building an institution during this time, yet his contributions were valuable to the continuing development of the land-grant colleges during their darkest hour. His address at Elmira, New York, in the wake of McCosh's assault, served notice that the land-grant institutions had in only several years become viable colleges with enrollments and resources on a scale with other colleges. His strategic advice to the colleges during the House investigation helped to shape the outcome. Equally important, Atherton had formed a close relationship with Justin Morrill and had become adept at influencing the legislative process.

Atherton's relationships with White, Gilman, and Bowman would also be intrinsically valuable—more for what he learned from and with them than for what was accomplished. Atherton would soon be the lone repository of their collective experience. In 1875, Gilman left California to become founding president at Johns Hopkins. Bowman was on especially fragile political ground at his home institution; in 1876, he asked Atherton for a confidential letter of recommendation for a post in Indiana,[73] and in 1879 the University of Kentucky trustees ended his regency, which severed his connection with the institution he had founded.[74] And White stepped down from the Cornell presidency in 1885.

Only Atherton would remain. He would, in fact, provide the bridge of experienced leadership for the land-grant movement from the futility of the 1870s to the promise of the late 1880s. His reputation as a land-grant advocate firmly established, he was positioned to assume a central role in the land-grant saga of the 1880s. Oddly, he had achieved this prominence without the platform of a college presidency. But his attendance at the Columbus convention of 1877 would help to bring such a platform his way.

Atherton Becomes a Land-Grant College President

The letter arrived unexpectedly, an unofficial inquiry from a tired acting president:

> I write to you hurriedly to make an inquiry on a matter of importance to me and possibly to you. We are, as you probably know, without a president, having been so for more than a year. Our Board elected two years ago a man without experience except in an academy of low grade and wanting in several essentials and found it necessary to get rid of him within a year. . . . I am personally very desirous that the right man should be found ready to enter on his duties by the opening of the fall session.
>
> A friend, who knew something of you from your attendance at our convention in Columbus, Ohio, some four years ago in connection with which meeting you will perhaps recall me—suggested that you might suit the work and the place. . . . The president has had $2,000 and a house; the salary will probably be increased for the right man.[75]

Little more than two months later, on July 22, 1882, Atherton was unanimously elected by the trustees as the seventh president of the Pennsylvania State College. He also, in the estimate of historian Wayland Dunaway, became the institution's "second founder." But it did not come easily. Atherton had joined an institution that represented, as much as any other, the multiple travails of the period. Dunaway characterized the eighteen years between the first president, Evan Pugh, and George Atherton as an "era of drifting and experiment," in which the school had come to resemble more a backwoods classical college than the advanced scientific institution Pugh had envisaged. In the years of drift, Penn State had consumed five presidents, whose tenures ranged from nine months to nine years. Dunaway noted that the three years before Atherton's arrival had been particularly chaotic:

> Within the short space of three years (1879–1882) troubles multiplied as never before: President Calder resigned under pressure, President Shortlidge served nine distressful months and retired under fire, the student attendance declined to a handful, debts accumulated, the College was attacked by the

Fig. 6. **Old Main, The Pennsylvania State College.** This was Penn State as Atherton first knew it in the 1880s. Predicated on the "Princeton Plan," the main building housed everything—classrooms, laboratories, student living quarters, faculty offices, library, chapel, and the president's office.

Grange and the press, two legislative investigations were held, the Trustees conducted an investigation on their own account, and the whole course of instruction was remodeled.[76]

Yet Atherton showed no hesitation in his decision to accept the call. "I understand full well that my path is not to be strewn with roses," he wrote to the president of the board, General James A. Beaver. "There will be alert and vigorous criticism at every step, for a good while at least; but if devotion and hard work, and singleness of purpose can accomplish anything, we will win."[77]

There is little evidence and even less speculation about Atherton's motives in accepting the presidency of the Pennsylvania State College. The most recent Penn State historian reports that the trustees "considered themselves extremely fortunate to have secured a man so familiar with and dedicated to the concept of land-grant education."[78] But the more curious issue is why a man who had declined at least two and possibly three presidencies in the previous decade waited so long and then accepted the reins of an institution in such desperate condition. Perhaps an offer had not presented itself since the mid to late 1870s and Atherton, at age forty-five, decided to avail himself of the first opportunity. Perhaps in the spring of 1882 Atherton felt himself out of sympathy with the new administration of President Merrill E. Gates at Rutgers, then only thirty-four years of age.[79] Perhaps Atherton felt a strong liking for General Beaver and others at Penn State. One wonders too whether Atherton was intrigued mainly by the challenge at Penn State or whether he came in part out of a desire for a presidential "platform" that would accommodate and even accelerate his land-grant advocacy. If this were so, the Pennsylvania State College would present at least one important advantage related to geography: despite its isolation in mid-state farmlands, it would still be within a day's striking distance, by rail, of the nation's capital. Penn State offered a proximity to Washington that an institution beyond the Alleghenies could not.

In any event, George Atherton was now positioned to embark on the first of what he considered to be his life's two most significant contributions: the "rehabilitation" of the Pennsylvania State College and his efforts to effect passage of the Hatch Act—and, to a lesser extent, his work with the second Morrill Act.[80]

The Hatch Act
and
"the Association"

GEORGE ATHERTON NEVER WROTE HIS MEMOIRS or autobiography, but he did leave behind part of a personal "memoranda," nine pages of which survive and are reproduced in facsimile in the Appendix. Written toward the end of his life, in 1905 or 1906, the memorandum reflects Atherton's effort to assay his professional contributions. His two most highly prized public services lay, he recalled, "in drafting and aiding to secure the passage of the so-called 'Hatch Act' [and] the rehabilitation of The Pennsylvania State College."[1]

Yet Atherton devoted most of the memorandum to detailing his role not at Penn State but in the Hatch Act, which established federally funded agricultural experiment stations as departments of land-grant colleges or in certain cases as independent entities. Perhaps his emphasis on the Hatch Act did not suggest a preference so much as an effort to bring to light an undertaking in which his role was much less apparent. As Atherton told it, he was the unequivocal prime mover, the individual most responsible for the success of the Hatch Act. His account is not corroborated in every detail by other evidence, but neither is it refuted.

Atherton's involvement in experiment station legislation began in 1883 and culminated in 1887 in the Hatch Act. He spent much of the winters of 1886 and 1887 in Washington, D.C. spearheading a legislative committee of three land-grant college presidents to move the bill that Atherton had rewritten thoroughly from earlier legislation through Congress. The story of the Hatch Act is exceedingly complex, and most references gloss over its intricacies. The most complete accounts are found in Alfred True's *History of Agricultural Experimentation and Research in the United States, 1607–1925* (1937) and Alan Marcus's meticulously researched *Agricultural Science and the Quest for Legitimacy* (1985). Yet neither work brings the range of Atherton's contributions to light, although True did acknowledge Atherton's central role in the process. So too did a contemporary observer: a U.S. senator who during the floor debate of the Hatch Act in 1887 referred to "the gentlemen who have devoted special attention to this subject, including and chief among whom is Mr. Atherton."[2]

The Hatch Act was a masterpiece of political compromise. Although the rising class of agricultural scientists eventually emerged as the chief beneficiary, the land-grant college presidents, the agricultural interests (represented most forcefully by the Grange), the senators (acting both on their beliefs and on their presumptions of state sentiment) got provisions they wanted and provisions they did not want. Even the Department of Agriculture, whose formal authority was actually reduced by the legislation, soon found it had gained more than it had lost. The five-year struggle to pass this experiment station legislation was tied inextricably to the beginning of the Association of American Agricultural Colleges and Experiment Stations—an ambivalent alliance of college presidents and experiment station directors who often worked toward mutually opposed goals regarding station structure and function.

The tension between the two groups did not abate during Atherton's lifetime. The evidence suggests that the colleges needed the experiment stations more than the experiment stations needed the colleges. The scientists found themselves overburdened with responsibilities for teaching and service, at the expense of research. Moreover, Hatch Act funds were sometimes used to support college needs that were not related to agricultural research. On the other hand, the college presidents—and Atherton in particular—tended to view the stations as federally funded academic departments.

The Hatch Act not only provided an underpinning for agricultural research and instruction, but also freed limited funds that had been allocated to agriculture for use by other academic programs. Equally important, it provided the "agricultural colleges" with the means to make substantial contributions to the well-being of their agricultural constituencies. During the preceding quarter-century, the powerful Grange and National Farmers' Alliance had denounced the land-grant colleges as failures and shams for their inability to attract agricultural students. With the Hatch Act came heightened prospects for mending fences with the farmers. On another front, the Hatch Act gave the colleges the means to function as the collective research laboratory for a new and rapidly expanding applied science; in gaining the stations, the colleges found a measure of sorely needed academic respectability in the emerging university movement—in which research was valued highly.

Most significant, however, was the precedent the Hatch Act provided: the federal government could use institutions of higher education as instruments of national policy. By effectively placing the stations in the land-grant college context, the Hatch Act provided a powerful impetus to the experiment station movement. In turn, according to Charles Rosenberg, the stations, "as much as any other single factor, [have] been responsible for the remarkable growth of productivity of twentieth-century American agriculture."[3]

The Rising Influence of Agricultural Science

By 1880, land-grant colleges had stalled in their efforts to secure legislation that would provide an additional endowment for basic educational operations. Interest in such a measure would continue, and new bills would appear from time to time throughout the 1880s, but a different legislative initiative began to preoccupy the land-grant college leadership: the effort to secure federal sponsorship for a national network of agricultural experiment stations. For the colleges, the central question would be that of locus of control: Would the stations be connected to the colleges or to the Department of Agriculture, or would they exist autonomously—responsible only to state boards of agriculture or to state legislatures? And aside from the issue of nominal or functional control, who would determine the research agenda? Farmers and agricultural organizations, the college presidents, the Department of Agriculture, or the fast-emerging class of agricultural scientists?

A coordinated network of research facilities had been a topic of the 1872 convention called by Agriculture Commissioner Frederick Watts. The impetus for such a system in the early 1880s came not from the college presidents, however, but from the newly self-conscious class of agricultural scientists. In June 1880, agricultural professors from midwestern land-grant colleges met at the University of Illinois to discuss mutual concerns. A year later, in June 1881, they met again at Michigan Agricultural College "to agree upon some plan for united and systematic agricultural experimentation." The convention endorsed the idea that the stations should be state-supported, the federal government already having done its share by establishing the colleges. Such a system, these "Teachers of Agriculture" believed, would not only benefit farmers, but also provide a better practical education for college students, by exposing them to research.[4]

The idea of agricultural experimentation at the land-grant colleges was hardly new. Demonstration and model farms were an original or early part of many colleges, and certainly of the self-professed agricultural colleges such as the Pennsylvania State College and Michigan Agricultural College (now Michigan State University). At first little more than garden plots designed to occupy students' time and labor or to provide a showpiece for visiting agriculturalists, these model farms quickly evolved into experimental facilities. Typically, they did little more than serve as test plots for crops and fertilizers, with chemical analysis being conducted in the college laboratory. But this arrangement was common to a number of land-grant colleges by 1875, when the nation's first agricultural experiment station was born.[5]

This first experiment station was established in Connecticut, connected to Wesleyan University at Middletown. The founding fathers were Samuel Johnson of Yale's Sheffield School (who had studied in Germany with Evan Pugh) and Wilbur O. Atwater, a professor of chemistry at Wesleyan who later became the first director of the Agriculture Department's Office of Experiment Stations in 1888. The station succeeded because of Atwater's political acumen in gaining the support of the farming community: he stressed the station's utility for fertilizer analysis and its promise for eradicating the blight of the unscrupulous or incompetent fertilizer manufacturers who preyed on farmers. Indeed, the station analyzed 162 samples of fertilizers in its first year of operation. Its value apparent, the station was moved from Wesleyan to the Sheffield School the year following, in 1877.[6]

On the West Coast, the California Experiment Station was getting started at roughly the same time. Its founder was Eugene W. Hilgard, a University of California agriculture professor regarded as one of the finest agricultural scientists of the day. His forte was soil analysis, and he examined the soil composition of the various regions of his state. By 1877, the legislature was sufficiently impressed to appropriate $5,000 to the station for the ensuing biennium and to double that sum in 1879.[7]

In Pennsylvania, Atherton began working at the state level for a station shortly after his arrival in the summer of 1882. He relied heavily on former Rutgers colleague George H. Cook for guidance, as well as on Whitman Jordan, a Penn State professor of agriculture who had previously worked at the Connecticut station and who would leave the college in 1885 to serve at posts in Maine, Wisconsin, and New York. The Pennsylvania legislature passed Atherton's experiment station bill in the spring of 1883, but Governor Robert E. Pattison vetoed it, claiming, "The farming communities of the state are absolutely indifferent about the existence of the College and do not believe it of any use."[8] In 1885, Pattison vetoed a second experiment station bill on the same grounds.

But elsewhere, experiment stations began to appear, encouraged by a coalition of interests: prominent farmers, state agricultural societies and boards of agriculture, and state legislatures. By 1887, fourteen states had organized stations, eight of which had been connected to land-grant colleges. In thirteen other states, equivalent work was being carried out with less formal organization.[9] These stations were as diverse as the conditions that nurtured them. The seventy state-sponsored German experiment stations provided a general example of the desired system but not a prototype. The differences between the fledgling American stations also indicated "the intense disagreement among investigators as to the form and function of agricultural research."[10]

That situation would soon be put on a corrective course. The emerging class of agricultural scientists met not only in 1880 and 1881, but also in 1882 at Iowa, in 1883 at Ohio, in 1884 at New York, and in 1885 at Indiana, in the informal organization known as "Teachers of Agriculture."[11] More important, they began to organize along disciplinary lines. The Association of Official Agricultural Chemists was established in 1880, its original agenda being to standardize tests and measurements across state lines. Similarly, a group of horticulturalists organized the Society for the Promotion of Agricultural Science at the 1880 meeting of the American Association for the Advancement of Science, in the belief "that the formation of a select society would help raise the level of agricultural science in the country."[12]

As agricultural scientists began to pull in one direction—toward their increasingly professional and exclusive disciplines—other forces began pulling in other directions. The Grange, for example, continued to grow more critical of land-grant colleges. Agricultural research, the Grange maintained, should fall under the control of agricultural organizations or the state, but not the land-grant colleges, which were viewed as abject failures by the farming community in general. The Grange, in fact, had launched its own investigation of the land-grant colleges in 1875, just as the House's more visible inquest was being brought to a close. The Grange's report condemned the institutions bitterly and urged the establishment of a permanent Grange committee on education to monitor the schools. The Grange also recommended that land-grant colleges be placed under the exclusive control of farmers nationwide.[13] No serious dislocations came from the critical reports of the Grange over the next several years, but the unrelenting criticism took its toll. The Grange had unequivocally declared itself a foe of the land-grant colleges; it would later direct its animus on the Hatch Act and the 1890 Morrill Act as well.

The militancy of the Grange was the outgrowth of a malaise that gripped American agriculture after the Panic of 1873. Soil infertility in the east, and drought and pestilence in the west, coupled with a general overproduction and consequent decline in commodity prices, brought unprecedented economic stress to the farmers. Such problems were confounded by what was seen as a disquieting internal rot in the rural communities: a visible dissatisfaction and frustration among farm families, manifesting itself in the frequent abandonment of farms; the inability to prevent farm children from leaving for the city; and the lack of esteem accorded farmers. A profound shift had occurred in American agriculture. Inside seventy years, the Jeffersonian ideal of the noble, independent citizen-farmer had been reduced to the caricature of a struggling, dependent "hayseed." No longer was it possible for the farmer to function without aid of some sort.[14]

From these conditions grew the demand for what Alan Marcus calls "systematic agriculture," as distinct from "scientific agriculture." Scientific agriculture, at least until it was claimed by the scientists, advocated that farmers needed to function as their own scientists. They were to experiment on their own tract, and from their understanding of nature apply the results of those experiments to improve their operations. Scientific agriculture saw farmers as a professional class, "in tune with the new age's spirit." Systematic agriculture, on the other hand, held science in high regard but disagreed that farmers should solve their own problems. Adherents saw systematic agriculture more as a business than a profession. They wanted farmers to follow a prescribed "system"—the laws of which would be determined by science—to produce satisfactory results. The argument between the two schools of thought centered not on the value of science per se but on which model farmers should emulate: scientist or businessman.

The influence of the scientific agriculturalists waned with the emergence of the professional agricultural scientists, who pointed to the folly of experimental work conducted by lay farmers. And in their agitation for experiment stations, the scientists found a natural ally in the systematic agriculturalists, who wanted the farmer to follow procedure. To the systematic agriculturalists, the station represented a facility in which to perform experiments that the individual farmer, lacking time and training, could not. To the scientists, the station represented an opportunity through which they could divorce themselves from actual farming practice, pursuing science from the standpoint of general principles rather than specific instances.[15]

The emergence of the scientists and their appropriation of the research function did not, however, resolve the question of who should control the research agenda. Not until the Hatch Act did that issue begin to resolve itself—in favor of the agricultural scientists.

As agricultural scientists were organizing themselves in the early 1880s, a meeting of a different sort was being planned. In July 1881, President James A. Garfield's new commissioner of agriculture, George B. Loring, issued a call for a convention. He invited a spectrum of leaders, from agricultural colleges, experiment stations, agricultural societies, and state boards of agriculture to explore ways in which the Department of Agriculture might become more useful to them. The convention, the first department-sponsored meeting in a decade, took place in January 1882, with a light turnout of fifty delegates. Agricultural scientists dominated the agenda; at least four scientific papers were read. The convention produced a split among the scientists in terms of where publicly funded agricultural experimentation should take place—at the land-grant colleges or within the Department of Agriculture. Atherton, though not in attendance, might have been pleased with the contribution of his Rutgers colleague George Cook, whose paper is reputed by one scholar to have "launched the college-station campus." Cook's views apparently carried the day. The convention authorized the Agriculture Department to solicit Congress on behalf of the agricultural colleges; the department was to lead the move to establish a college-station connection that the Department would administer.

Although the agriculture commissioner afterward introduced two bills to establish stations sponsored by the Department of Agriculture, the most significant outcome of the convention was that Seaman A. Knapp, then a professor of agriculture at Iowa Agricultural College in Ames, soon drafted a bill "to establish national experiment stations in connection with the agricultural colleges." This bill became H.R. 6110, the so-called "Carpenter bill," introduced by Iowa Representative Cyrus C. Carpenter in the U.S. House on May 8, 1882. With this bill, the legislative history of the Hatch Act had begun.[16] Knapp's bill, which Atherton would eventually rework, contained six parts. First, it connected the "national experiment stations" to "each of the agricultural colleges" for a larger purpose: to "enable" the Department of Agriculture to "fulfill the design and perform the duties for which it was established," that being in part "to acquire and diffuse among the people . . . useful information on subjects connected with agriculture."

The bill laid out a broad agenda for station research, including the physiology of plants and animals and their pathologies, the chemical composition of crop plants, soil and water analysis, cattle nutrition, and other topics "bearing directly on the agricultural industry." In what became the bill's most controversial provision, the stations were to be placed "under the general control of the Commissioner of Agriculture, who shall have power to employ a professor for each . . . college." These professors would function as "superintendents of the experiment stations" and would make "such reports to the Commissioner . . . as he may direct." The professors were, however, free to "act in concert" with the president and faculties of the colleges to which they were assigned, under rules and regulations to be determined by the commissioner of agriculture and the college presidents.[17] In addition, the salary of the agriculture professor was to be paid directly by the Department of Agriculture.

In sum, the Carpenter bill would have made the experiment stations instruments of the Department of Agriculture, and the colleges would have maintained virtually no control over the station's operation or its research agenda. Referred to the House Committee on Agriculture, the bill died.

In January 1883 came the second of Loring's department-sponsored conventions. The convention was more heavily attended than its predecessors, drawing 120 delegates—including Atherton, only six months into his Penn State presidency. The convention focused on experiment station legislation. Knapp introduced a resolution in support of the Carpenter bill, which was endorsed by the convention. Knapp also moved to appoint a committee of five, headed by himself and President Theophilus C. Abbot of Michigan Agricultural College, to present a statement on the legislation for the House Agriculture Committee—a maneuver also endorsed by the convention. The three additional members of Knapp's committee included Stephen D. Lee, president of Mississippi Agricultural College; Paul A. Chadbourne, president of Massachusetts Agricultural College; and Emerson E. White, president of Purdue University, but none of them was in attendance at the convention.[18] In the fall of 1883, the station movement received an added boost when the president of the Grange expressed his support for "properly conceived" agricultural experiment stations.

By that time, Knapp had modified the Carpenter bill and presented it to Iowa Representative Adoniram J. Holmes, who had taken Carpenter's seat in the November 1883 election. At the beginning of the Forty-eighth Congress in December 1883, Holmes introduced Knapp's modified bill as H.R. 447. The bill's principal difference was that it placed the stations under the general control of "the regents or trustees of said . . . colleges," not the commissioner of agriculture. Further, the bill gave the authority for employing the agriculture professor to the colleges instead of to the Department of Agriculture. Yet the bill kept the Agriculture Department in control of the stations' research agendas, which were now to be determined by "the Commissioner of Agriculture, the president of the college . . . and the professor in charge of said station." Unlike its predecessor, the bill called for an annual appropriation of $15,000 to the stations, to be drawn quarterly from the U.S. treasury, a process that required the endorsement of the commissioner of agriculture, among others. Finally, the bill required the state legislature to pass an act accepting the trust before the college could begin drawing funds.[19]

Knapp also issued a circular on the heels of the Holmes bill's introduction. He noted that the Carpenter bill had been "substantially the same" as the Holmes bill, and also said that the Holmes bill "was perfected" at the January 1883 meeting of "delegates from the several Agricultural and Mechanical Colleges" by the five-man committee, previously identified. He also argued that a national network of stations would provide the means for overcoming the diversity of climatic conditions across the nation, as well as the most efficient mechanism for approaching the enormous research agenda then building in the agricultural sciences. His reasons for connecting the stations to the colleges included the economic benefits of using existing college facilities and the pedagogical utility of the stations in providing "object lessons" for the students.[20] Knapp's enthusiasm apparently led him to take some liberties in the circular. In fact, Marcus accused Knapp of falsifying information in the circular to gain college support for the bill:

> First, he never acknowledged that he had drafted the measure or had had it introduced during the preceding Congress. Instead, he maintained that the bill was a product of the 1883 conclave, stating that it was "perfected" there. . . . Second, he misrepresented the Washington gathering entirely. He identified it as "a meeting of the delegates from the several Agricultural and Mechanical Colleges." He [also] implied that the circular was an agreed-upon committee document, representing the collective wisdom of its membership of five college presidents.[21]

Despite Knapp's concessions to the colleges in redrafting the Carpenter bill into the Holmes bill, college presidents and agricultural scientists alike remained distressed over the measure. The scientists objected to the degree of control still vested in the commissioner of agriculture. Especially pointed criticism came from Henry P. Armsby, professor of agriculture at the University of Wisconsin and a former student of Samuel Johnson at the Sheffield School (and future director of Penn State's experiment station). Armsby wanted stations to "aim to advance agricultural science in general, without regard to obtaining immediately useful results." He also observed that no scientists worthy of the name would "consent to conduct that station according to a plan laid out in Washington."[22] And college presidents, for the most part, also objected to the authority the Holmes bill vested in the commissioner of agriculture.

According to Marcus, Knapp's intention was precisely to limit the control the colleges—presidents and scientists alike—could wield over the stations. In fact, Knapp's circular boasted that the Holmes bill "wisely gives to the Commissioner of Agriculture such a relation to these stations as will systematize their work, and will avoid too much repetition of experiments at different stations." Knapp was an advocate of systematic farming, believing that esoteric research of the kind Armsby espoused would not solve the fundamental problems of American agriculture.[23] Indeed, Knapp's major contribution to American agriculture was the County Demonstration Agent System. This invention for diffusion of agricultural knowledge is the cornerstone of the cooperative extension service, in which county agents translate research findings into practical procedures for the farming community.[24]

The Struggle for the Hatch Act, and the Preliminary Association Convention

The first six months of 1884 saw a major revision of the Holmes bill, a process in which George Atherton played the leading role. A handful of college presidents and scientists met with members of the House Agriculture Committee, persuading them to reject the Holmes bill and accept a substitute. The land-grant leaders objected to the Holmes bill because "it seemed to make the stations virtually branches of the Department of Agriculture."[25] Atherton's memorandum (see Appendix), which tells a tale of almost unilateral action on his part, provides a closer look at the process. After the gubernatorial veto of the experiment station bill in the Pennsylvania General Assembly in the spring of 1883, Atherton's attention was drawn to the Carpenter bill, which had been introduced almost a year earlier, in May 1882. Atherton traveled to Washington, D.C., to introduce himself to the bill's sponsor and ascertain his plans for the measure:

> He [Carpenter] very frankly told me that he had not introduced
> his bill with the idea of securing its passage at once, but

rather as a means of directing public attention to the subject; that the thought was a wholly new one for him, and had been suggested by some testimony before a Committee of which he was a member, with reference to the growing importance of scientific tests in every branch of industry, and that the query had presented itself to his mind, why the same method could not be successfully applied in Agriculture, he being evidently quite informed as to what was already being done in Germany, France, and England.

He told me, however, that while he did not expect himself to secure the passage of any bill during that Congress, and that he expected to close his term of service at the expiration of the Congress . . . he proposed to undertake to enlist the interest of [his] successor [A. J. Holmes] in this project.

Soon after the opening of the first session of the following Congress [the Forty-eighth Congress, in December 1883], I visited Washington and sought out the new member from Iowa, Mr. A. J. Holmes of the Tenth District. He furnished me a copy of a bill [H.R. 447] which he had already introduced [on December 10] in pursuance of the suggestion of his predecessor, which, after a very thorough examination, I decided was altogether ineffective and unworkable. At that time I received no suggestion as to the authorship of the bill, but assumed that Mr. Holmes was the author, and felt, therefore, a degree of hesitation about making suggestions of change. Mr. Holmes, however, entered very cordially into the matter and gave me the largest possible freedom in modifying the bill to suit my own views. After I had done so, he secured me a hearing before the Agricultural Committee, of which Mr. Hatch of Missouri was then Chairman, and accompanied me at the hearing [no published record of this hearing exists]. The Committee had before it the original "Holmes Bill," and I therefore addressed my remarks and criticisms to that, in connection with a discussion of the general subject. The Committee gave me a very attentive hearing, and, at the close, asked if I would prepare and present to them a bill embodying my suggestions. This was, of course, precisely what was desired by both Mr. Holmes and myself. I subjected the matter to further careful review, and shortly had a second hearing before the Committee, when the modified bill was approved and referred to a sub-committee, of which Mr. [William] Cullen of Illinois was the Chairman.

Without going further into this detail, which is given for the sake of showing my intimate identification with the first stages of the preparation of the "Hatch Act," I may say briefly that the bill was reported favorably to the whole committee by Mr. Cullen, and that Mr. Cullen died directly after the close of that session of Congress, and then I cast about as to the best method of starting anew. During all this early process, I had worked without a confidant, and without consultation with any one, except in the later stages of it, when I took up the matter with Dr. Cook of New Jersey, who, from that time on, was my one trusted counselor and confidant, and who was identified with every stage of the movement until its successful consummation.... [Atherton later added that he] had changed the original crude form of the bill prepared by or for Mr. Holmes in such a way as to make the stations branches of those colleges....

In all this I do not mean at all to disparage the services, or to underestimate the influence, of others, and it is fair to say that Professor Knapp, then of Iowa, after the passage of the [Hatch] bill was secured claimed that he had personally done all things which I have above stated as done by myself. As to that, I have only to say that I never knew Professor Knapp in the matter from the beginning to the end of the affair, except that after the "Hatch Act" was well under way I received copies of a printed circular from Professor Knapp, advocating the passage of the "Holmes Bill."[26]

Atherton's reminiscence bears scrutiny, however, as several of his points seem puzzling. The historical record, at least that provided by True and by Marcus, and a hackneyed account by Knapp's biographer, indicates that Knapp indeed authored both the original Carpenter bill (H.R. 6110) and its revised successor, the Holmes bill (H.R. 447). Neither True, Knoblauch and associates, nor Marcus, however, provides any evidence that refutes Atherton's claim to rewriting the Holmes bill into the Cullen bill.[27] Unfortunately, no documentation exists for the two House Agriculture Committee hearings on the Holmes bill in the spring of 1884, at which Atherton made the persuasive case against the measure.[28]

The problematical aspects of Atherton's account lie in his implication of unilateral action and his professed ignorance of Seaman Knapp's activity with the Carpenter and Holmes bills. For one thing, Atherton attended the January 1883 Washington convention, at which Knapp played a leading role. The convention endorsed the Carpenter bill and appointed a committee of five, with Knapp at the head, to press for legislative action. For Atherton to say "I never knew Professor Knapp in the matter from the beginning to the end of the affair" seems to defy the historical record. Perhaps he dated the "beginning" of the affair on his own terms, when he rewrote the Holmes bill. Even so, during the 1885 preliminary convention of the Association of American Agricultural Colleges and Experiment Stations, Atherton and Knapp served together on two committees, and Knapp exhorted the delegates to endorse the Cullen bill, which Atherton had authored.

Another unresolved aspect of Atherton's account involves the House Agriculture Committee hearings in the spring of 1884. It seems strange that neither Knapp nor his committee of college presidents—the individuals ostensibly responsible for the experiment station bills—was ever called to testify, but the evidence does not attest to their participation. At the Association's 1885 preliminary convention, Atherton's colleague George Cook of Rutgers gave an account of the hearings. Cook corroborated Atherton's account, but added that he and two others—one from Ohio State, the other from the Sheffield School—also presented testimony (though not necessarily at the same time as Atherton). Cook said the committee was at first indifferent, but noted that "the subject grew upon them" and that they gave it their unanimous endorsement.[29] Further, a regional agricultural newspaper also mentioned the names of three land-grant college representatives who testified; none of them, however, was a member of the Knapp committee.[30]

In any event, the mantle of leadership on experimentation station legislation passed from Knapp to Atherton in the spring of 1884, and after the convention of 1885, Knapp's involvement in the process ended entirely. The transition would be of critical importance to the land-grant college and experiment station movements, because Atherton and Knapp held antithetical views on the fundamental purpose of land-grant colleges. Atherton favored a liberal interpretation of the 1862 Morrill Act, in which agriculture was only a part of a broad educational mandate. Knapp, by contrast, thought agriculture should predominate. At the 1885 convention, he submitted a paper in which he charged that most of the revenues intended for agriculture and the mechanic arts had been "absorbed in general education to the exclusion of the main purpose."[31] As will be shown later, Atherton and Knapp also clashed over convention priorities. Perhaps the philosophical differences between them caused Atherton to ignore Knapp's early role in experiment station legislation.

Atherton's account was supported by the *New England Homestead,* but its story was printed in response to a sharp letter from Atherton to the editor, Herbert O. Myrick. Atherton had criticized the influential agricultural newspaper for printing an account in which the credit for the Hatch Act had been given mainly to the agricultural press. The *Homestead*'s corrected story ran thus:

> ...In the 48th Congress Hon. A. J. Holmes of Iowa introduced the same bill, but being occupied with other matters nothing was done about it until Dr. G. W. Atherton ...obtained a copy of the bill and re-wrote it, making it practically a new bill, though following out the original idea. At this time it was found that not even the subcommittee of the committee on agriculture, to which the bill had been referred, knew of its existence. Mr. Holmes and Dr. Atherton, however, presented the new bill to them at an official hearing, at which Prof. W. H. Brewer of Conn., Prof. George H. Cook and Hon. Thomas H. Dudley of New Jersey were also present. The committee adopted the Atherton bill as a substitute for the original, and it went on the House calendar as No. 7498, report No. 2034, with a favorable recommendation from the committee....[32]

When questioned by others about his role in the passage of the Hatch Act, Atherton reiterated this account without appreciable deviation. In a letter written thirteen years after the fact to his former professor of agriculture, Whitman Jordan, then director of the New York state experiment station at Geneva, Atherton said: "It is not quite correct to say that I drew the bill because I used as a foundation for it one which had already been introduced [the Holmes bill]. Of that, however, I changed the title and the substance so completely that all the distinctive provisions of the act as finally passed were my own, and nothing of the original bill was retained except a few general provisions."[33]

In 1903, in response to an individual seeking to learn about the "role of the original committee of five" [most likely the legislative committee appointed at the 1883 convention and chaired by Knapp], Atherton said, "No such Committee as you refer to was appointed, at least not for the purpose you name." The Hatch Act, he recalled, "was little more than a vague and formless proposition, which the author [apparently Carpenter] himself told me he did not expect to press, but which he hoped would be followed up by his successor [Holmes]." Holmes drafted a more ambitious but "entirely unworkable bill," which Atherton "re-wrought . . . from title to conclusion." All of Atherton's changes were accepted. The modified bill was referred to a House subcommittee chaired by Representative Cullen and reported back favorably.[34]

The Cullen bill, introduced July 2, 1884, contained many substantive changes from the Holmes bill. Thematically, the Cullen bill constricted the authority of the Agriculture Department and enlarged that of the colleges. The Holmes bill purported to "enable" the Agriculture Department to fulfill its mandated duties; the Cullen bill offered only to "aid" the department in that respect. Atherton also added an important teleological mandate to the stations in respect to agricultural science. Where the Holmes bill concerned itself mainly with the "systematic agriculture" concern of enabling the Department of Agriculture to disseminate information to farmers, the Cullen bill went much further. It added that the stations would also "promote scientific investigation and experiment respecting the principles and applications of agricultural science." The Cullen bill, unlike the Holmes bill, explicitly recognized that agricultural science must have a theoretical dimension as well as an applied one, that it must be driven by the esoteric search for governing laws and principles as well as by the utilitarian demands of farmers. In addition, Atherton's Cullen bill did not merely "connect" the stations to the colleges, but it subordinated them, as the Holmes bill did not do. The stations were henceforth to be regarded as "a department" of the college.

When Knapp transformed the Carpenter bill into the Holmes bill, he had removed the stations from the direct control of the Department of Agriculture and placed them under the college regents or trustees. Atherton kept this provision substantially intact in the Cullen bill. In a marked departure from the Holmes bill, however, Atherton stripped the Agriculture Department of any formal authority to determine the stations' research agenda. Nothing in the act, he wrote, "shall be construed to authorize said Commissioner to control or direct the work or management of any such station except as to the standard of valuation of commercial fertilizers."

In other departures from the Holmes bill, Atherton required the stations to make annual reports to the governor of their state, with an additional copy to be forwarded to the U.S. commissioner of agriculture. He also limited the Agriculture Department to a facilitative rather than authoritative role in helping to establish "uniformity of methods and results in the work of said stations." In addition to setting the aforementioned standard of valuation for fertilizers, the department was to furnish forms for the tabulation of experimental results. The commissioner also was free to suggest "such lines of inquiry as to him shall seem most important . . . and to furnish such advice and assistance as will best promote the purposes of this act." With that advisory role, the commissioner's power stopped.

Atherton also required that the stations communicate their research findings periodically to the public. Strangely enough, the Holmes bill, with its bias toward systematic agriculture, did not contain such a requirement. In the Cullen bill, the stations were to publish bulletins or progress reports every three months and to send them to each newspaper in the state. To support the expense of such a measure, Atherton reserved the federal franking privilege for the bulletins.

Following the Holmes bill, Atherton called for an annual appropriation of $15,000, to be drawn quarterly from the U.S. treasury. But there the similarities stopped. In the first appropriation, to begin July 1, 1885, Atherton provided that up to $3,000 could be spent to "erect, enlarge or repair" the station's physical plant. He also provided up to $750 for similar expenditures in subsequent appropriations. Finally, in a concession to economy or as a spur to station productivity, he required that stations with annual expenditures under $15,000 return the balance to the U.S. treasury in the form of a proportionately reduced appropriation for the ensuing year.[35]

There is no direct evidence of Atherton's having written the three-page report (No. 2034) accompanying the Cullen bill.[36] He did not claim authorship, as he did for the longer report (No. 848) that accompanied the Hatch bill. Nevertheless, it is highly probable that Atherton's hand was involved, for the arguments evoke Atherton's style. The report established that its object was "to aid agriculture." Using only part of Knapp's earlier argument, it spoke of the variability of soil and climate across the nation. Unlike Knapp's circular, it stressed that dispersing state experiment stations would be more effective than expanding the research capability of a centralized federal department. The report pointed to increased foreign competition in the production and export of agricultural products and made a strong case for the efficiency of the extant stations. Echoing Atherton's method, the report also discussed the return the colleges had made on the federal investment and stressed their scientific utility in social terms: "Many thousands of young men educated in science have already gone out from their colleges to engage in the practical duties of life." Finally, the report added that the stations would "increase the efficiency of these colleges in their relations to agriculture," a statement that strongly suggests Atherton's thinking.

Atherton's next step in promoting the Cullen bill was to join with Cook in producing a circular urging the bill's passage, which contained some similarities to the report but some important differences as well.[37] Their argument centered on how the stations would benefit the farmer and spoke of the futility intrinsic to "scientific farming," in which the farmer was expected to function as his own scientist. Atherton's penchant for economic data showed itself when he compared the relatively small federal expenditure ($15,000 per year per station, or $570,000 in all) against the scope of American agriculture. He stated that 44 percent of the working population was engaged in agriculture, adding that $10 billion was invested in farmlands and $400 million in implements and machinery, all of it generating agricultural products valued at $2.2 billion annually. Finally, the circular provided a defense of the land-grant colleges: "The colleges have done excellent work, and have given a large return to the country for the gifts by which they were established." Atherton and Cook also foresaw an instructional role for the stations on their respective campuses, a role that would translate itself into benefits for farmers. "The studies begun by the students in college," they wrote, "are carried on by the practical farmer in the field, and the college professors will be quickened in their duties by seeing the useful purposes to which their sciences are applied."

Despite Atherton and Cook's promotional efforts, and the strong messages of support sent to Congress by the land-grant colleges, the Cullen bill did not reach the House floor for debate in the Forty-eighth Congress. An unfriendly House faction was pressing for another investigation of the colleges, which did not materialize. A debate over the Cullen bill, intended to give the colleges total control over the stations, might have prompted the anti-college faction to press more vigorously for the investigation. Nevertheless, a group of college presidents journeyed to the nation's capital in the winter of 1884–85 to lobby for the bill, but Congress did not act on the measure.[38]

The new administration of President Grover Cleveland came to Washington, D.C., in March 1885, and with it a new commissioner of agriculture, Norman J. Colman. A longtime member of the Missouri State Board of Agriculture, Colman was publisher of the St. Louis-based agricultural newspaper, *Colman's Rural World.* The new commissioner lost no time in calling for a convention of delegates from agricultural colleges, experiment stations, state boards of agriculture, and agricultural societies. He intended that the convention focus on agricultural instruction in the public schools, the issue of experiment station legislation, and working relationships with state and federal agencies.[39] On July 8–10, 1885, what would come to be known as the "preliminary convention" of the Association of American Agricultural Colleges and Experiment Stations began its proceedings. No one would play a more prominent role, or come out of it with a higher standing, than George Atherton, one of ten college presidents in attendance.

Colman appointed a five-person committee on business—all but one of them college presidents—to keep the convention on track: Atherton; Seaman Knapp; Henry E. Alvord, then manager of the private experimental station Houghton Farm in Orange County, New York; Merritt C. Fernald, president of Maine State Agricultural College; and Edwin Willits, the new president of Michigan Agricultural College. Colman also appointed five vice-presidents "of this association": Atherton; Willits; Stephen D. Lee, president of Mississippi Agricultural College; George T. Fairchild, president of Kansas State Agricultural College; and Professor C. H. Dwinelle, of the University of California. Most consequential, however, was that Colman also appointed a committee on legislation to pursue the convention's agenda with Congress, consisting of Atherton, Willits, and Lee.[40] As H. C. Knoblauch and associates observed, "no figure at these conventions showed greater skill in winning a position on key committees than President George W. Atherton."[41]

The convention focused immediately on agriculture experiment stations and the Cullen bill. Knapp noted the tampering the House Agriculture Committee and the Atherton group had done with the Holmes bill to create the Cullen bill. "I think they have made some mistakes and I think they have made some improvements," he said.

Fig. 7. **The Preliminary Convention.** Delegates to the "preliminary convention" of the Association of American Agricultural Colleges and Experiment Stations, July 8–10, 1885, Washington, D.C. George W. Atherton is in the first row, third from left. Seaman Knapp stands two rows directly above Atherton.

But he recognized it as a "grand bill" that would do "excellent work" and urged the convention to endorse it, which it did unanimously.[42]

With the Cullen bill, Knapp and Atherton had no quarrel. Yet on other matters—not the least of which were the convention's priorities— they split sharply. After a long evening's speech by Willits on industrial education, Atherton moved to adjourn and pick up the discussion the next morning. Knapp preferred to begin the discussion immediately, so that more time would be left on the morrow for the item he wanted to discuss: "how can we practically co-operate with the Department of Agriculture in carrying on this experimental work?" To Atherton, who had virtually written the Department of Agriculture out of the Cullen bill, the topic was of ancillary importance. "First, we came here to see what each other are doing, and how we can learn from one another to do better," he said, "and secondly, as a natural result of that, how we can coordinate our work, not only with the institutions but with the Department of Agriculture, and not at all with a view to subordinate all others to the one question which President Knapp suggests."[43] Atherton was not opposed to cooperation with the department, but he sought to use the convention for a larger purpose. The possibility of creating a permanent organization had occurred to him, and he sought to generate discussions on a variety of issues and problems that concerned college presidents.[44]

Evidently he succeeded. The delegates found the time to discuss, for example, the creation of a bureau that would serve as an information clearinghouse between the Department of Agriculture and the colleges. There was some fear that the bureau might try "to arrange with the different experiment stations as to what particular class of experiments each one should make." Atherton noted that the concern was valid, and for that reason it was decided to omit such a directive in the resolution passed by the convention to establish what would eventually become the Office of Experiment Stations, founded in 1888 as a bureau of the Department of Agriculture.[45]

Finally, the convention resolved to perpetuate the "association" and formed an executive committee to work with the commissioner of agriculture in determining the date and agenda of the next convention. Atherton was named chairman of this executive committee, and he appointed five others: Knapp; Cook; Selim Peabody, president of the University of Illinois; George W. Curtis, a professor at Texas A&M; and James S. Newman, a professor at the State University of Alabama.

As Atherton had hoped, the convention covered a range of other topics. Delegates moved to restrict the seed distribution program of the Department of Agriculture, citing the problems of indiscriminate distribution and urging that the department use the colleges as the intermediary in this program. Delegates also urged that the Department of War appoint land-grant college graduates currently serving in the military to teach military science at the colleges. In addition, they asked the War Department to establish meteorological signal stations at the colleges so they could provide a weather service to their agricultural constituents. Delegates also entered into a wide-ranging discussion of the difficulties of attracting farm boys to the colleges, and broached the topic of establishing forestry experiment stations at the colleges. And though they began to talk about the efficacy of agricultural instruction in the public schools, Atherton derailed the discussion in the interests of time.

The convention seemed to end on a positive note. Colman said he wanted to meet annually. Atherton added that he had "never attended [a convention] which seems to be composed of more earnest men, or to have accomplished more substantially the results we aimed at."[46] He had much to be gratified about. He came out of the 1885 convention positioned, at the very least, as first among equals. He had received a unanimous endorsement of his Cullen bill and in other ways succeeded in strengthening the autonomy and independence of the colleges vis-à-vis the Department of Agriculture, while working out "cooperative" arrangements with the department when he thought it suited the colleges' interests. Not least, he had also established the idea that the primary value of the Association lay in the opportunity to learn from the experience of member colleges, and that their first and best resource was each other. The colleges' relationships to the agencies of government were important, but secondarily so, he had emphasized. He did not want the colleges to be transformed into vassal states of the Department of Agriculture.

Most significant, however, was that Atherton's informal legislative role had become legitimatized. He had been appointed by the commissioner of agriculture, with his colleagues Willits and Lee, to carry out the Association's legislative agenda: the enactment of the Cullen bill. His work in Congress would now carry the weight of the Association — however inchoate — behind it. In addition, as chairman of the executive committee, Atherton was empowered to determine the time, place, and agenda of the next meeting. But his attention in the coming months would focus not so much on the consolidation of the new association as it would on the passage of the experiment station bill, an accomplishment that would require intensive effort lasting another year and a half.

Atherton's skill in promoting legislation was nowhere more amply demonstrated than in the first few months of the Forty-ninth Congress, the first session of which opened in December 1885. His first step was to produce a show of congressional support for the Cullen bill. In October 1885 he wrote to the delegates of the convention, asking each to work with his congressmen to "introduce the bill himself (as several others will), or to prepare himself to give it an active support and advocacy."[47]

The new session of Congress produced the flurry of bills Atherton had sought. Prompted by Stephen D. Lee of Atherton's legislative committee, Senator James Z. George of Mississippi introduced the Cullen bill as S. 372 on December 10, 1885. Holmes of Iowa reintroduced his bill, II.R. 643, shortly thereafter. Then, between January 5 and January 7, 1886, came Allen's H.R. 1321, Heard's H.R. 1374, Buchanan's H.R. 1496, Outhwaite's H.R. 1904, Curtin's H.R. 2039, Pettibone's H.R. 2268, La Follette's H.R. 2748, and Hatch's H.R. 2933.[48]

Atherton's tactic now was to select the most effective sponsor, which he determined to be William H. Hatch, a congressman from Missouri. Hatch had acceded to the chairmanship of the IIouse Agriculture Committee during the first session of the Forty-eighth Congress; in the spring of 1884 he had tapped his subcommittee chairman, William Cullen, to handle the experiment station legislation. Atherton's 1905–6 memorandum provides the sequence of events:

> With Dr. Cook's knowledge and full assent, I undertook to secure the services of Mr. Hatch as a sponsor for the bill. I venture to say that neither he nor any other member of the Committee, when the matter was first presented to him [presumably in 1884], had the remotest notion of what was meant by an "Agricultural Experiment Station," but he soon showed an apt and appreciative grasp of the main purposes of such Stations, and gave me his personal assurance that he would undertake to secure the passage of the bill. From that time forward and of set purpose, we everywhere spoke of it as the "Hatch Act." At Mr. Hatch's request, I wrote the report [No. 848] which he for his Committee presented to the House to accompany the bill, the only change being the insertion by someone (whose name I never asked) of the short paragraph which very properly recognizes the work of Laws and Gilbert at Rothamsted, though their establishment was not, technically speaking, called an "Experiment Station." As soon as the movement was well under way, we sought the cooperation of all Land Grant Colleges (I had changed the original crude form of the bill prepared by or for Mr. Holmes in such a way as to make the Stations branches of those colleges) and most efficient service was rendered by correspondence and, in a few cases, by personal visits to Washington. Among the presidents of Colleges who made such visits I recall President Adams of Cornell, President Goodell of Massachusetts, President Gates of New Jersey, President Willits of Michigan, and, I think, President Patterson of Kentucky.
>
> After the bill was passed by Congress, Mr. Hatch requested

those of us who were then in Washington to go with him to ask the favorable action of President Cleveland. Mr. Hatch called upon me to present the matter to the President, which I did. He gave us a very attentive and careful hearing, and shortly after (March 2, 1887) signed the bill.[49]

In a March 5, 1887, letter to Herbert Myrick, editor of the *New England Homestead,* Atherton took vigorous exception to an earlier account Myrick had printed. In it Myrick had given most of the credit for the Hatch Act to the agricultural press and also painted an inaccurate picture that portrayed Hatch as the "father" of experiment station legislation. Wrote Atherton:

> I have spent a good deal of time, for three years and more, in working up the measure, with others; I put it into working shape and was first to waken the attention of the Congress to its importance. So far from William Hatch being the "Father" of the measure, he had no hand whatever in preparing or introducing it. He did not even know, in the 48th Congress, that there was such a measure referred to his committee. . . . His great merit is, that he grew more and more impressed with its importance, and, when the 49th Congress opened, took vigorous hold of it. His service in its behalf is simply incalculable. But is not credit done to those who [indecipherable] support for its passage in the House and Senate, before you ever heard of the measure, and Mr. Hatch had already pledged to me and to others his hearty support which he has since given. But to secure this was a two years' work, and you yourself expressed to me your surprise at the amount of work . . . which you found to have been done, when you came to take this subject up in your papers. What you have done came at a most fortunate time. . . . You have awakened a public interest . . . which has helped to give the final push. . . .
>
> About matters of this kind, I have never troubled myself to inquire who was entitled to the most credit. . . . But I insist that you shall not, without protest, carry off the honors that are due others.[50]

And in a 1903 letter Atherton noted that he alone had interviewed Hatch and "secured his promise to father the Bill in the House."

Atherton then "took pains to label it everywhere the 'Hatch Bill,' for the sake of securing for it the prestige that Mr. Hatch had then won."[51] But Atherton probably painted an overly gracious picture of Hatch's enthusiasm for the bill. The measure failed to come up for debate on the House floor in the first session of the Forty-ninth Congress, due largely, as Alvord charged, to Hatch's declining interest in the legislation.[52]

The Hatch bill moved quickly through the preliminary stages of the process, however. After the hearing described by Atherton, the bill was reported back favorably, with only minor amendments, on March 3, 1886. Atherton's accompanying report (Report No. 848) contained many of the basic arguments and language found in the report for the Cullen bill. But Atherton went much further in providing a comprehensive description of the "scientific" and "practical" research that had been undertaken by the sixty-seven German experiment stations up to that time. His strategy was to overwhelm the reader with the scope and depth of agricultural science research and to imply how valuable it would be to have a similar network examining problems peculiar to the United States. He also provided a detailed description of the agricultural research emphases at nine extant experiment stations and/or land-grant colleges.

Despite the onslaught of data on agricultural research, Atherton used the report to point out that the land-grant college mission extended far beyond agriculture: "It should be borne in mind that experiment work is only an incidental part of their proper vocation.... Their work cannot be restricted to agriculture." In fact, Atherton implied that the agricultural research the colleges had already conducted came in response "to deeply felt public need" and at great cost to the colleges themselves. Indeed, the colleges had been forced to compromise their broad educational mandate "by diverting to this use resources which were already inadequate for their strictly educational work."[53]

To Atherton and his coterie of presidents, the Hatch Act would not only help to render the colleges more responsive to an antagonistic agricultural constituency, but also bolster the colleges by underwriting agricultural research and instruction (or so they desired) so that the institutions could apply the funds they were devoting to agriculture to other areas. This is not to imply that Atherton and his colleagues developed a hidden agenda in regard to the Hatch Act. It is to say only that they wanted the stations on their own terms: as subordinate departments functioning in the context of broadly structured, scientifically oriented public colleges. But they were not unaware of the positive implications for their other academic programs should the federal government subsidize the colleges' agricultural "departments."

After the initial work attendant to introducing bills, negotiating the committee hearings, writing the report, and seeing the bill favorably reported to the whole House on March 3, 1886, Atherton found that the legislative process had stalled. The Hatch Act did not come to a debate, much less a vote, during the first session, which adjourned in July 1886. Another important bill introduced by Hatch's committee—to promote the Department of Agriculture to cabinet status—crowded the station bill off the House calendar.[54] The Atherton group blamed Hatch himself, however. Shortly after the Hatch bill had been reported to the whole House, President Charles K. Adams of Cornell informed Atherton that "a general apathy exists and nobody seems to think it his particular business to champion the cause."[55] In July, Henry Alvord wrote Atherton that he had "no faith in General Hatch's interest or action on that subject" and said, "My opinion of him has certainly now been fully justified. We have got to find a man like Cullen, who will make the bill his special aim, watch over its progress and push it to final issue."[56] Meanwhile, the Senate Agriculture Committee, under George, had reported the Cullen bill (S. 372) favorably to that chamber on April 21, and a brief discussion of the measure had begun just before Congress adjourned.[57]

The final push for passage of the Hatch bill came in late fall of 1886, in anticipation of the start of the second session of the Forty-ninth Congress. The bill's enactment did not come easily. Agricultural interests, the Grange in particular, began to exert their influence. The commissioner of agriculture, Norman Colman, tried to shape the legislation more to his liking. Atherton and his colleagues were on the scene for much of the winter of 1887, as the legislative theater shifted from the House to the Senate. Despite his careful stage-management of the legislation since the 1885 convention, Atherton and his committee soon found themselves fighting a defensive battle, as the issue became that of who would control the experiment stations—the colleges, the state, the agricultural interests, or the Department of Agriculture.

In a circular dated December 1, 1886, calling for "renewed interest" in the bill's behalf, Atherton noted that he expected a House vote on the measure before the holiday recess. He added, "Those of us who are in the best position to judge believe it can become a law before

March fourth, if its friends will use proper efforts." Atherton's prophecy was realized, but not quite in the manner he had expected.[58]

In November 1886, the Grange announced its support for the Hatch bill, pending certain alterations. First, it recommended that federal funds go directly to the experiment stations existing independently of land-grant colleges, which affected about half the fifteen stations then in existence. (Particularly in the Northeast, most stations operated under independent boards and not in conjunction with colleges.) The second recommendation was to funnel the federal funds directly to state boards of agriculture, which would determine where the station funds should go. This plan permitted a recision of funds should the land-grant college administering the station ever be found wanting. And states without a college were free to establish a station without even having to connect it to a college.[59] In short, the Grange proposals severely undermined the college-station nexus.

The commissioner of agriculture also wanted the state to determine which institution would receive the funds. He proposed the establishment of a special central office to act as a clearinghouse. He also proposed that $5,000 in the first year and $1,000 in following years be used for station construction and maintenance. This was in some respects a threat to the colleges, for it provided the states with considerable means to build a new facility. The states thus would be less motivated to use a college's facilities for the sake of economy.

Added to this was the interest of the agricultural press, exhorting for the bill's passage. Agricultural organizations besieged Congress with petitions for the bill's enactment. Most ominous for the colleges, however, was the Grange's decision to send a delegation to Washington, D.C., "to provide a counterbalance to the committee of college presidents."[60]

The House did not take up the Hatch bill when the session opened, as Atherton had anticipated. On January 17, 1887, the Senate began debating the bill. The first argument came over a clause Atherton had inserted into the Cullen bill, giving the commissioner of agriculture the authority "to determine annually a standard of valuation of the ingredients of commercial fertilizers." Senator George Hoar, who in the 1870s had championed the common school legislation in the U.S. House, objected to the idea, claiming that the differences in local soil and climatic conditions would render a national standard useless.[61]

Attuned to the general dissatisfaction with this idea, Atherton had prepared an entirely new section for substitution. Atherton's amendment, introduced by Senator George F. Edmunds of Vermont, left out all references to fertilizers. It provided what appeared to be a limited concession to the commissioner of agriculture's desire for some authority in determining the research agenda of the stations. However, the clause precluded him from mandating the agenda without the consent of the station. Atherton's amendment called for the commissioner to "lay out certain lines of work and methods" for the stations, to an extent that would consume "at least" 15 percent of their appropriation. To become effective, the commissioner's suggestions required the approval of a station's "commission," composed of its various directors. This amendment also opened the doors, albeit indirectly, for the creation of a national fertilizer standard to facilitate uniform analysis. Ultimately, however, the Atherton amendment was not incorporated, having been deemed to give excessive authority to the Department of Agriculture.[62]

Other objections arose during the Senate debate, many of them related to the degree of federal control the bill implied. The intention of the bill to funnel the appropriation directly from the federal treasury to the experiment station upset Senator Joseph R. Hawley of Connecticut, who believed the funds should be sent to the state for disbursement. Senator John J. Ingalls of Kansas objected not to the fact that a federal appropriation would be sent to his state's college, but to the attachment of conditions with the money. Senator Henry L. Dawes of Massachusetts, reflecting the Grange's position, sought to amend the bill so that experiment stations existing independently of land-grant colleges would benefit from the act—to which Senator Morrill objected strenuously. Nevertheless, sentiment was strong to provide the states with the latitude to make the decision as to where the funds ought to go.

Other objections arose over the perceived federal intrusion into what was deemed to be the states' prerogative: public education. Hawley argued that it was "substantially a reconstruction of a State college without the permission of the state." Days later, sharp arguments about whether the colleges were providing adequate agricultural instruction took place, with Morrill reminding the Senate that the colleges were never intended to "force every student enrolled to study agriculture—merely to provide them with the opportunity to do so."[63]

In the interim between January 17 and January 26, when the Senate again debated the measure, the Grange and Atherton's legislative committee met several times to reach a compromise over the issue of station control. In fact, some evidence attests to Atherton's "consultation with the agriculturalists" before the Senate debates began.[64] In any event, one provision of the compromise was to allow the states to award the funds to stations established under independent boards, as the Grange had wanted.[65]

After the debate picked up again on January 26, the Senate agreed to two other amendments. It removed all references to fertilizer valuations and extended the benefits of the act to "agricultural departments" of state universities as well as to the land-grant or "agricultural colleges." Atherton's amendment and all references to "aiding" the Department of Agriculture were also dropped, in deference to those objecting to excessive federal control.[66] Though the final measure provided more autonomy for the college vis-à-vis the Department of Agriculture, Atherton and his colleagues emerged from the fray with a bill that had overturned the land-grant colleges' exclusive claim to the stations.

With its emendations, Senate bill 372 passed the Senate without a recorded vote on January 27, 1887.[67] The bill came back to the House two days later and was referred to Hatch's Agriculture Committee. It came to the full House for final action on February 25 and passed overwhelmingly without debate, 152 to 12. "Those [the Senate's] amendments are not entirely unacceptable to individual members upon the floor or to a part of the Committee on Agriculture," Hatch said, "but in view of the few remaining days of the session the Committee on Agriculture have instructed me to present the bill as it passed in the Senate."[68] At Hatch's arrangement, Atherton explained the fine points of the act to President Grover Cleveland, who signed it into law on March 2, 1887.

Except for the Grange amendment—which allowed the states to apply the funds to independent stations and to use their discretion in determining whether future agricultural schools should be awarded station funds—the Hatch Act retained much of Atherton's original intent, as he expressed it in the Cullen bill. For example, it required that stations established in conjunction with the colleges be subordinate to the larger institutions, a critical relationship to Atherton. And Atherton's conception of agricultural science—to promote "scientific investigation and experiment respecting the principles and application of agricultural science" in addition to solving the practical problems of farmers—also stood intact.

The authority of the commissioner of agriculture also was held in check, even more so than Atherton had thought prudent. With the imperative of setting a standard valuation for fertilizers now removed, and with the amendment giving him the right to determine "at least 15 percent" of the station's research agenda (with local consent) also defeated, the commissioner's role had been reduced to less than even the Cullen bill had intended. Atherton was willing to entertain a station role limited to "aiding" the Agriculture Department in acquiring and disseminating information, but even that had been removed. Now the commissioner was permitted only to furnish forms for tabulating experimental results and to advise stations about certain lines of research they might undertake. There his role ended. Atherton's provision that bulletins be published every three months was kept, as was the stations' franking privilege for distributing them.

The source of the annual $15,000 appropriation was altered. It was now to come from proceeds generated by sales of public lands, rather than directly from the U.S. treasury. Atherton's construction and maintenance provision — $3,000 the first year, $750 a year thereafter — also was maintained. Further, the Senate retained his provision to deduct from the ensuing year's appropriation those funds left unspent from the current year.[69] There was a final deficiency, however. The act authorized money but failed to appropriate it, or so the secretary of the treasury ruled. An intensive lobbying effort was required to produce the special act of February 1, 1888, to start the flow of Hatch Act funds. An entire year's research agenda was disrupted by the absence of the expected funds.

In the meantime, the on-site work required to shepherd the Hatch bill through Congress had been prodigious. Willits, Atherton's colleague on the legislative committee, reported that he had spent seven weeks in Washington, D.C., during the winter of 1885–86, when the Hatch bill was introduced, and ten days in the winter of 1887 — only to produce an act "in mutilated form." Atherton left no account of his investment of time, but as de facto leader of the three-man committee, it is likely he spent at least as much time in Washington as did Willits. Atherton had the advantage of proximity (Willits worked in Michigan) as well as the added desire to see the bill he had recreated brought to fruition. And as desecrated as the act may have seemed to them at the time, it would probably have emerged in a form of little relevance to the land-grant colleges had not Atherton and Willits been at hand.[70]

Implications of the Hatch Act,
and the Association's Founding Convention

Atherton was greatly disturbed by the treasury secretary's ruling that the Hatch Act failed to appropriate funds. The practical effect of such a ruling was to deter for another year the operation, if not the establishment, of stations and the conduct of field experiments at many land-grant colleges. In a letter to the treasury secretary in mid-March 1887, Atherton asked him to reverse his ruling in view of clear congressional intent to provide a continuing annual appropriation. He pointed to a legal precedent in which similar contradictions were resolved by "a reference to the journals of Congress," and he urged the treasury secretary to inspect the record.[71] His letter, however, was to no avail.

Atherton's next step was to call a meeting of delegates from agricultural colleges and experiment stations, the last meeting of which had occurred in July 1885. The campaign for the Hatch Act had precluded such a meeting, but with its passage, and with questions of interpretation and implementation looming large, Atherton called for a meeting of delegates on April 13–14, 1887, in Washington, D.C.[72] For reasons unknown, the convention did not materialize.

As chairman of the executive committee, Atherton found out that a fall meeting best suited the delegates' schedule and issued a circular calling for a convention on October 18–20, 1887, at the Department of Agriculture. The circular promised the attendance of the commissioner of agriculture, a report from the committee on legislation, and at least three papers relating to experiment stations: Cook's "Limitations of Experiment Work," Atwater's "Coordination of Work in Agricultural Experimenting," and Johnson's "Successful Conduct of Experiment Stations."

The delegates focused on adopting a plan for implementing the Hatch Act at land-grant colleges with experiment stations. The adoption of the four-point plan has been characterized by one scholar as a victory for the scientists and a defeat for the presidents,[73] although an earlier account portrayed the convention as being dominated by the presidents.[74] Indeed, the committee of five that came up with the plan included four college presidents. In any event, the convention adopted the plan, which was designed to ensure (1) that Hatch Act funds were used exclusively to advance agricultural research and experimentation,

(2) that the station's financial records were kept separate from the college's, (3) that the station would be directed by a "recognized official head . . . on an equal footing with the other heads of departments . . . whose time shall be chiefly devoted to this department," and (4) that the publications of the station be kept separate from those of the college.[75]

The third point—that there would be a department head for the station—consumed almost a day of discussion. The scientists insisted that this measure would ensure that each college-station would employ at least one full-time research scientist, preventing a redirection of Hatch Act funds elsewhere. Atherton and Willits, joined by Adams of Cornell, argued against such a measure. The appropriation of college funds, they felt, was the president's, not the scientists', prerogative. They favored a plan calling for a controlling board of directors for the station rather than a single director or department head, but their argument did not prevail.[76]

The convention also organized itself into a permanent organization: the Association of American Agricultural Colleges and Experiment Stations (or the Association), the first peer organization of higher education institutions in the nation. There is no evidence to suggest why the misnomer (as Atherton and other presidents had long claimed) of "Agricultural Colleges" was selected. Perhaps the colleges sought to identify themselves in the strongest possible ways as the natural complement to the experiment stations, creating a nexus in nomenclature that was absent from the legislation. The Hatch Act did not create an organic relationship between colleges and stations, except in instances where the colleges already had established stations. Stations existing independently of land-grant colleges could continue to do so. Furthermore, states in which no station existed were also free to establish stations however they wished; the act did not require that a station be placed under the control of a land-grant college.

The name might also have represented an effort to mollify the Grange and other antagonistic agricultural organizations and to identify strongly with the Department of Agriculture, itself the object of a grass-roots legislative effort to attain cabinet status. At the very least, the name suggested a united front of two distinct but roughly equivalent and functionally related institutions working to address the problems of American agriculture.

That equivalence was borne out in the Association's constitution, which Atherton had drafted. Each college receiving funds from the

1862 Morrill Act was entitled to one vote, as was each experiment station "established under State or Congressional authority."[77] The constitution called for a slate of officers to include a president, five vice-presidents, and a secretary-treasurer. The association also established an executive committee composed of the president, the secretary-treasurer, and five additional members, not necessarily the five vice-presidents. The executive committee was empowered to select its own chairman from any of its members. The executive committee elected at the founding convention included George Atherton, Charles Adams of Cornell, Edwin Willits of Michigan, James Patterson of Kentucky, Charles Dabney of Tennessee, Charles Thorne of Ohio, and Henry Alvord, then of Massachusetts, as chairman. Atherton, who had been serving as chairman of the executive committee, was elected as the founding president of the association and, he recalled, "re-elected the second year for the expressed purpose of recognizing his services in securing the passage of the 'Hatch Act.' "[78]

Whatever its several perceived imperfections at the time—depending on one's point of view—the Hatch Act is regarded as landmark legislation for a number of reasons. First, despite the attempt to limit the Department of Agriculture's power, the act set in motion the forces that vastly increased that power. What had been a single central agency was now the clearinghouse for a national network of agricultural research facilities, and the Department's authority vis-à-vis the stations began to gradually increase. The Adams Act of 1906 would mark the culmination of the Agriculture Department's power in Atherton's lifetime. Through it, the stations would see their annual federal annuity double, but the department would exact the authority to control precisely how the additional funds were used.[79]

The attempt of the Grange to perpetuate, at the discretion of the state, independent experiment stations also backfired. The practical effect of the Hatch Act was to meld the stations into the colleges, and very quickly so. At the time of the Hatch Act, eight stations were connected to land-grant colleges, and seven existed independently; systematic agricultural research without a designated station was being conducted in thirteen states, mainly at the land-grant colleges. In 1888, Louisiana set the pace, taking its two existing independent stations, creating a third, and attaching all three to its land-grant college. In addition, new experiment stations were created under the auspices of land-grant colleges in northern states where independent stations had also existed: Massachusetts, New Jersey, and Connecticut.

In twenty-four other states and one territory, experiment stations were established at land-grant colleges. By 1893, fifty-five stations were in operation nationwide, forty-nine of which received Hatch Act funds. By 1906, the year of Atherton's death, sixty stations existed, fifty-five of which had an attachment of some sort to land-grant colleges.[80]

The Hatch Act also legitimatized agricultural science as an intrinsic part of the entire agricultural enterprise and helped to establish scientists as the source of knowledge and the engine of agricultural productivity. Not only had the scientists established themselves as a professional class, but their value was beginning to be appreciated by the entire agricultural community. The payoff would not be immediate, not in the nineteenth century at least, but the work of the station scientists would provide the underpinning for American agricultural productivity in the twentieth century.

Despite the Grange amendment, the Hatch Act also placed the federal government's imprimatur firmly on the land-grant colleges. Atherton and his colleagues had argued for fifteen years that the Morrill Act of 1862 implied a continuing federal relationship with the colleges; the Congress that had brought the "national schools of science" into being, they charged, had a continuing responsibility to nurture them. The Hatch Act gave great credence to their argument. Now they "possessed what amounted to a federal commission to serve as the site for American agricultural science."[81]

Important as it was, the Hatch Act may have been overvalued by some scholars. Earle Ross, for instance, states categorically: "The stations brought system and gave direction to the colleges, and more than any other factor assured their continuation,"[82] but that argument is too facile. The colleges found the Hatch Act problematical. While the act provided a sorely needed financial undergirding, it did so in only one area, agricultural research, in which many colleges had already been making gradual progress. Indeed, the Pennsylvania State College had been conducting rudimentary plant variety and fertilizer tests for nearly thirty years before the Hatch Act.[83] The Hatch Act did very little, in a direct and immediate way, for agricultural instruction, the colleges' Achilles' heel with agricultural groups. Many experiment station scientists were required to provide instruction as well as research, but the apparent strengthening of the instructional component did not trigger a concomitant increase in agricultural students. By the late nineteenth century, no more than 2 percent of the total college-going population chose to study agriculture, and less than 2 percent of college graduates chose agriculture as a career.[84]

If the Hatch Act "assured" the colleges' continuation, it did so, at least for the time being, in unintended fashion. In many instances, the colleges appropriated Hatch Act funds for other purposes. Some did it subtly, others blatantly, "charging insurance, a portion of the president's salary, students' laboratory supplies—in one case, even a carpet, to the Hatch fund."[85] Indeed, a number of presidents, though not Atherton, also assumed the title of station director, which might have galled some of their station's staff. Henry Alvord took the titles of president and station director at Maryland Agricultural College though he was an agricultural researcher by vocation. Henry H. Goodell of Massachusetts, an ancient and modern language professor by discipline, also retained both titles. So did George Fairchild of Kansas State, Charles L. Ingersoll of Colorado, and Hiram Hadley of New Mexico, among others.[86]

Aside from the instances of dubious allocation of funds, the Hatch Act benefited the colleges in another way: by freeing them to use the funds previously spent on agricultural instruction and research for other academic programs. In a real sense, the Hatch Act provided to the colleges a federally subsidized academic "department"—agriculture. In fact, Atherton had suggested that agriculture was but an "incidental" (to use his word) part of the total land-grant college mission and that the colleges had diverted a disproportionate share of their own resources to serving the demands of their agricultural constituencies.

These points are made not to denigrate the importance of the Hatch Act for land-grant colleges but to place it in its proper perspective. Critical as the act was, it was not—in and of itself—the saving grace of the land-grant movement. Indeed, the act's greatest significance lay in what it did for American agriculture. The colleges would require a broader program of assistance before they could begin to emerge as consequential collegiate institutions. This assistance would come with the Morrill Act of 1890.

Curiously, when Atherton discussed the implications of the Hatch Act, one of the two accomplishments of which he was most proud—he omitted any mention of the measure's impact on the land-grant colleges. Instead, he valued the act for its contributions to agricultural science and to the agencies thereof:

> The results of this measure have been far beyond the most sanguine expectations of those who were interested in securing

its passage. . . . These Stations have secured the confidence of the great body of the Agricultural people on the one side and of those who are engaged in scientific investigation on the other side. They have revolutionized the character and scope of the Agricultural press. . . . They have greatly enlarged, if not revolutionized, the work and shaped the methods of the . . . Department of Agriculture, and they have given an impulse to the action of European and other foreign governments in the same direction to such an extent that there is today no more promising field of research in any branch of applied science than those which relate directly to the development of Agriculture.[87]

But the telling blow to Ross's contention that the Hatch Act was key to assuring the colleges' continuation may have been delivered by the Association's executive committee in its testimony for the 1890 Morrill Act: "These stations, while they have increased the responsibility and usefulness of the colleges, have not given the colleges any added resources for their own proper work."[88]

The Second Morrill Act

NO ONE WAS ENTIRELY SATISFIED with the compromise that was the Hatch Act, so the necessity of amending the legislation to include language that would appropriate the funds annually gave rise to the idea of improving the act through additional amendments when Congress reconvened in December 1887. At its annual meeting that same year, the Grange had condemned the Hatch Act altogether. It recommended that colleges found to be "in violation" of the 1862 Morrill Act be penalized by having their experiment stations placed under the direct control of the Department of Agriculture. Because in the Grange's eyes most if not all land-grant institutions had defied the intent of the Morrill Act, that recommendation would have destroyed the college-station relationship. Even for those rare colleges found to be in compliance with the act, the Grange nevertheless would have placed their stations under supervision of the Department of Agriculture.[1]

The commissioner of agriculture, Norman Colman, also sought

changes that would expand the role of his department beyond that of handmaiden to the stations. He wanted to establish a central experiment station in Washington, D.C., that would focus on research questions of national concern. He also wanted the authority—implicitly denied him by the act—to coordinate the work of the stations, or at least to be a part of that process.[2] At its October 1887 convention, the Association of American Agricultural Colleges and Experiment Stations had agreed that an informational clearinghouse within the Department of Agriculture would be desirable, but it expressed concern about federal control over the research agenda.

George Atherton and his colleagues also sought to amend the bill, although, beyond the necessity of specifying an annual appropriation, the nature of their desired emendation is unknown. In any event, Senator William Hatch himself seemed willing to entertain Atherton's suggestions. In December 1887 he offered to "meet . . . at an early day and confer personally in regard to the further legislation necessary to perfect the Experimentation Bill."[3]

Atherton and others on the Association's executive committee worked assiduously to bring about the amendment that would start the flow of Hatch Act funds. On January 1, 1888, the executive committee set up a field office in Washington, D.C., with "one to three members" continuously on duty. On January 18, the House amended the act to authorize the annual appropriations, and on January 30 the Senate concurred. Henry Alvord later reported to the full Association that "but for the presence in Washington of the . . . representatives of this Association . . . the desired appropriation would not have been made in time for the respective stations to have organized for the agricultural season of 1888."[4] Beyond the authorization of funds, however, Congress was unwilling to amend the act. From time to time, the Association would discuss the possibility of changes but pull back just as quickly, deferring to sentiments expressed by President Merrill Gates of Rutgers: "Let us not attempt the task of tinkering with a measure of that kind until we have worked under it long enough to find out how it works."[5]

Although the issue of Hatch Act emendation was largely resolved by the winter of 1888, the question of station operation was not. The Association's October 1887 convention had laid out broad guidelines for using Hatch Act funds, while providing a strong measure of station autonomy within the college context. But the more prosaic issues of station operation were yet to be addressed. The Association had asked its three scientific presenters—George Cook, Wilbur Atwater, and Samuel Johnson—to prepare a report on station operation. The trio concluded that the stations' mission must be broad enough to accommodate several functions. They recommended that stations address themselves to "things immediately useful," of "direct practical importance," and that they give such matters a disproportionate amount of attention. They also urged that "the highest scientific ideal" be maintained, and admonished that the future of the stations would depend on their ability to conduct serious research and make contributions of permanent value. The stations also were reminded of their duty to teach as well as experiment, and to bring that information "home" to the farmer, thus ensuring the needed measure of public support.[6]

Yet the report stopped short of discussing some important particulars. For example, it specified no procedures by which the commissioner of agriculture might implement his advisory powers, it avoided any suggestions as to how the working relationship between station and college might be best effected, and it offered no advice for working with the farm population.

In part because of the shortcomings of the report, the questions of station operation and of the college-station relationship would loom large during Atherton's two-year Association presidency. It would not be the smoothest of tenures, largely because of the Association's tendency to divide members into two camps: college presidents and experiment station scientists.

Atherton's founding presidency began at the October 1887 convention. The Association did not meet again until January 1–3, 1889, in Knoxville, Tennessee, where Atherton was reelected to another one-year term. The third annual convention took place only eleven months later, November 12–15, 1889, in Washington, D.C. During that time, Atherton's leadership was tested, but he used his office effectively to advance his vision of the Association. He strived to preserve a unity of college and station interests that he deemed essential if the Association were to successfully manage their emerging relationships with the federal government and with each other.

Atherton considered college-station unity important for several reasons. First was the fluid situation in the nation's capital. In October 1888, the Office of Experiment Stations was formed within the Department of Agriculture in response to the Hatch Act, and soon after, in February 1889, the department itself was elevated to cabinet status.[7]

Second, Atherton viewed the experiment station as a subsidiary of the college, not as a co-equal institution. He believed disunity would prove inimical to college interests, though it might be not quite so injurious to the stations. Finally, from the standpoint of educational theory, Atherton believed the college's teaching function and the station's research function complemented each other perfectly, and that thus a yoking of the two would improve each other's effectiveness.

In the meantime, station directors were seeking to transform the association into a professional scientific organization. To an extent they succeeded, though not as fully as they might have preferred. In addition, by the time of the 1889 Washington convention, there already was a feeling among some college presidents that the time had come to bow out of the Association and give it over to the station scientists, the essential work of establishing the stations having been completed. Such were the forces with which Atherton had to contend, but he did that successfully. In fact, he held the Association together during the November 1889 convention, preserving an organization that was on the verge of splitting into mutually exclusive sections.[8]

Atherton also figured prominently in securing the passage of the second Morrill Act, which he considered one of his most significant accomplishments. Introduced with little warning on March 25, 1890 (although Atherton may have had something to do with its introduction at that time), the bill galvanized the Association's executive committee members. Their first reaction was to turn to Atherton for guidance. With his help, and with the assistance of a cadre of land-grant presidents, the bill was signed into law only five months later, on August 30, 1890. The act would do for the colleges what the Hatch Act could not. It provided annual appropriations beginning at $15,000 and eventually leveling off at $25,000 for "instruction in agriculture, the mechanic arts, the English language, and the various branches of mathematical, physical, natural and economic science . . . and to the facilities for such instruction."

With the financial and psychological stimulus provided by the 1890 Morrill Act, the colleges' permanence would be assured.

Atherton's Association Presidency
and the Association Agenda

The founding convention of the Association of American Agricultural Colleges and Experiment Stations in October 1887 focused mainly on discussing the Hatch Act. The second annual convention, held in Knoxville, Tennessee, on January 1–3, 1889, was by contrast dedicated to defining the organization: What was the Association to be and to do, and how should it organize itself to accomplish its objectives? Atherton charted a sublime course in his presidential address: "What is the meaning of this Association and what is its future?" As he saw it, the Association's mission was to facilitate accumulation of knowledge about the fundamental processes of life itself and to put that knowledge to work in the service of mankind.

Atherton first used his address to define land-grant institutions in the broadest sense. He stressed that the 1862 Morrill Act required the colleges to teach such "branches of learning" as are related to agriculture and the mechanic arts. To Atherton, this not only excluded a purely vocational approach to teaching agriculture and engineering, but also meant an emphasis on teaching the undergirding scientific disciplines. For agriculture, these disciplines included "the natural and physical sciences, chemistry, botany, zoology, biology, etc."; for engineering, they included "the mathematical and physical sciences."

The Hatch Act, he suggested, should be interpreted in a similar spirit, along the broader lines the 1862 Morrill Act intended. The purpose of the experiment stations was "not to teach" (in terms of providing general instruction to farmers), but to investigate "the hidden secrets of the laws of disease as well as the laws of health; the laws of death . . . as well as the laws of life throughout the whole realm of nature." As Atherton saw it, the charge of the experiment stations was grandly scientific rather than immediately practical. Basic science must be pursued first and foremost, and applications would develop therefrom. "What is the great and mysterious force that we call life?" he asked rhetorically. "What is the secret of all these forces? These, and such as these, are the questions which the experiment stations—or, as I should prefer to call them, the research stations—are called to investigate."

Finally, Atherton spoke to the core purpose of the Association: "What higher ambition for man can there be than this: to bring himself into the presence of the very thoughts of the Creator, to see with the creative vision and to use his intelligence for the elevation and help of his fellow man! That I say with all reverence is the true aim and genius of this Association." On a more prosaic level, he noted that the Association already represented some 350 to 400 men "engaged in this grand mission." Their purpose in meeting was "to compare results and to encourage one another, to point out difficulties and indicate lines of work for the future." The relationship with the Department of Agriculture, he said, would benefit both the Association and the Agriculture Department.[9]

Atherton's purpose in such a speech, devoid of particulars, was to create a sense of unity among presidents and scientists alike based on sharing the most profound mission: an investigation into the essence of life and nature, an understanding of which would usher in a new age of progress. It is not likely that Atherton spoke in these terms merely to mollify the scientists, because his conception of collegiate purpose was to instill an understanding of broad and basic principles. The experiment stations, being a "department" of the college, must reflect the same broad purpose.

The Association spent considerable time discussing the relationship of the experiment stations to the Department of Agriculture. The Office of Experiment Stations had been established only three months prior to the convention, and delegates suggested that it could help best by acting as a bureau of information, serving as a clearinghouse and exchange between the stations, and focusing on universal problems of agricultural research methodology.[10] The new director of the office, Wilbur O. Atwater, formerly of the Connecticut Agricultural Experiment Station, noted that his budget was small and that his operation required further funding before it could begin to function effectively as a conveyor of scientific information to the stations.

The Association also voiced concern about lodging excessive power in a central federal agency such as the Department of Agriculture, remaining wary of the department's desire to control the research agenda. Although Atwater, a "station man" himself, could reassure his colleagues that he had no such intention, they were quick to remind him that the newly elected U.S. President, Benjamin Harrison, would be appointing a new commissioner (soon to be secretary) of agriculture. That new official could take the department in an entirely different direction. Delegates also expressed anxiety over the potential of the Office of Experiment Stations for transforming itself into a large, central experiment station, supplanting the role of the state stations. Despite that concern, the delegates had no problem with the scientific work being conducted by the Department of Agriculture, considering it to be complementary to their work in the field. In fact, the Association resolved that the department be maintained "as a scientific and economic department, on a basis analogous to those of the Geological and Coastal surveys, the Smithsonian Institution, National Museum, and weather service, and free from all political influences and considerations."[11]

The high drama of the Knoxville convention came in the form of a motion from Henry P. Armsby, director of Pennsylvania State College's

Fig. 8. **Henry Prentiss Armsby.**

experiment station, to amend the Association's constitution. Armsby intended to split the organization into two permanent sections. The first would be the "experiment station section," for station directors and their scientists. Armsby also wanted the sections to meet separately, discussing the interests of each in isolation from the other. Armsby felt the time had come to move beyond the focus on broad administrative and policy questions, and he considered it essential for the development of the stations to bring station researchers and directors into their own meetings to "talk shop."[12]

His proposal sparked a sharp reaction. "I do not think the time has come to split the Association into two associations of presidents on the one hand and directors on the other," said Charles Dabney, who functioned both as president of the University of Tennessee and as director of its experiment station. The Association voted to defer the matter until the next convention, on the condition that Armsby furnish a copy of the proposed amendment to the director of each station and the president of each college.[13]

The Atherton-Armsby polarity epitomized the tensions within the Association, because the two men wielded a disproportionate influence over the organization. In 1902, for example, Alvord reported:

> Twenty-one states have been represented once on the board of officers. . . . One state has been represented four times—the State of Pennsylvania. This state has had presidents twice [Atherton for two terms, Armsby for one], Vice-president once [Armsby], and secretary and treasurer three times [Armsby], and members of the executive committee three times [Atherton twice, Armsby once].[14]

Despite their differences over the structure and function of the Association, Atherton held Armsby in high professional regard. When Atherton recruited Armsby from the University of Wisconsin in 1887 to direct the new experiment station at the Pennsylvania State College, he knew he had attracted one of the premier agricultural scientists in the United States. In fact, Atherton's recruitment of Armsby was the culmination of a four-year effort. Atherton first angled for Armsby in the spring of 1883, anticipating that Penn State would get its state-funded experiment station momentarily. Armsby expressed strong interest in coming, noting, "My tastes are for experimental work rather than for teaching,"[15] but the governor's veto of Penn State's experiment station bill ended that possibility. Atherton's confidant, George Cook of Rutgers, soon afterward confirmed Armsby's reputation, and thus Atherton never lost sight of his future station director.[16] It was Armsby, however, who wrote to Atherton just after the Hatch Act was signed into law, to congratulate him and suggest that he would consider coming to Penn State, if invited, to accept the directorship of its new experiment station.[17]

Only thirty-four years old in 1887, Armsby came to the Pennsylvania State College with impeccable credentials: bachelor's degrees from Worcester Polytechnic Institute and from Yale; a Ph.D., also from Yale, from the Sheffield School under Samuel Johnson; additional study at the University of Leipzig, where he had begun research into what would become his field of renown, animal nutrition. Returning to the States in 1881, he served as professor of agricultural chemistry and vice-president of Connecticut Agricultural College at Storrs. From 1883 to 1887, he was associate director of Wisconsin's experiment station. Along the way, he had written one of the first scientific books on animal nutrition and digestion, *Manual of Cattle Feeding* (1880).[18]

A champion of science for its own sake, Armsby found himself at the head of a four-man agricultural department at the Pennsylvania State College, handling instruction as well as research and administration. He might have tensed a bit when Atherton said in his annual report for 1889 that he hoped to see the station "become more and more a department of instruction, so as to concentrate in it all the work of the College on the agricultural side."[19] At Knoxville, Atherton had sounded quite an opposite theme, charging the stations with a mission of basic scientific research. Yet Atherton would turn about at the November 1889 convention and rationalize that the teaching function, as well as the research function, was intrinsic to the experiment station.

Despite their differences of opinion, Atherton and Armsby were similar in other respects. Both were fiercely dedicated to their professions, and both insisted that their respective lines of work—land-grant education and agricultural science—be carried out in the most sublime fashion. Neither man was a narrow vocationalist, bound by a limited vision.

Their philosophical differences over the role of the experiment station never broke out into open warfare on the campus of the Pennsylvania State College, but tension did manifest itself from time to time, especially over the issue of station resources and finances. "For the past two years, I think that every one connected with our work has felt that we have carried it on at a disadvantage and has experienced a constant sense of effort and strain," Armsby wrote in 1896 to the executive committee of the college's board of trustees, for which Atherton was secretary. "I very much hope that it may be possible to better this condition of things and particularly to so increase the number of assistants." Things did not improve, largely because of the vagaries of state funding and of income derived from fertilizer analysis. Six months later, Armsby was forced to cut his staff from eighteen to sixteen and to reduce the salaries of others who remained. "There is a more or less prevalent feeling that the college is not devoting a due proportion of its funds to agriculture," he said. Nevertheless, Armsby and Atherton maintained a proper Victorian deference toward each other through-out a working relationship that spanned nearly two decades. Had the relationship become untenable, Armsby would not have remained at Penn State.[20]

Armsby, for his part, might have been pleased with Atherton's devo-tion to the cause of agricultural science. Atherton not only viewed the emerging discipline in the same elevated light as did Armsby,

Fig. 9. **Agricultural Experiment Station, The Pennsylvania State College.** The facility as it appeared in Henry Armsby's day. Built in 1888, and much altered through the years, the building remains in use today.

but he had worked relentlessly to help it mature. Atherton's pivotal work in the Hatch Act was well-known to Armsby, but his contributions had gone beyond that. In 1884, for example, Atherton, Dabney, and Alvord formed an association for publishing the new *American Journal for Agricultural Science*.[21] In the busy winter of 1887, when Atherton was leading the Association's Hatch Act campaign in Washington, D.C., he found the time to address the Ithaca Farmers' Institute. There he told the farmers: "It is not wise to keep our agricultural colleges purely trade schools. . . . We do not want a peasant class, nor a peasant education."[22]

In the winter of 1889, unbeknown to Atherton, a delegation of Association leaders met with President-elect Harrison to urge Atherton's nomination as U.S. secretary of agriculture. But James A. Beaver, then governor of Pennsylvania and president of the Pennsylvania State College board of trustees, wrote a shrewd letter to Harrison that may have destroyed Atherton's nomination:

> We need him here in Pennsylvania, and I would be very loathe to see him leave us. Although better fitted for the position . . . than any person of whom I have knowledge, it is nevertheless true that local and geographical reasons may (and perhaps ought to) weigh against his appointment. It is generally understood that Pennsylvania is to have another representative in your cabinet. . . . This fact would weight against the appointment of Dr. Atherton.[23]

Finally, in the spring of 1890, Atherton accepted a special assignment from Secretary of Agriculture Jeremiah M. Rusk to inspect and advise four southern experiment stations at Blacksburg, Virginia; Raleigh, North Carolina; Columbia, South Carolina; and Lake City, Florida, and to report his findings to the secretary upon his return. (Atherton was paid $10 a day plus expenses.)[24]

In sum, few land-grant college presidents could approach Atherton's knowledge of agricultural policy and of experimentation station structure and function. His working knowledge of the House and Senate agriculture committees, the legislative process, and the Department of Agriculture did not go unappreciated among experiment station scientists, including Armsby.

Atherton's leadership skills for keeping the Association intact were put to the test again at its third convention, November 12–15, 1889, in Washington, D.C. Armsby reintroduced his resolution to split the Association into a college section and a station section, noting that the intention was to accommodate the Association's functional dichotomy between administrative issues and scientific-technical issues. Armsby noted further that, on the station side, the chemists, botanists, and entomologists had already begun meeting informally at Association conventions to address the technical questions relevant to their disciplines. "But it is not only the chemists, botanists, and entomologists who need these discussions," Armsby declared. "The agriculturalists and [station] directors need them as well. They need to consider methods of experimenting as well as methods of administering affairs. . . . Those interested in agricultural instruction feel, I suppose, the need of discussing methods of teaching."[25]

For the sake of economy and scientific stimulation, Armsby wanted to group the agricultural disciplines together in one large section—a format that would hold particular advantages for station directors. "I, as a director, want to know what the horticulturalists, chemists, botanists, and agriculturalists are talking about," he said. "We want something more than printed results. We want to know the tone and spirit of the meetings. We want to hear the specialists talk and know what topics are uppermost in their minds."[26] Armsby also argued against the strong impulse to subdivide along disciplinary lines, as was already happening informally.

Others reacted sharply to Armsby's schismatic proposal, including some scientists. An agriculturalist at the University of Illinois station, George E. Morrow, said, "We ought to magnify the common interests rather than by subdivision risk what we recognize as a danger—the narrowing of the influence of the Association." Charles Dabney, president of the University of Tennessee, observed that the Association stood "at a crisis in its history": "It seems to me this should be a grand Association. It represents agricultural education and agricultural investigation in America."[27]

With his proposal, Armsby had hoped to drive a wedge between research and instruction, believing that the latter compromised the efficiency of the former. In fact, as one account suggests, his proposal brought to fruition might have revived the impulse for independent stations pursuing their own research agenda with little concern for the problems of the practical farmers.[28] To many of the college presidents, though not necessarily Atherton, a purely scientific mission for the stations was anathema—certainly not the way to please their states' agricultural constituencies. And despite his idealized view of the stations as basic science research units, Atherton was keenly alert to the political implications of their research agendas. Although he "thoroughly sympathized" with the intent of Armsby's proposal, he deemed its adoption a "serious mistake." He reminded the convention, "We have an outside relation, we must not forget—a relation to Congress and to the public, as we represent all the interests mentioned in the Hatch Act."[29] Finally, many of the college presidents were also carrying the title of station director, so they were hardly predisposed to a sectional format requiring them to be in two places at once—though Armsby had hoped to force their choice.

Atherton's carefully structured presidential speech, a clarion call for unity, helped further in precluding a division of the Association into mutually exclusive sections. First, he defined the college-station relationship as inseparable: "In the eye of the law wherever college and station exist as a part of the same organization the college is the station and the station is a department of the college." Stations, he added, had been "placed directly under the control of the college . . . or agricultural departments of colleges." In an interpretation that might have infuriated the Grange, Atherton considered the Hatch Act to be a form of institutional aid: "That intent was to enable the colleges to carry on such lines of experiment and research as it had been found they were not able to do with sources accruing from the original land grant."

He presented, once again, his liberal view of the 1862 Morrill Act and aligned with it his lofty sense of experiment station purpose: "to inquire into the operations of nature by the most searching processes and appliances which science can furnish, and, on the other hand, to subject the processes and the inductions of science to the tests of nature, in her free operations." Discussing the history of European stations, he emphasized the importance of taking the initial steps of the American system "from a right starting-point and in a right direction." The precedents in station policy and procedure, he offered, would be "of lasting influence in shaping the attitude and development both of the stations and colleges."

Then, his theme: The history of the land-grant movement, the law, and "the natural fitness of things" had conspired "to bring the colleges and the stations into close and intimate relations, and to make their work mutually helpful and their prosperity mutually dependent." With that evocation of determinism, Atherton proceeded to defuse the Armsby initiative of transforming the stations into exclusive research operations, but he departed from fact when he spoke of the intentions of senators in modifying the Hatch Act. They had, he averred, "no other thought that the stations they were establishing should be identified with teaching institutions." In fact, the compromise between the Grange and the Association had preserved the autonomy of independent stations. Nevertheless, Atherton pointed to the colleges—with "lands, buildings, libraries, apparatus, and . . . the only body of men who could be summoned to the new service of research"—as the natural complement to the stations. "A separation of the two . . . would have been for many years extremely injurious to the best interests of both," he claimed.

Just as the colleges and stations were designed to function in seamless complementarity, he suggested, so were the teaching and research designed to function within the experiment station. In addition to his perception of stations as basic science research units, Atherton viewed the station as a federally subsidized academic department of the college, and such a conception would naturally incorporate the teaching function. Now Atherton would rationalize his view. Pointing to pedagogical theory and practice, he maintained that "the mutually stimulating relations of teaching and investigation have often been dwelt upon by those who have been practically engaged in the two directions, as well as by all who have made a study of the philosophy of education." Thus, experiment stations should actively seek to enlist the services of the college's active teachers. As for the colleges, they "could do themselves no greater injury than to withhold their active teachers from participation in the work of research . . . in the stations." He then invoked the example of the German university, where "the teacher has been the investigator, and the investigator has been the teacher." "Thus it may ever be," he intoned. "Let the college investigate that it may teach well, and the station teach that it may investigate well, and this two-fold cord shall not easily be broken."[30]

To resolve the schismatic issue, the Association voted to establish not two sections, as Armsby had wanted, but five "permanent committees"— agriculture, botany, chemistry, entomology, and horticulture. The scientific exclusivity Armsby had sought was diluted by a provision entitling "each institution represented in the Association" (meaning each college as well as each station) to representation on each of the five permanent committees. Later, the Association added a sixth "standing committee" on college management, and Atherton was named chairman.[31]

In terms of the balance of power within the Association, the November 1889 convention created a watershed. If the Hatch Act of 1887 represented an unadulterated victory for the agricultural scientists and a compromise for the college presidents, the Washington convention of 1889 constituted a triumph of the college presidents and a setback for the agricultural scientists of the Armsby school. But the factions were not so clearly defined as the foregoing may suggest. Not every agricultural professor was a consummate researcher like Armsby. Even within the smaller universe of "station men" who attended Association meetings, Armsby's was a minority viewpoint. His voice was, however, the wave of the future, as stations eventually would succeed in divesting themselves of any classroom or instructional duties. And in 1903 would come the split into the two sections Armsby had desired.

For the time being, there was great utility in keeping the fledgling Association strongly unified. The new assistant secretary of agriculture, for example, had come from the Association's ranks: Edwin Willits, formerly the president of Michigan Agricultural College and a key participant on Atherton's Hatch Act legislative committee. With another from its ranks having been chosen to direct the new Office of Experiment Stations, Wilbur Atwater, the Association was already beginning to shape the character, and by implication the policy, of a Department of Agriculture that had just been elevated to cabinet status. The Association's executive committee was not reluctant to boast that "it is really owing to the existence of this Association and its active influence that the scientific divisions of the Department hold their present satisfactory status, and that a selection was made of an Assistant Secretary of that Department so fully in harmony with this Association."[32] Yet Assistant Secretary of Agriculture Willits, who attended the convention, might have galled Armsby with his views on still another function for the new experiment stations, public service: "I believe that they should go to the people in their territory, not only by means of bulletins and the press, but in persons and in voice."[33]

Important work was accomplished in determining a division of labor between the experiment stations and the Office of Experiment Stations. Wilbur Atwater, director of the office, suggested that the primary obligation was to "confine its work to a comparatively limited number of important problems which it may reasonably hope to solve to the lasting benefit of the agriculture of its state." This immediacy, however, created the danger of failing to pursue "the larger and more profound problems and to study them in the way that will be in the long run most effective and most creditable." It was this latter function—of studying the larger scientific and methodological questions—that Atwater proceeded to stake out for the Office of Experiment Stations.[34]

For Atherton, it was time to step down from a two-term presidency and go off the executive committee. He did, however, assume the chairmanship of the new Committee on College Management (later the Committee on College Work). He left Washington, D.C., with a sense of gratification at having helped reshape the Association in a way that would allow for technical discussions while preserving its essential unity and future effectiveness. "The seeds of disintegration would very soon have begun to germinate had not some such reorganization as has been provided for here been effected," he said in his parting message.[35]

Campaign for the Second Morrill Act

In his personal memorandum of 1905–6, Atherton briefly described his role in the passage of the 1890 Morrill Act. He claimed credit for helping to father the Morrill "educational fund" bills whose genealogy stretched back to 1872, and there is evidence that he substantially modified, if not actually drafted, two of Morrill's bills introduced in 1873 and 1875.[36] The successful Morrill bill of 1890, however, differed in one important way from all its predecessors, and the difference led to its passage: it contained no provision to aid the nation's common schools, as had all of Morrill's previous educational fund bills. Ironically, Morrill, a master legislative tactician, subsequently received criticism for his "lack of political foresight" in combining aid to common schools and land-grant colleges in a string of unsuccessful bills over an eighteen-year period.[37]

But this time Morrill approached the matter differently. On March 25, 1890, he introduced Senate bill 3256, which in the fashion of its predecessors provided that the proceeds of public-land sales and a portion of revenue from land-grant railroad companies be used for land-grant colleges and public education. It differed, however, in that it gave the colleges rather than the public schools preferential treatment. Each college was to receive $25,000 a year from the federal sources. On April 30, a substitute bill (S. 3714) was introduced, intended to aid only the land-grant colleges, and no mention of the public schools. Atherton claimed no credit in the writing of either bill, but he was actively involved in their promotion. He recalled:

> I was able to render a public service of almost equal importance [to the Hatch Act] in aiding to secure the passage of the "Morrill Act" of 1890. I had been closely associated with Senator Morrill ever since 1873, when he accepted as his own a bill which I drafted and which, with modifications, was kept alive Congress after Congress until the final passage of the Act of 1890. In that case, however, Mr. Morrill is entitled to full credit for the conception of this measure, and my own service consisted of a protracted and exacting legislative campaign, together with a body of able and devoted associates after Mr. Morrill had given up all hope of securing the passage of his bill during that Congress.[38]

Credit for the 1890 Morrill Act belonged, as Atherton suggested, to a cadre of land-grant college presidents from the Association of American Agricultural Colleges and Experiment Stations. At its fourth annual convention in November 1890, the executive committee reported that the Association had "materially contributed to the early enactment of the law" and had received a letter from Morrill in which he expressed his appreciation. Indeed, the Association was caught off guard by the introduction of the first bill and was subsequently surprised at how quickly its substitute moved through both houses of Congress—in just four months. Without specifying names, the executive committee cited the efforts of Association members who traveled to Washington to help with the lobbying effort:

> One made journeys of 1,000 miles each five times during the season. Another visited Washington eight times, occupying at least three days on each trip. Several practically surrendered their summer vacation and held themselves in readiness to respond to the call of the committee for work either at Washington or in their respective states. Among the most active

and effective workers were some who were unable to leave their homes.[39]

The linchpin of the legislative campaign was Henry E. Alvord, chairman of the executive committee and currently president of Maryland Agricultural College in College Park, on the outskirts of the District of Columbia. Other prominent participants were Merrill Gates, a vice-president of the Association and president of Rutgers (and, before year's end, the new president of Amherst College); Henry H. Goodell, president of Massachusetts Agricultural College; James H. Smart, president of the Association and president of Purdue; James K. Patterson, president of the State College of Kentucky; and William H. Scott, a member of the executive committee and president of Ohio State University. But no one save Alvord played a more strategic role than Atherton, who had just stepped down as president of the Association.

The college presidents mounted a shrewd campaign. Mindful of

Fig. 10.   **Henry Elijah Alvord.**

the roadblocks to the Hatch Act set up by the Grange, they met early on with the powerful farm organization and agreed to an amendment specifying the use for the funds. They also created a ubiquitous presence on Capitol Hill that, to at least one representative, seemed more like a swarm:

> I tell you, Mr. Speaker, that the only lobby I have seen at this session of Congress was the educational lobby, composed of the presidents of the agricultural institutions. They have haunted the corridors of the Capitol; they have stood sentinel at the door of the Committee on education; they have even interrupted the solemn deliberation of that body by imprudent and impudent communications.... My God, if there is any eagerness in the world it is possessed by these gentlemen who are presidents of these agricultural colleges.[40]

The story of the second Morrill Act began only two weeks after the Association's 1889 Washington convention. In early December, Morrill wrote to Atherton for guidance in the matter of legislation. He noted that President Harrison had promised not to "specially recommend" a bill by Senator William Blair of New Hampshire to aid common schools via direct payments from the U.S. treasury. Notwithstanding that pledge, Morrill said it was evident that Harrison preferred Blair's bill to the one Morrill was intending to introduce, which would provide revenue from public-land sales for land-grant colleges as well as for common schools. "I know nothing at all about what you and your friends have done upon the subject," Morrill said. "Please advise me at your earliest convenience."[41]

Several days later, Blair introduced a new common school bill in the Senate, a bill much along the lines of previous initiatives. Since the early 1870s, Blair, along with Senator George Hoar of Massachusetts, had functioned as the legislative champions of the common school movement, much as Morrill had served as the legislative godfather of the land-grant colleges.[42] Blair's bill (S. 185) attempted to provide $77 million from the U.S. treasury over eight years to establish and maintain public schools (common schools, grades 1–8). The funds were to be distributed to the states on the basis of their respective illiteracy rates.[43]

Like its predecessors, the Blair bill was defeated, on March 20 by a vote of 31 to 37. Senators objected to federal intrusion into what was

deemed to be the states' prerogative. They also found particularly
odious a provision calling for federal inspection of the common schools.
One senator noted that the Blair bill ventured into far deeper constitutional waters than the 1862 Morrill Act, which did not enter into the
"established system of common schools." Instead, "it established an
entirely distinct institution in each State . . . and then said that after-
wards it should be continued in accordance with the legislation of the
State. There was no inspection provided for."[44]

As a negative example, the Blair bill and the debate it sparked in
the Senate may have helped to smooth the way for Morrill's proposal.
In any case, Morrill's new bill, Senate bill 3256, was introduced on
March 25, only five days after the defeat of the Blair bill. A letter from
Alvord to Atherton suggested that the timing may have been more
than coincidence:

> It must have been just about the time of your last Washington
> visit — that the new Morrill Bill appeared — and I have it in
> my bones that the two events were somewhat related! At all
> events — said Bill had had your attention 'ere this. What should
> our Association do in the premises? Should we organize a
> vigorous supporting campaign at once? It is too important a
> subject to handle by correspondence between members of a
> widely scattered committee. Had I better not call the execu-
> tive committee to meet in Washington (and a few others) to
> consider this carefully?[45]

At Atherton's suggestion, the executive committee called a meeting
for April 23. The college presidents were also able to meet with
Morrill and Blair, who as chairman of the Senate Education and
Labor Committees would be key in getting the measure through
that body. Atherton could not attend the meeting, but Alvord reported to him, "The Morrill Bill is dead — beyond resurrection — in
its duplex form." It was evident that the provision to aid common
schools would ruin the bill in the Senate, especially in the wake
of the Blair bill's defeat. Added Alvord: "Whether we shall draw the
[new] bill, or help Blair and his Committee to do it — or leave it
all to them — or wait and hope for Senator Morrill to see new light
and make a new simple college bill, is the question remaining to
be decided this week."[46]

Morrill was wounded by the reluctance of Blair's committee to report his bill favorably. Henry Goodell of Massachusetts Agricultural College noted a "very delicate situation between Morrill and Blair," and Merrill Gates of Rutgers confirmed the situation. Gates, James Smart of Purdue, and Morrill's private secretary met, and the presidents were assured that Morrill would draft another bill, omitting the common school provision. After meeting with Morrill the next day, Gates reported that Morrill "would do what he could for us," although the senator did not seem disposed to pressing the matter. The presidents on site (Alvord, Gates, Goodell, Patterson, and Smart) concluded that their confidence now lay with the Senate Committee on Education and Labor rather than with Morrill.[47]

The Association presidents immediately drafted a letter to Blair's committee, stating that increased federal support was needed for two reasons: the increasing cost of scientific equipment and the "great increase in the number of students within the last few years." The subcommittee observed that the Hatch Act, "while increasing the responsibility and usefulness of the colleges," did not provide the institutions with "any added resources for their own proper work."[48]

However sympathetic Blair might have been, it was Morrill who introduced the substitute bill, Senate bill 3714, on April 30. The measure purported to establish an education fund and to apply the proceeds "of the public lands and receipts from certain land-grant railroad companies to the more complete endowment and support of colleges for the advancement of scientific and industrial education."[49] The bill, with no provision for the common schools, was referred to Blair's committee.

Blair quickly scheduled hearings on the measure, and Atherton left for Washington, D.C. By this time, the Grange had gotten wind of the bill, and Joseph H. Brigham, the grand master, showed up to testify. The Grange insisted on a short amendment that would specify where the funds were to be applied: "to instruction in agriculture and the mechanic arts and the facilities for such instruction." Blair's committee concurred, adding that the amendment had been endorsed by the land-grant college presidents who "manifested great zeal and anxiety about the bill, because these representatives of the farmers said that the farming interest felt that in many of the States these funds were being diverted from agricultural education."[50]

Other than that, the Association presidents were pleased with the hearings. They issued a circular reporting that "a very friendly feeling" emerged toward the colleges, "together with a recognition of their further needs."[51] And Alvord reported to Atherton in mid-May that the committee had made "no material change in the construction of the bill" and that "most of the amendments are those which were suggested while you were here two weeks ago."[52]

The committee report to accompany the bill, written by Blair, reflected the fine hand of the college presidents. The bill was intended to place the colleges "on a basis of assured support for all time." The report acknowledged the "long period of struggle" through which the colleges had passed. It also paid notice to their broad mission, encompassing not only agriculture "but scientific education as applied to the mechanical arts." Most significant, the report declared the colleges to be "the chief agencies through and by which the new and practical industrial education of the people is to be accomplished." It also noted that the cost of equipping the institutions was "at least ten times greater than that of an ordinary classical institution." The report added a cautionary note, however, about the expected decline in revenue from public-land sales, but declared the income from railroad revenue to be sufficient "for the next half century at least."[53]

Floor debate opened on June 14, 1890, resuming on June 21 and June 23, when the bill was passed. Initial opposition came on constitutional grounds, objecting to the federal intrusion of states' prerogatives. A section of the bill requiring the colleges to submit detailed annual reports to the secretaries of agriculture and the interior was deemed to "give the Federal Government supervision of education in the States." On another front, Senator Hoar of Massachusetts offered to amend the bill to include under the act whatever colleges—land-grant or otherwise—the states might deem appropriate. The Hoar amendment drew a stiff protest from the college presidents.[54]

The presidents also managed to revise the Grange amendment to which they had consented in early May. Now, the funds would be applied not only "to instruction in agriculture and the mechanic arts and the facilities for such instruction," but also to "the various branches of mathematical, physical, natural, and economic science, with special references to their applications in the industries of life, and in a thorough training in the English language." The Senate agreed to the addition, but the discussion prompted sharp opposition to what was perceived as an attempt by the federal government to prescribe the curriculum and to wrest control of the land-grant colleges from the states. Morrill rejoined that the amendment "is but a mere amplification of the original law," adding that the act of 1862 had specified broad areas of instruction as well.[55] Nevertheless, on Morrill's own motion, the entire amendment, now deemed superfluous, was stricken from the bill.[56]

In other revisions, the Senate removed as a revenue source the payments to the federal government from land-grant railroad companies. The contradictory section forbidding payment of funds to a state that maintained a segregated land-grant college, but considering the maintenance of separate land-grant colleges for blacks and whites to be compliant with the act, stood intact. A slight amendment was accepted to liberalize the definition of a black institution, most of which were below college grade, in order to qualify for the receipt of funds.[57]

The Morrill bill was passed by the Senate without a recorded vote on June 23.

The excision of the amendment to which the Grange and the college presidents had agreed—and that the presidents later tried to broaden—now began to cause problems. Senate bill 3714 intended to provide only "for the more complete endowment and maintenance of colleges for the benefit of agriculture and the mechanic arts." The National Farmers' Alliance had no complaint about the removal of the amendment, but the Grange reacted angrily at the new, less specific directive, voicing its displeasure to the House Education Committee. Buttonholing committee members after a morning session with Grange officials on July 2, Alvord found them unwilling to talk. He did manage to confer with John Trimble, secretary of the national Grange, and learned that the grand master, Joseph H. Brigham, was coming to Washington, D.C., to agitate further.[58]

The Senate's passage of the Morrill bill and the impending change of legislative theater brought a dramatic gathering of forces to Capitol Hill, none more impressive than those mounted by the Association. In the last week of June, the land-grant presidents stalking the halls of Congress included Gates, of New Jersey; Fairchild, of Kansas; Dabney, of Tennessee; William I. Chamberlain, of Iowa; Louis McLouth, of South Dakota; Peabody, of Illinois; Goodell, of Massachusetts; a proxy sent by Merritt C. Fernald, of Maine; the omnipresent Alvord; and of course Atherton.[59]

And from the university above Cayuga's waters came a voice from the past eager to do battle. With Charles Adams in England, Andrew White was temporarily attending to the president's duties at Cornell. "I see by the papers that the new Morrill Bill has passed the Senate: what are the prospects of its passing the House?" he wrote Atherton.

"Is there any opposition, and if so, in what quarter? And what can be done here to help matters along?" White was sensitive, however, to the "old jealousy" Cornell could stir up among certain elite private institutions in its reference group. He was wary of taking too prominent an interest in the measure for fear of awakening dormant antagonism.[60]

White did ask Atherton for the names of members of the House Education Committee and pledged to bring his influence to bear in quiet ways. White later reported that he had written to his congressman and other legislators. He seemed to think the Grange incursion of no real import, and had said as much to Morrill: "If this amendment simply restricts the appropriation to Agriculture and the Mechanic Arts, or to branches relating to Agriculture, so be it. The great point is, not to jeopardize the bill, and to accept whatever amendments are necessary."[61] But that was easy for White to say, given Cornell's endowment. By the end of July, White told Atherton that his congressman had assured him of the bill's success. Meanwhile, Alvord was managing the Association's campaign in Washington, D.C. He started to lay groundwork with the Grange, trying to arrange a meeting with Brigham. Alvord was also coordinating the arrival of college presidents to meet with key congressmen. "I did hope you would be here for a day before the end of the week for consultation," he wrote Atherton on July 26, "but greatly prefer your coming next week."[62]

The threat from the Grange was growing. An Association circular of August 6 warned members that Grange officials "are using their influence to secure a postponement of the bill until next session." The circular urged members to communicate with their congressmen and "ask that the bill be passed as it came from the Senate, and has been reported by the House Committee, with the 'Granger Amendment' added."[63] The next day, Alexis Cope, secretary of Ohio State University, met with Grange Secretary Trimble. Both agreed that Atherton needed to meet with Ohio Representative John D. Taylor, a friend of Brigham, and deter him from introducing amendments that would dictate the use of existing college funds theoretically freed for other uses by the infusion of new Morrill funds.[64] Atherton visited Taylor and apparently dissuaded him from introducing anything beyond the Grange amendment. On August 12, Alvord urged Atherton to come to Washington again, as "the Grangers have been ploughing deeper than we thought. . . . Both Goodell and Cope thought you ought to see Taylor, not too soon, but in time to get to him again if work with or for him was found necessary before action in the House."[65]

Atherton stayed in Washington, D.C., the entire week before the House took up the bill on August 19. He, Alvord, Goodell, and William H. Scott, president of Ohio State, met with Grange officials and agreed to support the restoration of the amendment that had been accepted, and then deleted, by the Senate. The amendment would direct funds not only for instruction in agriculture and the mechanic arts, and for facilities for their instruction, but also in the broader areas the college presidents had wanted: "the English language and the various branches of mathematical, physical, natural, and economic science." Atherton tried also to get Trimble to appear in the House chamber to show his support for the bill, but Trimble declined.[66]

The House disposed of the bill in one day, on August 19. Taylor noted that he had intended to introduce an amendment restricting use of the money to agricultural education but had not anticipated the persuasive powers of the land-grant presidents. As Taylor told it:

> Afterward, when it became known that I expected to propose this amendment in the House a number of gentlemen connected with the agricultural colleges . . . and also a number of gentlemen representing the agricultural interests of the country came here for the purpose of agreeing . . . upon some amendment which would not defeat the bill and which would be satisfactory to all of the friends of the measure. There was at first great anxiety that the bill should pass as it came from the Senate, as the Senate might not agree to the amendments the House would make. . . . I said to these gentlemen that I would insist on making an amendment, and after considerable consultation the amendment which I have proposed was agreed upon. . . .
>
> The amendment I have proposed has the approval of Henry E. Alvord, . . . W. H. Scott, . . . H. H. Goodell, . . . George Atherton, . . . John Trimble, . . . Mortimer Whitehead, lecturer National Grange. . . . I hold in my hand a paper prepared and signed by all of these gentlemen approving the amendment I propose.[67]

Taylor earlier had made it clear he wanted none of the funds currently used to support agricultural instruction to be diverted to the classical languages, or to any other area he deemed inappropriate for an "agricultural" college. As the amendment turned out, the funds could be applied only "to instruction in agriculture, the mechanic arts, the English language and the various branches of mathematical, physical, natural, and economic science, with special reference to their applications to the industries of life, and to facilities for such instruction."

The House debate spilled out mainly along party lines, with Democrats in opposition to the measure. The obligatory objection to excessive federal intrusion in state affairs was presented, replete with a reading of James Buchanan's 1859 veto message for the original Morrill bill. It was parried, however, by a reading of the 1862 Morrill Act and the Hatch Act, noting that the college and experiment stations had been established for some time and that the new act was designed "simply to increase to a limited extent the amount of the annual appropriations—that and nothing more." Some concern was voiced over the rapid diminution of public lands, and the continuing efficacy of public-land sales as the source of revenue for the act. But public-land sales were deemed sufficient to fund the measure for years to come, and the provision stood.

Support for the measure was overwhelming. One representative even sought to exonerate the overeager land-grant presidents:

> A few presidents of agricultural colleges come here in the interest of what? of colleges designed to give special education to those who labor on the farm and to mechanics in the shop. There is such an immense difference between such gentlemen coming in the interests of such institutions and lobbyists paid $10,000 a year . . . by railroad companies to look after their steals.[68]

The bill passed the House, 135 to 39. The Senate concurred with the amendments, and the president signed the act on August 30, precisely four months after its introduction. Cope wrote jubilantly to Atherton: "Too much praise cannot be given to Major Alvord and yourself for your wise and prudent direction of the forces which have wrought so noble a result. Some day we will build a monument to you."[69] If time spent working in Washington, D.C., were any indication of Atherton's contributions, a monument might have been in order. Between May 1 and August 20, Atherton had made eleven trips to Washington, totaling thirty-six days.[70]

Five years later, from the pulpit of the Association's presidency, Alvord was to recount the story of the "Grange Amendment." The

Grange had claimed credit for "saving" the bill from being utilized for deviant purposes by the land-grant colleges, and Alvord aimed to correct the record. In his version, the National Farmers' Alliance and the Grange were "freely consulted" by the Association's committee of presidents and invited to attend the committee hearings (presumably the House hearings in the summer of 1890). The Alliance officials were cooperative, but the Grange representatives seemed distrustful. Alvord continued:

> To show their good faith, and as a wholly voluntary act, the Association representatives proposed this now famous amendment, while the bill was before the Committee on Education of the House. . . . I have the original draft of that amendment in my possession; it was first written by one college president who cared more for object than form; was carefully trimmed and punctuated by another college president, and cordially adopted by others on the committee, none of these being Grangers, although entirely friendly to that order and its general work. The Association committee did not believe this amendment necessary, but willingly proposed it and supported it consistently until adopted. The House Committee on Education did not like the amendment and the House itself was inclined to reject it. The lightest intimation or even indifference on the part of its authors and supporters would have led to its rejection and passage of the bill just as framed by the Senate. Nothing could be further from the truth than the allegation that "The Agricultural College Presidents" . . . were insincere in this matter. They worked faithfully for its adoption when inaction or absence would have caused its defeat. Therefore, instead of this limiting amendment being of Grange origin, opposed by the colleges, and the salvation of this bill, the plain facts are that it originated with college men and their honest support from first to last.[71]

Aftermath, Implications, and the Association's 1890 Convention

Until 1890, the land-grant colleges had related mainly to the Department of Agriculture—the federal administrative agency to which they owed their fealty. The Morrill Act of 1890 brought the colleges into a closer relationship with another federal department: the Bureau of Education, then a part of the Department of the Interior. It was the secretary of the interior, in fact, who held the power of the purse and to whom the colleges were now accountable in terms of the disbursement of Morrill Act funds and the proper use thereof. The secretary of the treasury made the actual payments to the states, but only after receiving the "warrant" from the secretary of the interior authorizing payment. If the secretary elected to withhold payment to a particular state, he was so to inform the President of the United States, and required to hold the payment in escrow until a final determination could be made. The college treasurer, in turn, was now required to make a detailed report of Morrill Act expenditures to the secretary of agriculture and the secretary of the interior.

The act also provided a penalty against the misapplication of funds. It required the offending state to pay back the misapplied funds and also withheld further appropriations until the problem had been corrected. Two areas in particular held the greatest potential for the misuse of funds: the curriculum, and racial segregation. Southern states could choose to comply with the act by establishing or designating a separate land-grant college for blacks that would qualify for a "just and equitable" division of funds, reserving the existing land-grant college exclusively for whites. Presumably, in states of the north and west, the land-grant colleges did not discriminate in their admission policies; if they did, they ran the risk of misapplying the funds. The act also forbade the expenditure of funds for the "purchase, erection, preservation, or repair of any buildings"—that being, theoretically, the responsibility of the states. But aside from specifying the eligible instructional areas, the act struck a chord of ambiguity in also permitting the expenditure of funds "to facilities for such instruction." College presidents would wrestle with this ambiguity at the Association's 1890 convention but would elect not to press for clarification.

In addition to the fiscal reports required from the college treasurer, the act also directed college presidents to make detailed annual reports regarding "the condition and progress" of their institutions. To be submitted to the secretaries of agriculture and the interior as well as to each sister land-grant college, these reports were required to provide statistical data relative to receipts and expenditures, the library, student enrollments, instructional staff, and any improvements and experiments made under the direction of the experiment stations.[72]

In short, the act introduced an increased measure of federal control and institutional accountability. It specified where and how money could be spent and required an annual reporting of those expenditures.

Atherton and Alvord had little time to celebrate the passage of the act, before procedural questions over the disbursements of funds required their attention. Visiting the treasury, Alvord was told that nothing could be done about the first payment of $15,000, due immediately, until the secretary of the interior had signed warrants authorizing release of the funds. Unfortunately, the secretary, John Noble, was vacationing in Richfield Springs, New York. Alvord noted a further complication arising from a meeting with the assistant secretary, George Chandler. Chandler told Alvord that the act had authorized the secretary "to investigate the educational privileges of the colored people of the South." Alvord implored Atherton to visit the secretary in Richfield Springs to clarify the situation, which Atherton did.[73]

By early October, Alvord told Atherton that the preliminary paperwork for twenty states had been completed and that Noble was prepared to sign the warrants the following week. The papers of the Pennsylvania State College were among those slated for quick action, and Atherton was elated "because we have recently borrowed funds in anticipation of prompt payment." By late November, after further bureaucratic mistakes had been rectified, Penn State and about fourteen other institutions began receiving the first payment.[74]

Atherton and Alvord were extremely anxious about the potential for rogue initiatives—especially from the Grange—to exclude land-grant colleges from receiving the benefits of the act or to qualify non-land-grant colleges for the new funds. Thus, they prepared a "Brief of Points" for Assistant Interior Secretary Chandler and distributed it as appropriate to various land-grant colleges. In their document, Atherton and Alvord interpreted the second Morrill Act as "a supplement to the Act of 1862." They were careful to note that the latter act applied only to institutions designated by their state legislatures to receive funds from the original act. Anticipating potential arguments to the contrary, Atherton and Alvord emphasized that the broad nature of the original act, and the power it gave to the various states to develop their land-grant colleges according to the demands of local conditions, had given rise to a disparate class of institutions: "Great variety has existed from the first, in the organization and designation of these institutions." They further emphasized that questions of institutional purpose and organization (e.g., whether a purely agricultural college, technical school, or institution of general science) had already been settled in the various states "and cannot now be raised to debar them from the benefits of the Act of 1890." Finally, in respect to the question of black colleges, Atherton and Alvord advised that states maintaining two separate institutions receive "at least the first annual appropriation, leaving subsequent action by the Secretary of the Interior to be determined on the basis of reports received."[75]

Atherton and Alvord's instincts about a renewed attempt to divorce land-grant colleges from the benefit of the 1890 Morrill funds proved accurate. At its annual meeting in 1891, the Grange declared the land-grant colleges to be "practically worthless" and implored Congress to separate the agricultural departments from existing colleges, establishing entirely new and purely agricultural institutions around them. "We further ask," the Grange added, "that all appropriations now paid to the combined institutions . . . be transferred to such separate distinct agricultural and mechanical colleges as may be established in the several states."[76]

At its fourth annual convention, held November 11–13, 1890, in Washington, D.C., the Association explored the ramifications of the 1890 Morrill Act. The Standing Committee on College Work, which Atherton chaired, hammered out a declaration of principles concerning the colleges' obligations under the new law. As finally approved, the declaration provided:

> That every college should keep a separate account for the income derived from the act.

> That the expenditures "should conform to a strict interpretation of the language of the law."

> That the secretary of the interior should speed the payments due the colleges. The first payment, for the year ending June 30, 1890, was "to be regarded . . . as an equipment fund." The second payment, $16,000, was also due and was to be used for "the expense of the current academic year," 1890–91.

> That the presidents' and treasurers' reports to the secretaries of agriculture and the interior should be made before September 1, 1891, for the preceding academic year.

That the colleges should press their respective state legislatures to take the required action necessary for institutional
receipt of the Morrill funds.

Finally, the Committee on College Work postponed a discussion on
the Association's responsibilities in the event of a misuse of federal
funds by a college or station.[77]

The 1890 Morrill Act contributed to the rapid development of
land-grant colleges in many ways. Of no small significance was the
sudden infusion of cash—nearly $50,000—like manna from heaven.
Despite bureaucratic delays and mix-ups, the majority of land-grant
colleges received a total of $48,000 within twelve to eighteen months of
the bill's enactment. The first payment, $15,000 for the year ending
June 30, 1890, was being mailed in November of that year. The second
payment, $16,000, for the 1890–91 year also was theoretically overdue,
as the act stipulated that payments for the ensuing academic year were
to be disbursed by July 31. The third payment, $17,000, for the 1891–92
year, was due theoretically by July 31, 1891, eleven months after the
act had been signed. A report by Interior Secretary Noble showed that
the three disbursements were made within about a year's time. For the
Pennsylvania State College, payments were ordered from the Interior
Department on November 5, 1890 (for the year ending June 30, 1890);
February 5, 1891 (for the 1890–91 year); and September 1, 1891 (for the
1891–92 year).[78]

Not every college received the funds as quickly as the interior
secretary's report had stated. In at least ten cases, the check was sent
from the U.S. treasury directly to the state treasurer with a cryptic
note. Not knowing what the checks were for, the state treasurers deposited
them, and in those states the colleges could not draw funds from the
state treasury without enabling legislation. Such incidents put added
pressure on Atherton and Alvord to ensure that the second round of
$16,000 payments was handled promptly and accurately, because that
was all those colleges would receive that year.[79]

The funds from the 1890 Morrill Act were to have a salutary effect
on curriculum development at land-grant colleges; they made it possible for the colleges to hire new faculty in the prescribed areas. Ross
reported that "contemporary official reports and college histories
alike emphasize the act as the turning point for that particular
institution."[80] Certainly that was the case at the Pennsylvania State
College. In his annual report for 1890, Atherton proclaimed that the

year was "one of the most important in the history of the institution and seems likely to be marked hereafter as one of the critical turning points in its progress." He noted further that the act would help generate appropriations from the state: "The more liberal support provided by Congress will also make it necessary to call upon the Legislature to continue the work it has already begun of providing necessary buildings and equipment."[81]

The act proved to be a particular boon for the engineering disciplines, which were becoming the mainstays at many land-grant colleges. At the Pennsylvania State College, the total instructional staff increased from twenty-eight in 1890–91 to forty by 1893–94, with the bulk of the new faculty being added in engineering. They were sorely needed. By 1893–94, some 128 of 181 undergraduates at Penn State (70 percent of the student body) were enrolled in engineering programs.[82]

The other important feature of the act was, as Atherton had intimated, to spur increased levels of state financial support. Up to 1890, state support—when it materialized at all—usually came earmarked for the construction and maintenance of buildings, the area from which Congress had precluded 1862 Morrill Act expenditures. Such support was critical to the development of the colleges. For example, the Pennsylvania State College received $100,000 in 1887—its first state money in a decade—for construction of new buildings. In 1889 and 1891, the legislature appropriated a total of $277,000 for building construction and maintenance.[83]

The 1890 Morrill Act—itself an implicit admission by Congress that the colleges could not live on their original endowments—ushered in a general reconsideration of the manner in which the states were supporting the institutions. The act helped to dispel the perception that the colleges needed no help in maintaining their educational programs, and state support for that purpose began to materialize. As Earle Ross said, "the decade following the second federal grant marked their full adoption as state institutions with the obligations entailed."[84]

State support began to rise considerably during the 1890s, registering a 500 percent increase between 1889 and 1890 and between 1899 and 1900, outdistancing federal support by nearly half a million dollars by the decade's end. In 1889–90, just before the second Morrill Act, thirty-six land-grant colleges reported a total of $506,254 in state funds, with an additional $405,297 in "productive funds," presumably from the original Morrill Act. (The same statistics did not include Hatch Act funds, which would have totaled $385,000 at the thirty-one schools that had experiment stations.) By mid-decade, total federal support to the sixty-one land-grant institutions still exceeded total state support. In 1894–95, the 1890 Morrill Act supplied $891,389 to the colleges, the Hatch Act provided $652,576, and annuities from the original Morrill Act amounted to $505,630. Together, those federal sources totaled $2,049,595, slightly more than the aggregated state funds of $1,860,245. By 1899–1900, however, the states and territories appropriated for the land-grant colleges a total of $2,916,837, while the amount received from the three federal sources amounted to $2,488,354.[85]

The 1890 Morrill Act also marked the establishment of a more formal relationship between the colleges and the agencies of the federal government. The act provided funds, but also specified conditions for their use and penalties for their misuse. And while the act would bring the colleges a more supportive relationship from their respective states, it also would crystallize the perception for many land-grant presidents that the colleges were essentially national institutions; they owed at least as much fealty to the federal government as to their states. And as the 1890s would show, the presidents increasingly saw their institutions as instruments of national policy, and accordingly the colleges came to view themselves as a class of colleges sharply differentiated from the old-line state universities that did not share the bounty of the Morrill acts.

Finally, the 1890 Morrill Act was not without its "democratizing" effect, in the strictest sense of extending higher education to previously excluded groups—in this case, blacks or African Americans. While the act presaged the separate-but-equal doctrine of *Plessy v. Ferguson* (1896) and reflected the ubiquitous Jim Crow color line, it also prompted the creation of new black land-grant colleges. Although seven of the seventeen black land-grant colleges had their origins prior to 1890, only three had offered agricultural instruction. After the second Morrill Act, five states named the existing state-supported black institution as the black land-grant college, six states established new colleges under state control, and six more designated existing private schools as the black land-grant institution. One historian, writing in the 1950s, likened the act to accomplishing "for the Negroes of the South what the first act in 1862 had accomplished for the men and women of other races."[86] That paternalistic view assumed those struggling colleges had resources equal to those of the segregated land-grant colleges and could confer an education of equivalent quality on their black matriculants who— thus armed—could use their educational advantage in the manner of their white counterparts to improve their station in life. Although the black land-grant colleges made important but limited contributions, they could hardly do for their race what civil disobedience, freedom marches, federal troops, and civil rights legislation would begin to do seventy years later.

6

The Association
and the
Emerging Federal Relationship

THE YEARS AROUND 1890 MARKED a turning point not only for the land-grant colleges but for the entire American university movement as well. The accumulation of huge fortunes now permitted philanthropy on a grand scale, which brought a number of important institutions into being. The birth of three universities in particular—Chicago, Clark, and Stanford—strengthened the demand for faculty members and heightened institutional competition for scientists and scholars. The experiments of the elective system and the graduate school had proven successful at such leading institutions as Harvard and Johns Hopkins, though neither innovation had taken hold at most land-grant colleges. Most telling, however, was that college and university enrollments began to rise sharply after 1890, and with increasing student attendance came increasing institutional aid, whether in the form of private gifts or legislative appropriations.[1]

For the land-grant colleges and experiment stations, the new decade ushered in an era of increased complexity as well. Although the

Hatch Act and the 1890 Morrill Act provided long-sought financial support, the colleges and the experiment stations found themselves enmeshed in a web of new or redefined relationships with the federal government, specifically with the departments of Agriculture, Interior (Education), and War. These departments could and did behave variously toward the colleges—at times strongly supportive, at others highly intrusive. Hardly static entities, the cabinet-level departments often swung on the force of their administrators' personalities. The Association of American Agricultural Colleges and Experiment Stations also found itself continually involved with the legislative branch of the federal government and, as appropriate, with the executive branch too.

Just as important, the colleges and experiment stations had yet to resolve their relationship with each other, not only on their respective campuses but also especially within the context of the Association. The balance of power, tilting toward the college presidents at the beginning of the 1890s, would shift haltingly into the station directors' camp just after the turn of the century, and the change would be reflected in revisions to the Association's constitution. The same dynamic would bring an accretion of support for Armsby's view—that stations should function primarily as scientific research units—and an erosion of sentiment for George Atherton's philosophy that stations should blend teaching as well as research in their mission (though in practice most stations did both long past Atherton's death).

The tenuous relationship between college and station was confounded further by the rapid development of both institutions. The stations grew in number from roughly forty in 1890 to fifty-five in 1906, by which time they had issued, in the aggregate, nearly 8,000 scientific, technical, or instructional publications.[2] On average, a station employed ten people, and as late as 1905, despite the growing realization of the importance of the research mission, half the station scientists were also employed as college teachers.[3] But prompted by a cadre of uncompromising scientists, Henry P. Armsby prominent among them, and by the courteous but unrelenting prodding of the Office of Experiment Stations, the stations were moving in an unmistakable direction: toward greater emphasis on original scientific research. That development was codified into an imperative by the Adams Act of 1906. Raising the stations' annual stipend from $15,000 to $30,000, the act required that the funds be used only for conducting original research programs or experiments bearing directly on the agricultural industry.

The colleges too were changing dramatically. By 1900, the sixty-five land-grant institutions enrolled 19,238 students in "collegiate classes" alone.[4] In structure and function, most of the colleges were moving toward de facto university status (some, of course, such as Cornell, Wisconsin, California, and Illinois, had already attained it), a direction reflected in the Association's focus on curricular concerns. In 1896, the Association adopted an ideal curriculum plan in which general education — including modern languages — constituted 40 percent of the coursework for the bachelor of science degree. Equally telling was that the college presidents in their annual addresses to the Association began extolling the virtues of humanistic education and railing against overspecialization — this in institutions where the great majority of students chose to study engineering. Toward decade's end, the Association explored new formats for graduate work and worked unsuccessfully to establish a capstone graduate school utilizing the federal scientific agencies in Washington, D.C. On a more modest scale, it successfully instituted a summer graduate school in agriculture at Ohio State in 1902 and at the University of Illinois in 1906.

Despite the tension between colleges and stations, and the consequent schismatic tendency of the Association, the organization weathered the trials of 1890–1905 without dissolving. The executive committee, composed mainly of presidents, worked to represent the interests of a unified association. It was not unusual for men like Atherton, Henry E. Alvord, and Henry H. Goodell to throw themselves into the service of station interests vis-à-vis federal agencies or congressional committees. Even Armsby, elected president in 1899, seemed to have come around to espouse Association unity, at least rhetorically: "This Association does not stand for two parallel but distinct sets of interests. It is not an Association of colleges and of experiment stations, but an Association of colleges and experiment stations — of college stations, if I may coin a word."[5]

George Atherton, having stepped down from a two-term presidency in 1890, continued to play a major role in the affairs of the Association over the last fifteen years of his life. He worked on a variety of legislative fronts, meeting both success and failure. He continued to serve in formal leadership posts, particularly on committees, and was returned to the executive committee in 1900 for two terms. Equally important, he continued his informal leadership role, serving as adviser to the Association's executive leadership. "Ever chief among the wisest of its counselors," as Henry C. White eulogized in 1906, Atherton worked intimately with the chairmen of the executive committee: Alvord (1887–94) and Goodell (1895–1902). Atherton's multifaceted activity on behalf of the Association, and especially on behalf of the interests of the college presidents, reflected the complexities of new relationships now thrust on an organization for which no precedent existed.

Fig. 11.   **Henry Hill Goodell.**

The College-Station Relationship and the Agriculture Department

At the Association's 1889 convention, Henry Armsby had proposed the establishment of mutually exclusive sections for college presidents

and station directors. Opposed by Atherton and others, the proposal
was defeated. Nevertheless, the station scientists began to strengthen
their hand over the next several years. In 1892, station directors
won a minor but important constitutional concession from the college
presidents. Their amendment provided that the station could appoint
delegates other than the station director to attend, and vote in, the
sectional meetings of the various agricultural disciplines.[6] The practical effect of this amendment was to encourage the attendance of station
scientists at Association conventions.

In 1893, a station director was elected for the first time as Association president: William A. Henry of the University of Wisconsin. In
his address, Henry articulated the view of the leading station directors—
that the stations' future lay in the unfettered conduct of scientific
research—and he criticized the stations for lack of preparation "so
essential to good scientific work." He called for stations to reduce the
turnover of their scientists and to exercise greater selectivity in research
projects: "Many of us are attempting to cover too large a field." Henry
also criticized college presidents who insisted on functioning as station directors. In a slap at the Atherton philosophy, he condemned
the "sloppy line of demarcation between the teacher and the researcher
at the stations."[7]

The impetus for scientific work came not only from within the
Association but also from without, and specifically from the Office
of Experiment Stations. Among the enduring contributions of the
Association's 1888 *Report of the Committee on Station Work,* co-authored
by Wilbur Atwater, George Cook, and Samuel Johnson, was the admo-
nition that the future viability of the stations "will depend upon what
they discover of permanent value, and this must come largely from
the most abstract and profound research; to forget this will be fatal."
Carrying this philosophy with him as the founding director of the
Department of Agriculture's Office of Experiment Stations from 1888
to 1891, Atwater deduced a structure and function for the stations that
came to be known as the "Atwater standard." The Atwater standard
called for a first-rate scientist as full-time station director; a staff of
highly trained scientists substantially free from undergraduate instruction and motivated to attain the level of excellence established by the
European stations; and an organization that set forth a selective research
agenda based on the station's particular strengths.[8]

The "Atwater standard" was maintained by Abram W. Harris, who
directed the office from 1891 to 1893, after which he left to assume the

presidency of what later became the University of Maine, and more particularly by Alfred C. True, who directed the office from 1893 to 1915. A professor of classics at Wesleyan University, True was brought by Atwater to the Office of Experiment Stations to edit its publications. As a nonscientist, True adopted a management style of gentle but persistent persuasion, praising the stations for their good work but never failing to remind them of the need to use Hatch Act funds essentially for scientific research.[9]

The first administration of the new cabinet-level department was highly profitable for the Association. The law that elevated the Department of Agriculture to cabinet-level status in February 1889 also provided for an assistant secretary of agriculture, to be appointed not by the secretary but by the President of the United States. The new President taking office in March 1889, Republican Benjamin Harrison, made selections for both positions that pleased the Association—after an Atherton-led committee visited the President-elect to make its case. The new secretary was Jeremiah M. Rusk, three-term governor of Wisconsin prior to his appointment. Rusk had aided the development of agriculture at the University of Wisconsin during his gubernatorial tenure and was supportive of the land-grant college idea as well as the experiment station movement. He divided the work of the Department of Agriculture into two major divisions: the executive, under his immediate direction; and the scientific, under the direction of the assistant secretary.[10]

The new assistant secretary, Edwin Willits, was an Association stalwart, having served as president of Michigan Agricultural College since 1885 and as a member of Atherton's Hatch Act legislative committee. With Rusk, Willits, and Atwater in the Office of Experiment Stations, the early relationship between the Agriculture Department and the Association was one of mutual support. The Association was not reluctant to lobby for increases in the department's congressional appropriation. As early as 1891, Atwater was asking Atherton to muster Association support for an increase from $15,000 to $20,000 in the appropriation for his office.[11]

The relationship changed dramatically with the second election of Democrat Grover Cleveland to the presidency of the United States in 1892. With the Harrison administration, Atherton and the executive committee had "staked out" the assistant secretaryship as being the Association's position, and Atherton moved to renew that claim with President Cleveland. Prompted by press reports about unacceptable candidates for both positions, Atherton and the executive committee began to maneuver quickly. Willits reminded him that had Cleveland been reelected in 1888, Representative William Hatch and Henry Alvord would have been promoted for the positions.[12] Atherton agreed that both men would be acceptable, especially Alvord in the post of assistant secretary. Hatch drew less enthusiasm, but he was actively seeking the post and the Association felt compelled to support him for his work in "fathering" the act that bore his name. "I think every one in the Association feels the obligation we are under to him," Goodell wrote to Atherton, "and would willingly do anything in his power if he only knew what to do and how to do it." In early February 1893, Atherton led an Association subcommittee that presented a slate of candidates to President Cleveland ("We depend on you to act as spokesman," Alvord told Atherton).[13]

But this was to no avail. Cleveland's choice for secretary was J. Sterling Morton of Nebraska, a staunch conservative who would soon prove to be an enemy of the Association. Morton came into office on the heels of the financial panic of 1893 and began cutting costs everywhere. He even tried his hand at supervising the stations, and humiliated one director for excessive expenditures in feeding his horses.[14]

Willits, of the opposite political party, was retained as Morton's assistant secretary through all of 1893, but only because he had been named director of the government's exhibits at the World's Columbian Exposition in Chicago in October of that year and was needed for on-site supervision. The Association did wield some influence in the choice of Willits's successor: Charles W. Dabney, another Association stalwart, who had served as president of the University of Tennessee and director of its experiment stations. But Dabney's appointment was not without its price to the Association.

Morton's animosity for the land-grant colleges and their experiment stations ran deep. Goodell wrote to Atherton a month after Morton's appointment that "there seems to be in his mind . . . a rooted antipathy to anything connected with college or station." Alvord reported that Morton called the stations "useless," and spoke of Morton's determination "to completely divorce the department from them, and have the station appropriation put in another bill." Alvord further noted that Morton sought "to throw the stations onto the states and rid the federal treasury of that load." Morton's animus stemmed from philosophical as well as budgetary considerations. He once challenged an employee to show him "a single instance where any good had resulted from any scientific man working under Government employ." By mid-summer, the situation had deteriorated to the point where Alvord asked Atherton to visit Morton. No evidence attests to Atherton's visit, but given Dabney's eventual appointment, such a visit by Atherton and others does not seem implausible.[15]

The concession Morton exacted was what one of his predecessors, Agriculture Commissioner George B. Loring, had also sought: direct control over part of the stations' research agenda. Morton wanted total control over a fixed percentage of the Hatch Act annuity, but Alvord and Goodell parried his initiative with the prospect of an angry Hatch—the stations' champion—in Congress.[16] Thus Morton was dissuaded from further attempting to secure prior control of a proportion of Hatch Act funds, which in any event would have required an amendment to the act.

Nevertheless, the secretary did secure, in the 1895 appropriations bill for the Department of Agriculture, "supervisory powers in connection with the expenditure of experiment station funds under the Hatch Act." The question of precisely how that supervision would work was unresolved, but the Association and the department had agreed on two possibilities: "critical examination of annual reports," which the Association deemed insufficient for obtaining an accurate appraisal of station work, and on-site inspections.[17]

Despite constant anxiety over federal intrusion, certain members of the Association welcomed the prospect of increased federal supervision through on-site inspections. Station directors believed the scrutiny would stop the diversion of Hatch Act funds for such dubious activities as the purchase of instructional equipment for other departments. Politically, the Association could not afford to ignore Morton's initiative. Alvord introduced a resolution approving the increased "measure of supervision" over expenditures, and the Association approved it, inviting "the closest scrutiny of the work of the stations by the Department of Agriculture, either by personal visitations of an agent of the Department, or such other method as the Secretary . . . may deem most efficient."[18]

The system of station inspections began in 1895, with True making thirty-five visits that year—and to good effect. The inspections gave this nonscientist the opportunity to examine all facets of station operation under the constraints of the local context. In the aggregate, the inspections gave True a comprehensive view of the entire national system of stations and enabled him to make recommendations from the broadest possible perspective.[19]

True was not reluctant to criticize, though he took pains to do so constructively by offering suggestions for more-efficient station procedures. At the 1893 convention, in reviewing the first five years of the Office of Experiment Stations, True interpreted its central function as facilitating creation of a literature for the agricultural sciences. A year later, True delivered his first critique. The "most frequent and serious" criticism was a "mingling" of Hatch Act funds "to the undue advantage of either the college or the stations." True also scored the growing practice of veiled advertising in station publications, "most often done by the use of pictures bearing the trademark or names of manufacturers." Finally, he cited "lack of unity" as a weakness. Station publications, he felt, were often issued in sloppily edited, haphazard format, with unclear sponsorship or affiliation, fueling a public perception of station impermanence.[20]

True's Office of Experiment Stations itself came under fire from the Association in 1895. Speaking as Association president, Alvord rebuked the Office for not living up to the original expectations of both Atwater and the Association. It was functioning, Alvord charged, as an uncritical publishing house for station work. Alvord wanted the Office to "act as an expert critic of the work, . . . a valuable service, which has been entirely lacking." He advised it to spend more time "visiting, advising, and criticizing, and less to the manufacture of bulletins, which . . . is encroaching directly upon a special function of the stations." Alvord also criticized the stations for weak management and called for an end to the practice of college presidents' "doubling" as station director.[21]

For station directors, 1895 marked the intensification of their drive for autonomy and independence. The stations' increased accountability to the Department of Agriculture, and Alvord's call for strong station management, galvanized the ad hoc Association committee charged with examining the president's speech and making recommendations therefrom. Led by Armsby and three other station directors, the committee forwarded a resolution (subsequently tabled for one year) that would have removed all aspects of station control from the college president. Instead, the station director would be "responsible to the governing board of the institution and representing the station in its relations to the public and the Department of Agriculture."[22]

Shortly before the 1896 convention, a circular from President Richard H. Jesse of the University of Missouri reminded colleagues that the schismatic proposal must be defeated: "It would make the Director of the Station independent of the President of the College," Jesse said. President James H. Smart of Purdue told Atherton he was not surprised at the effort to create friction between the stations and the colleges. "The station men have been in the saddle for some time," Smart said. "Unless the college presidents wake up an immense amount of mischief will be done. The Association has been turned over largely to station men and if they succeed in their present attempt it will injure the stations very much and annoy the college authorities."[23]

At the 1896 convention, Atherton parried consideration of the proposal by suggesting, instead, a comprehensive effort to amend the Association's constitution. He asked for the appointment of a special committee to report on the matter and to submit a draft of a revision at the next convention. Atherton's plan would have precluded action on the amended constitution until 1898. Under the rules of the constitution, the revised constitution and any new amendments approved at the 1897 convention would have to be tabled for a year before a vote could be taken. Yet Atherton's proposal was accepted, as was his choice of a committee: Alvord, Goodell, and Smart—college presidents all.

By June 1897, the Alvord committee approached Atherton with four propositions. The most radical, and the one that was recommended to the full Association, proposed to eliminate all sections entirely. Instead, the Association would become a conference of college presidents and station directors meeting only in general or joint sessions. Station scientists—the agriculturists, chemists, horticulturalists, entomologists, and others—would be ineligible, having to rely instead on their own professional societies for stimulation.[24]

In introducing the revision, Alvord noted that it was intended to bring the Association back to its original purpose: to consider problems related to the internal affairs of colleges and stations, the federal and state governments, other institutions, and new legislation. It was also designed to make the Association more manageable. "If the sections are continued," Alvord said, "the natural tendency will be to increase the number, . . . [making it] more difficult than it is now to select and limit attendance."[25]

The proposal for the revised constitution had turned on its head the earlier recommendation of the Armsby committee that the Association endorse the idea of station directors as the functional co-equals of college presidents. Instead, the Alvord proposition, endorsed by Atherton, attempted to create a new organization in which presidents and station directors would meet conjointly, the presidents never again losing sight of the directors. The proposal now had to lie on the table for a year.

Station directors of Armsby's persuasion might have been even more frustrated by a survey of experiment stations presented by the Section on Agriculture and Chemistry. Of the thirty-five stations surveyed, the average station, employing 9.18 people, was found to be engaged in a variety of activities. On average, only 1.86 people on staff devoted full time to the station (presumably doing research). The average number of staff dividing their time between teaching and research was 6.26. In addition, staff were delivering an average of sixty-nine public addresses per year, and 21 percent of their writing effort was devoted to instructional literature. Whitman Jordan, the station director at Geneva, New York, who wrote the report, concluded that the stations' research mission was being forsaken "for the utilization of existing knowledge through popular instruction and attention to the business side of farm practice." He did acknowledge, however, that the American station was organized under political conditions much different from those of the European stations, which gave rise to differences in its mission.[26]

Yet the implication, for the more aggressive station directors, was clear. Despite their efforts and those of the Office of Experiment Stations to create strong scientific research units, the Atherton philosophy reigned supreme in terms of general station operation. Yet not every station scientist necessarily disagreed with Atherton's position. The station director at Illinois, George E. Morrow, had echoed Atherton's philosophy in a convention address in 1894: "In exceptional cases it has been thought best to separate them [the colleges and stations]," Morrow said, "but I wish to emphasize . . . that, as a rule, an intimate union is best for both; that the teacher should investigate and the investigator teach."[27] Indeed, even so venerable an agricultural scientist as Samuel Johnson, in his president's address in 1896, said stations must justify themselves first to practical farmers, securing their confidence before indulging in abstract research.[28]

The 1898 convention saw the overwhelming defeat of the Alvord committee's constitutional revision, 44 to 8, but not before a spirited debate between Armsby and Atherton over the merits of the proposition.[29] Armsby argued for retention of the sections. To him the essential question was whether the Association should devote itself solely to administrative matters or should also accommodate the discussion of technical issues. "The discussion of these technical questions has been a great help to me," he said, adding that the system of sections had generally "worked well." The value of the sectional discussions, he observed, lay in the opportunity for scientists to discuss their work in the context of the experiment station. The chemist who attended Association conventions did so "as the chemist of an experiment station; he is interested not in questions of pure chemistry, but in the applications of chemistry to the purposes of agriculture." And Armsby struck an important teleological note in asserting that administrative work was not an end in itself: "it is simply a means to put these institutions in good working order to handle the technical questions."

Atherton argued that the amendments would bring the Association back to its original purpose and "its proper work." He pointed out that the Association antedated the Hatch Act and that its true purpose was to support colleges that were "to sustain a wholly new relation to the Government of the United States on the one hand and the governments of the States on the other hand." Questions involving the proper balance between the two levels of government "led the colleges to feel that they ought to form an association to discuss the new questions." To Atherton, the Association had been drifting away from such a focus.

Yet Atherton's envisioned regrouping was not for old time's sake. It was necessary, he maintained, because of the emergence of two profound questions of educational policy: how to unify the whole system of public education from top to bottom; and how to overcome the aversion in the East, the center of population, to providing public funds for education. "The questions which agricultural colleges have been formed to meet and deal with are large enough to call forth all our best energy," he said, "and, in my judgment, we ought to eliminate everything that can possibly interfere with the discharge of these high duties." But Atherton's argument failed to carry the day, and the Association rejected the constitutional revision that would have eliminated the sections.

The 1898 convention also served to introduce the new secretary of agriculture, James Wilson, to the Association. Stating his intention to provide as much support as possible, Wilson implied that, in contrast to the policies of his predecessor, his department would assume a laissez-faire attitude toward the stations. "There is no 'royal road' for the college or the experiment station to follow," he said. "When we sum up the results attained, we shall find that one man has taught us one thing, one college has taught us another thing, one experiment station has taught us still another, and thus we shall eventually arrive at the best methods for teaching the farmer's boy and the mechanic's son."[30]

"Tama Jim" Wilson was not as trusting to circumstance as his speech might have suggested. His sixteen-year tenure, 1897–1913, spurred a vast expansion of the Department of Agriculture into the world's outstanding scientific research organization. The entire thrust of the department under Wilson was toward scientific research that would increase crop production and facilitate livestock management. New bureaus, established around groups of talented scientists, began to take large strides. Major scientific advances were made in the identification and study of viruses, in plant genetics, and in reforestation studies. Wilson's department also championed the controversial consumer-protection legislation of the Progressive era: the Meat Inspection Act and the Food and Drug Act. In statistical terms, Wilson's department grew from a staff of 2,444 and a budget of $3.6 million in 1897, to a staff of 11,043 and a budget of $21.2 million by 1912,[31] but his penchant for expansion and control posed serious problems for the Association.

In the Office of Experiment Stations, True had been working patiently with the stations, pointing out mistakes and gently nudging them ever closer to the Atwater standard. In 1896, he called for stability in the composition of the stations' boards of directors, in order to preclude abrupt shifts in station policy and research programs. He also urged stations to do a better job of keeping records in their experimental work and suggested that they might begin maintaining general records of local conditions (soils, climate, land use) to aid future researchers. True continued to inveigh against advertisements in station publications, believing that the practice compromised the stations' scientific integrity.[32] In 1899, True grew more strict: the U.S. attorney general ruled in favor of his position that Hatch Act funds could not be applied to anything related to academic instruction, but the ruling did not stop such abuses.[33]

Armsby's championing of the "section" format in the debate with Atherton helped to secure his election as Association president at the 1898 convention. His 1899 president's address—delivered at San Francisco in a conclave Atherton did not attend—sounded a theme of reconciliation.[34] He explained that the Hatch Act had broadened the conception of the German model by making the new stations "departments of educational institutions." Armsby called for recognition that the station "in its broadest and most fundamental conception, is an educational institution, . . . an institution for higher education in agriculture." Recalling the ideal of the "separate station," Armsby exhorted his colleagues to "discard this notion and recognize the station unreservedly as an integral part of the agricultural college." Armsby still maintained that the station should be divorced from undergraduate instruction, but he did concede that graduate instruction was a useful adjunct for the station.

In Atherton's absence, another committee was appointed to study the constitution and suggest revisions at the next convention. "There is a strong feeling in this body that under this constitution the Association is not flourishing as it should," a delegate said. The committee appointed to remedy the situation consisted of four college presidents, including Goodell of Massachusetts and Patterson of Kentucky, and one station director, Henry of Wisconsin.

The convention of 1900 was a celebration of the twenty-fifth anniversary of the American experiment station. Appropriately, the convention met both at Middletown, Connecticut, where the Wesleyan University station under Atwater and Johnson was inaugurated in 1875, and in New Haven, home to the Sheffield School. The entire conclave was imbued with a sense of history. It gave vent to retrospectives of the experiment station movement and to the land-grant college experience as well. The patron saint of the colleges, Justin Morrill, had died on December 28, 1898, and Atherton had been appointed by the Association to deliver the eulogy at this convention.

Whitman Jordan, the station director at Geneva, New York, traced the history of the station movement and related a personal anecdote suggesting that American stations had finally arrived. He noted that a distinguished German agricultural scientist had recently visited his station to study its respiration apparatus and was soon to examine "one of similar construction soon to be completed at Pennsylvania State College." Jordan found it moving that, "at the end of only twenty-five years of our organized effort, Germany is coming to the United States for instruction."

However retrospective its mood, the convention kept one eye on the future. Jordan, too, turned from the past to launch a devastating critique: the organization of the stations as departments of land-grant colleges "cannot be regarded as so far wholly satisfactory." He excoriated the colleges for requiring "double duty" of their station scientists and called for a station director "who is that and nothing more." He condemned the stations for eagerly accepting the "duties of inspection" of commercial products for farmers and chastised them for focusing on short-term experiments that yielded immediate results: "The literature of agricultural science is already cluttered with so-called practical conclusions that in a brief time will be swept into the rubbish corner." He lamented that "anything like scientific research . . . occupies a decidedly minor place in our station literature," and he advocated adoption of a new research agenda to approach "the large and difficult problems which we have avoided because they looked so formidable."[35] Compared with Armsby's softer tones of the year previous, Jordan's call to arms energized the more aggressive station directors to renew their efforts at reshaping the Association's structure.

Fig. 12.   **Whitman H. Jordan.**

In a related matter, the new committee on cooperative work between the Department of Agriculture and the experiment stations reported that the two had begun to engage in some joint research projects. The committee foreshadowed Secretary James Wilson's "annexation impulse" when it added that station autonomy should be preserved in this emerging relationship: "stations should in no sense become extensions of the divisions of the Department for purposes of experimental work.... Your committee would therefore deem it desirable ... that the agreement take the form of a formal contract."[36]

Finally, the committee to revise the constitution brought forth its proposal.[37] The major amendment was to streamline its five sections (college work, agriculture and chemistry, horticulture and botany, entomology, and mechanic arts) into three: college work, agriculture, and mechanic arts. Atherton protested vigorously on procedural grounds. He argued, successfully, that the proposed revisions should have been advanced at the previous convention and then circulated again in the call for the current convention. In this case, the procedure had not been followed. The committee had been appointed at the previous convention, but no proposals had been laid on the table at that time; instead, the committee had assembled its plan privately, broaching it in the call for the convention. But Atherton's was a Pyrrhic victory. In the debate that he prompted, one delegate had proposed an amendment to organize the association "into sections upon college work and experiment-station work."

As it turned out, the constitutional revision of 1901 was minor. The Association kept its five sections, but in an amendment regarding the election of officers made the process more democratic. Previously, nominations for officers had been made by a special committee in closed session; now they would be made from the floor, reducing somewhat the power of the presidents. In addition, the Association voted to table a resolution that flew in the face of the Atherton philosophy: that the director and heads of divisions of station work should, if possible, "devote their whole time to the work of investigation."[38]

The schism Atherton had staved off for so long finally occurred in 1903. The year previous, William A. Henry of the Wisconsin station had introduced a constitutional amendment to divide the Association into a section on college work and administration, and another on experiment station work. In a concession to the presidents, Henry also had proposed that the five-man executive committee contain three members from the college section and two from the station group. In the weeks before the 1903 convention, Henry C. White, president of the University of Georgia and chairman of the executive committee, reminded Atherton that his help would be needed in fighting the proposal: "We shall need your leadership," White said. "You must not forget that I have held place in the Executive Committee for the year only, in the expectation and with the understanding that the 'Old Guard' or their legitimate successors should control the Association's affairs."[39]

Atherton seemed indisposed to another battle, however. He said he was "largely indifferent" to the proposed changes. He deemed them an "unsatisfactory compromise," but had resigned himself to accepting them on the grounds that they "may serve to hold the Association together a while longer, and possibly pave the way for putting things hereafter on a better footing." He confessed, however, that he was "not very sanguine on this point."[40] At the convention, Atherton in fact moved for acceptance of the new constitution, and the motion passed overwhelmingly, 53 to 1.

The revised structure enthralled the directors. They called a meeting of their new section in the wake of the convention, agreeing not to subdivide but to focus on two general areas: station administration, and "the methods and appliances" of research. "We look upon this unification as a very important advance and as affording a great opportunity for promoting the efficiency of the experiment-station enterprise," their report noted.[41]

The proposal Armsby had brought forth fourteen years earlier, and Atherton had parried for as long a time, was finally ratified. The Association had not been destroyed, but station directors emerged in a position co-equal with the college presidents. Their true objective, however, was a format that would give them the opportunity to intermingle privately and discuss mutual concerns. In most respects, the station directors' concerns were not different from other professionalizing groups during this era, particularly in their emphasis on raising professional standards and achieving autonomy. Galvanized by their success, the station directors would bring renewed vitality to the Association. With the specter of an aggressive Department of Agriculture now threatening to supplant the stations as the loci of American agricultural science, that new vitality would soon be called on.

The Adams Act

The agricultural experiment stations found themselves in a dilemma during the first few years of the twentieth century. The farm economy had recovered from the downturn of the mid-1890s, and farmers began putting more pressure on the experiment stations for information and help in solving practical problems. Coupled with the pressure from the colleges for classroom teaching, the stations could devote few resources to substantive scientific research. Although state funding for the stations had begun to increase, it was usually designated for substations or local experiments.[42] And Hatch Act funds had remained constant.

Yet the demands for the conduct of scientific research increased as well. The Office of Experiment Stations pointed to the need for increased federal funding for station research and in 1902 urged that whatever funds materialized should be reserved "for larger and more thorough experiments in many lines." The impetus for scientific work also grew from the stations themselves and from the professionalizing class of scientists they were attracting. The number of station scientists increased by more than 100 percent between 1889 and 1905, from 402 to 845, though the increase varied considerably from state to state. The new breed of station scientist, by the early twentieth century, was more likely to have received his graduate training at a land-grant college and to have trained under someone like Armsby, Henry, Jordan, or Morrow. The younger scientists also tended to view themselves as professionals, with a stature equivalent to that of their fellow scientists and academicians on the campus. And with their professionalism came the realization that their true mission had little to do with serving as experimental handmaidens to local farmers.[43]

Within the Association, the sentiment had developed that experiment stations could no longer progress—much less compete with the emergent research prowess of the Department of Agriculture—without additional funding. At its 1902 convention, the Association asked the executive committee to "urge upon Congress . . . that the appropriations . . . under the Hatch Act be increased by the sum of $15,000 annually [to $30,000 per year]."[44] However, the committee reported a year later that it would be "unwise to attempt to secure action of this character by the Fifty-Seventh Congress."[45]

Just after the 1903 convention, Henry of the Wisconsin station, convalescing in Washington, D.C., visited Wisconsin Representative

Henry C. Adams and another colleague. "I told them of the dire poverty of our experiment stations," Henry said, "pointing out how the original Hatch Act gift had accomplished a vast deal of good, [and] how there was need for more agricultural research, which could not be undertaken with our present funds, and closed by telling them that our experiment stations needed another gift. . . . Mr. Adams grasped the situation at once."[46]

Adams conferred with True, who framed a bill that Adams introduced in January 1904. In language that mimicked the Hatch Act, the bill provided an additional $15,000 per year to the stations, but with two important changes. The new money was limited "only to paying the necessary expenses of conducting original researches or experiments" with no provision for "diffusing . . . practical information," as the Hatch Act had done. And in the fashion of the 1890 Morrill Act, the Adams bill provided the $15,000 increase gradually: $5,000 the first year, and thereafter an incremental increase of $2,000 per year until the $30,000 ceiling had been reached. Adams got the bill on the calendar and to the floor for debate in a matter of weeks. Despite his impassioned pleas—and the show of support by letters from twenty-three station directors, printed in the *Congressional Record*—the bill did not come to a vote before Congress adjourned in March.[47]

Perhaps it was good it did not. The original version of the Adams bill was, in the opinion of Atherton and Henry White's executive committee, seriously flawed. Atherton wrote to Adams in mid-February that the bill had been written so as "to ignore the Institution to which the Experiment Station is by law a branch, and placed the Director in immediate relations with the Secretary of Agriculture, and, to a considerable extent, under his direction." Atherton construed the bill to be a departure from the intent of the Hatch Act that would "awaken the most serious antagonism throughout the country."[48]

At the same time, the Association's attention was riveted by another matter. In its annual appropriation bill, the Department of Agriculture quietly had inserted a clause authorizing the agriculture secretary to coordinate the work of the experiment stations with the Department of Agriculture. The department proposed that such an arrangement would prevent unnecessary duplication of work, increase the efficiency of the stations and the Department of Agriculture, and systematize agricultural research. Here, plain and simple, was a plan to absorb the stations into Wilson's burgeoning department. Atherton wrote Goodell that the move confirmed his apprehension "that the

Department is trying to reach out its hands into every State and Territory in such a way as practically to annex the Stations." Atherton also wrote to Pennsylvania's U.S. Senator Boise Penrose, calling Wilson an "ambitious and not overscrupulous secretary, building up enormous political power."[49]

The Association's executive committee did not learn of this maneuver until the bill had passed the House without a dissenting vote. The committee then wired the chairman of the Senate Agriculture Committee, who assured them that the Senate would reject or modify the clause. Committee members visited Washington, D.C., conferring with the agriculture committees of both houses and securing a unanimous agreement to reject the clause. For the Association—particularly the college presidents—the Department of Agriculture's bold annexation plan evinced the need to strengthen the stations. Aside from the obvious threat that the stations would be absorbed, it was increasingly apparent that the stations were in danger of being overshadowed completely by the Department of Agriculture. The executive committee observed that, in recent years, the department had given rise to "a number of bureaus of purely scientific research, . . . a field of endeavor which formerly was occupied by the State Stations."[50]

Wilson later tried to repatriate himself with the Association. In late 1904, after the death of Assistant Secretary of Agriculture Joseph H. Brigham, former master of the national Grange, the Association requested Secretary Wilson and President Theodore Roosevelt to place a station scientist in the post, as had been done in the Rusk and Morton administrations. Atherton particularly favored Armsby for the post, but the eventual choice was Willet M. Hays, a station scientist at the University of Minnesota and a candidate who was thoroughly acceptable to the Association. And at the 1905 convention, Atherton's last, Wilson told the Association he wanted to help strengthen the stations: "The Federal government is not giving the station men money enough. . . . I am earnestly urging upon Congress to give the stations more money to enable them to do their work."[51] Earlier that year, in hearings of the House Agriculture Committee, Wilson had argued unsuccessfully that the department could conduct state research programs more efficiently than the stations, but in fact he inadvertently made a strong case for increased funding for the stations when he said the department was doing much of the work stations could do—if only they had greater resources at their disposal.[52]

Adams reintroduced his bill in December 1905; it passed both houses of Congress with relative ease and was signed into law by President Theodore Roosevelt on March 16, 1906. With the act came an implicit repudiation of the Atherton station philosophy enunciated in 1889, a philosophy born of political necessity as well as educational theory: that teaching, as well as research, was an essential part of the stations' mission. Instead, the Adams Act codified the Atwater standard—and the scientific research philosophy of Armsby, Henry, and Jordan—toward which True had been trying to prod the stations for more than a decade.

The Department of Agriculture, after years of frustration with the disbursement of Hatch Act funds for dubious station activities, instituted an important new procedure to ensure that the annuities would be used "only to paying the necessary expenses of conducting original researches or experiments." In a circular to station directors, Wilson required a new system of accountability. Each station was to outline annually the research programs to which Adams Act funds would be applied. Further, Wilson precluded changes in these programs "until the problems under investigation have been solved, or their solution definitely shown to be impracticable."[53]

This mandate, to be executed by True in the Office of Experiment Stations, inaugurated the "project approach" to federally sponsored scientific research. True asked the station directors to draw up "definite and specific projects for the use of the Adams fund and to submit these in advance for his approval." Each project was to state the area of concern, the specific problem to be addressed, and the specific experiments and methods that would yield a solution, along with cost estimates. This approach was gradually expanded to include research conducted under original Hatch funds as well as state funds.[54]

More profound, perhaps, was that the Adams Act further legitimatized the principle of federal funding for scientific research—in a matrix of decentralized research units. The full implications of this pattern for the conduct of national science policy would become evident after World War II. In terms of agricultural science, these arrangements encouraged station scientists to work at the highest level of their disciplines, and it gave them the means to conduct the basic research leading to publication in scientific journals and enhanced academic recognition. Despite the tighter accountability under which they were to operate, the experiment stations gained new vigor. They had parried the thrust of Wilson's aggressive Department of Agriculture, winning a strategic victory in their often ambivalent relationship with an increasingly powerful federal agency.[55] Beyond the psychological lift and immediate financial impact, the Adams Act also began to stimulate substantial funding increases in some states for research along similar lines.

Yet to whatever extent the Adams Act marked a "strategic victory" for the Association and especially for the stations, it also heralded the introduction of direct federal control into higher education. The stations, still legally regarded as departments of the colleges, now needed prior approval for part of their research agenda before they could proceed.

For the scientists, this was perfectly acceptable. After nearly twenty years, they had finally freed themselves from college interference. The stations now benefited from a steady stream of federal funding that had taken away the colleges' voice in how the funds were to be used. With the Adams Act, agricultural experiment stations cast their lot with the U.S. Department of Agriculture, exchanging direct accountability for direct funding. The new relationship was reflected in subsequent legislation: the Purnell Act of 1925, for "the more complete endowment of agricultural experiment stations"; the Bankhead-Jones Act of 1935, "to provide for research into basic laws and principles relating to agriculture"; the amendment of the Bankhead-Jones Act and the Agricultural Marketing Act of 1946 "to provide for further research into basic laws and principles relating to agriculture and to improve . . . the marketing and distribution of agricultural products"; and the amended Hatch Act of 1955, which consolidated all these acts "for the support of agricultural experiment stations."[56]

For the Association, the irony of the Adams Act is that this "strategic victory" also represented a tacit defeat in terms of the Association's ability to resolve its own problems. The Association found that it took an act of Congress to do what it had been unable to for so many years: resolve the fundamental debate about station mission and station accountability, which had remained a divisive issue after nearly two decades.

The Mechanic Arts

The Association's preoccupation with the affairs of agricultural research and education did not bode well for the other fork of industrial education: the mechanic arts. Engineering faculty felt uncomfortable with the Association, for the Association paid little attention to the engineers. For good or ill, the Association's cachet in Washington, D.C., was agriculture—itself a remarkably strong focus of national policy from the Civil War through World War I. Engineering, by contrast, could claim virtually no constituency. Despite its fast growth as a profession in a rapidly industrializing America, its formally trained practitioners were relatively few in number, particularly when compared with the number of "practitioners" in agriculture. There was a sense that engineers were critical to the development of the nation but that the problem was solving itself according to the demands of an insatiable job market.

Ironically, however, engineering (mechanical, civil, electrical, and to a lesser extent mining and chemical) and not agriculture was the mainstay at a majority of land-grant institutions. Agricultural enrollments remained slight through the 1890s at most of the colleges, but engineering enrollments soared. For example, at the Pennsylvania State College about 70 percent of the 1893–94 student body had elected to study engineering. In 1900, a list prepared by Penn State's engineering dean showed that the schools with the largest undergraduate engineering enrollments were, with one exception, all land-grant institutions: Cornell, 754; California, 729; MIT, 535; Purdue, 450; Ohio State, 330; Wisconsin, 328; Iowa State, 311; Illinois, 287; Missouri, 214; and Penn State, 209. There were a few notable omissions from the list, however. Columbia the same year enrolled 414 students in its school of "applied science," Michigan enrolled 280 in its engineering curriculum, and Minnesota, a land-grant university, enrolled 209 in engineering.[57]

Nonetheless, the bulk of engineering students were found at land-grant colleges—indeed, it is fair to say that they dominated the campuses. Of the 15,841 "collegiate" students enrolled at the sixty-five land-grant universities in 1901, some 9,232 (nearly 60 percent) were in engineering.[58] Moreover, with the students often came money; at Penn State, $680,000 was received from the state between 1887 and 1897 for engineering facilities alone.[59]

The Association first called for a mechanic arts section in 1892, recognizing the prominent position that engineering had come to occupy in many of the land-grant colleges. The same year, when the Association met in Chicago in conjunction with the World's Columbian Exposition, the new Section on Mechanic Arts held its first meeting.

More important, engineers that same year and in the same place founded their own independent organization, the Society for the Promotion of Engineering Education. The engineers also had their own professional organizations: the American Society of Civil Engineers, the American Society of Mechanical Engineers, and the American Institute of Electrical Engineers. It was to these organizations—not to the Association—that engineers looked to resolve their professional issues and carry out their legislative agenda.

By 1894, the Association's Section on Mechanic Arts was already discontented. The section's report had not been printed in the general convention program, and the engineers interpreted the mistake as an intentional slight. The chairman of the section suggested the Association might change its name to the Association of American Agricultural and Mechanical Colleges, but the suggestion was ignored.[60] The year following, the engineers asked for delegate status but realized their request would be to no avail: "Most of our men interested in the mechanic arts are indifferent toward doing work for the Association, claiming that the Association is essentially agricultural and it is the intention of the agriculturists to keep it within such limits."[61]

Things began to improve over the next few years. In early February 1896, a Senate bill (S. 2301) was introduced to establish engineering experiment stations, much along the lines of the agricultural experiment stations. Another bill had been introduced the same year to establish naval engineering programs at the land-grant colleges, but a survey by the Section on Mechanic Arts showed that, of the two, the Association overwhelmingly preferred the engineering experiment station bill. Such a bill was deemed to have positive implications for engineering programs at the colleges, which (another section survey showed) varied in quality. At the bottom end were colleges "having a course of study scarcely better than that of the high school," and at the other end were those "whose requirements for admission would demand the completion of a first-class high-school course." Finally, the section discussed ways to attract more engineers to Association conventions. Of the 199 men registered as delegates and visitors at the 1896 convention, 12 were identifiable as engineers—and this was flood tide in the short life of the section.[62]

The Association appointed a special committee in 1896 to promote the engineering experiment station bill, but after two years the committee reported no progress. It was evident the bill was not an Association priority, the committee reported.[63] A year later, the committee chairman suggested that engineering programs might not yet be ready for experiment stations, as "most of the experimental work in this department was largely being done by the students instead of by the investigators."[64]

By 1901, there were indications that some engineers were prepared to abolish the section, which happened two years later by dint of the 1903 constitutional revision creating only two sections in the Association. After a brief life of ten years, the Association's engineering section would be moribund until 1919. The engineering experiment station movement, such as it was, would remove itself to the state level, where it met with only limited success. Industry was prospering sufficiently, and there were no strong demands for such facilities. Nevertheless, Illinois established a station in 1902, and Iowa State followed suit in 1904. In 1909, Pennsylvania State College trustees approved the creation of an experiment station within the School of Engineering, but because no provisions were made to finance the unit, the school restricted its activity to producing bulletins prepared by engineering instructors.[65]

The Land-Grant College Curriculum

No more important issue presented itself to the Association than that of curriculum, a subject that deeply interested Atherton. As the Association viewed it, the issue of curriculum reform contained several dimensions. Foremost was the question of balance between technical and general or liberal arts coursework, a burning issue that brought the presidents' educational philosophies to bear on the subject. Most of them had been educated in the liberal arts tradition and were extremely sensitive to charges that their institutions were turning out vocationalists. For years, Atherton had insisted that the mandate of the Morrill Act was essentially liberal. "While the College will keep this practical aim constantly in view," he said in his 1883 inaugural address at the Pennsylvania State College, it will also try to effect the "harmonious and symmetrical development of all the faculties which distinguishes the thoroughly educated from the half-educated. Not simply the artisan, but the scholar; not simply the scholar, but the man."

Even at so auspicious an event for technical education as the dedication of Penn State's new engineering building in 1893, in which the governor and the trustees' chairman bespoke the glories of engineering education, Atherton reminded the audience that the nation would not achieve greatness merely by educating technicians:

> I hear a louder cry than that which has been named. I, too, hear the coming century asking for the Engineer, the Electrician . . . but, when I see a republic like ours, whose foundations are and must be laid in the intelligence of the people, when I see in the midst of it this seething ferment of unrest that is taking possession of the hearts and minds of men, I conceive that one of the highest, if not the very highest, duties of an institution of this kind is to train men for citizenship, and to me the cry of the coming century is, "Give me the Engineer, Give me the Electrician," but above all, "Give me the all-around, well-trained man."[66]

Atherton and other land-grant presidents took seriously the idea that the Morrill Act's true intention was the liberal education of the industrial classes. This interpretation took on an especially important meaning in the context of the land-grant college. The prevailing assumption was that, unlike the students attracted to the older, elite eastern colleges, the matriculants at land-grant institutions tended to bring with them deficient educational backgrounds. It could not be assumed that these students had been exposed to "the best that has been thought and said" in their educational preparation, and thus it became the duty of the land-grant college curriculum to ensure that such an exposure took place.

Land-grant college presidents came to deal with the issue of curriculum from another direction—that of standardizing a land-grant curriculum to ensure a minimal level of liberal education. The colleges sought to ensure that, despite varying local conditions, their bachelor of science degree would represent a certain standard of curricular breadth, depth, and by implication quality, no matter where the degree was obtained. Surveys showed that, even in the mid-1890s, some land-grant institutions were only nominally "colleges," providing instruction on what was mainly a secondary level. Through the Association, the college presidents attempted to correct the situation. They worked to bring the land-grant colleges, as a system of institutions, into academic respectability by developing and advocating a revised curriculum for member institutions. In this important respect, the Association assumed the function of an accrediting body.

In 1894, the Association's Section on College Work discussed the issue of variability in entrance requirements and in baccalaureate degree coursework and successfully urged the appointment of a committee to conduct a comprehensive study of the situation. Chaired by Charles S. Murkland, president of the New Hampshire College of Agriculture and Mechanic Arts, the committee included Atherton; Abram W. Harris, president of Maine State College; John M. McBryde, president of the Virginia Polytechnic Institute at Blacksburg; and Thomas F. Hunt, a professor of agriculture at Ohio State.[67]

At the 1896 convention, the Section on College Work unveiled a study conducted by Joseph E. Stubbs, president of Nevada Agricultural College, on entrance requirements. He reported that of the 46 land-grant colleges two-thirds had preparatory departments and that, of those, the majority (18) required either one or two years of work. The variability in prerequisite coursework for admission to the freshman class was dismaying. Only one subject, U.S. history, was required by all 46 institutions. In English, only 18 colleges required standard high-school preparation; 28 required only eighth- or ninth-grade work. Most institutions (38) required arithmetic and algebra (34), but at that point the requirements dropped off considerably. Especially telling was that scientific prerequisites were few. Only 9 colleges required chemistry, the sine qua non of the agricultural sciences, and only 8 required botany, but 17 required physiology and 15 required physics. No college required Latin or Greek, but 8 required proficiency in French or German.

The study concluded that the land-grant colleges were divided into two classes: the first admitted students from eighth or ninth grade and then shunted them into the agriculture curriculum, which became "in the main a technical high-school course of study"; the second required completion of a high-school course of study for admission to its freshman class and then "seeks to maintain strong four-year courses in agriculture, and in the applied science courses."[68]

Such a bifurcation raised a serious legal issue, as noted by both the Stubbs study and the Committee on Entrance Requirements, Courses of Study, and Degrees. Because the land-grant institutions were required by law to be "collegiate in scope," the Committee on Entrance Requirements—on which Atherton served—recommended a cluster of courses designed to ensure, in the face of varying local conditions, uniformity in "scope and character." The committee noted that current educational conditions across the nation made it impossible to require of land-grant college students "that their liberal training should be acquired in preparatory schools," so they should include in their coursework "certain elements of a liberal or general education." Consequently, the committee recommended that certain general studies courses be required for the bachelor's degree: mathematics through algebra, geometry, and trigonometry; physics and chemistry, with laboratory work in each; English for at least two years; a modern language, four years; mental science and logic or moral science, one year; social, political, or economic science, one year; and a course in constitutional law—the latter courses recommended by Atherton.

Theoretically, the committee stated, those general education requirements should consume about 1,285 hours of coursework over the four years. Since the total number of hours for a bachelor's degree would come to 3,600 (assuming fifteen hours a week plus ten hours of laboratory work over eight eighteen-week semesters), the general education component should "comprise about two-fifths of the work required for a bachelor's degree."

As for entrance requirements, the committee recommended a standard series and, in a concession to the newer institutions in the West, a minimum series. The maximum standard called for completion of prerequisite courses in physical geography; U.S. history; arithmetic, including metrics; algebra through quadratics; English grammar and composition; plane geometry; one foreign language; one of the natural sciences; and ancient, general, or English history. The minimum standard called for physical geography; U.S. history; arithmetic, including metrics; algebra through quadratics; and English grammar and composition.

In all, the committee recommended and the Association endorsed four main recommendations: (1) that a standard and minimum series of entrance requirements be adopted; (2) that approximately fifteen hours of coursework (lectures and recitations) and ten hours of laboratory be required each week over a thirty-six-week academic year; (3) that the general education component—about 40 percent of all coursework—be adopted as part of the curriculum; and (4) that the degree of bachelor of science be recognized as the standard degree conferred by the colleges of the Association. The fourth recommendation implicitly called for an end to the bachelor of agriculture degree, to which even the agriculturists in the Association readily acceded because of the degree's inferior connotation. Although certain presidents objected to the modern language requirement, the report was adopted by a vote of 34 to 11. Education Commissioner William T. Harris, also in attendance, called the plan "a very wise report."[69] The following year, 1897, brought a recommended revision by another committee to the agriculture curriculum. In response to the 1896 report, the committee called for 1,746 hours in the 3,600-hour baccalaureate program to be devoted to agriculture (486 hours) and such related subjects as horticulture and forestry, veterinary science, agricultural chemistry, botany, zoology, physiology, geology, meteorology, and drawing.[70]

The curriculum reform plan of 1896—although it carried no real authority and contained no punitive measures—also represented a reaction to the rapid subdivision of disciplines and the perceived tendency toward overspecialization. The new theory of higher education, as Enoch A. Bryant of the State College of Washington pointed out in an 1898 address, contained among its tenets the propositions that it was no longer essential to cover the whole field of human knowledge, even in an elementary way, and that adequate investigation of one or a few subjects, with the acquisition of the scientific method and the power of independent investigation, was "better than superficial study of many subjects."[71] However much the Association's college presidents agreed with those propositions, each had his own strong views on what land-grant colleges needed to inculcate above all else. In sum, the presidents called for a curriculum that delivered a strong measure of humanistic, moral, and citizenship education.

To a surprising extent, the values of liberal education were revered among land-grant leaders. In 1900, for example, Association President Joseph E. Stubbs of Nevada sounded the call for liberal culture: "The exaltation of ethical values is of the most worth in modern education," he said. "From our secondary and even our higher education . . . we must exclude all overparticularization and all overspecialization. Our first aim shall be to make men endowed with the great social virtues. The useful must be incarnated with the true and the beautiful in a personality."[72] The following year, Association President Abram W. Harris of Maine credited the land-grant colleges with passing "from the narrow and particular to the broad and general."[73] Association President James K. Patterson in 1903 called for citizenship training, which he defined as a steeping in the history and lore of the United States: "The moral and religious tone of the country upon which the greatness of the nation will depend will be influenced largely by the moral and religious tone which pervades the colleges and universities which compose this Association."[74]

Graduate Training and the National University Idea

Graduate study at the land-grant colleges was in its infancy during the 1890s. Where it did exist, it came in the form of advanced work usually under the auspices of the agricultural experiment stations. By 1901, the sixty-five land-grant institutions reported a "post-graduate" enrollment of 495 students. Coupled with the 15,814 undergraduates, graduate enrollment constituted roughly 3 percent of the total.[75] Such a proportion was consistent with the 2.4 percent share of national higher education enrollments claimed by graduate students at the turn of the century, yet significantly below the nearly 9 percent share that graduate students represented at the fifteen leading research universities of the day.[76]

The subject of graduate work was, however, of great concern to Association members, most of whom were aware of the necessity for advanced work in the scientific and technical fields. Faced with the constraints at their own institutions, they devised a novel solution: a graduate study consortium composed of the federal scientific agencies in Washington, D.C., with the Smithsonian Institution as the administrative center of the program. The Association also flirted with the resuscitated national university movement of the 1890s championed by John W. Hoyt. Both efforts, although doomed to fail, shed light on the concerns of land-grant leaders for developing an infrastructure to provide advanced graduate work.

The movement for a graduate center in the nation's capital began in 1897 with the appointment of committee to devise a proposal by which graduate students of land-grant and other colleges "may have access to and the use" of the Library of Congress, the Smithsonian Institute, the National Museum, and the scientific bureaus of the various cabinet-level departments in Washington, D.C.[77] The next year, the committee reported some success, mainly in the form of receptivity for the idea on the part of certain department heads, the most enthusiastic being Agriculture Secretary Wilson. By 1899, True reported to the Association that the Department of Agriculture, in cooperation with the Civil Service Commission, was planning to accept graduate student interns from the colleges to study in the various scientific bureaus. The Civil Service viewed the plan as an experiment; if successful, the commission would "be inclined to favor its extension to other branches of government."[78] The larger plan, dependent on the Smithsonian Institution, had begun to go awry, however. The Smithsonian considered itself "scarcely broad enough to embrace the work proposed," and by 1903 the dream had died.

The Committee on Graduate Study did manage to create—under Association auspices—a summer Graduate School in Agriculture that traveled from institution to institution. The first such school was held at Ohio State in 1902 and was a "decided success," with seventy-five students. The next school was convened at the University of Illinois in the summer of 1906.

The national university movement, its genealogy stretching back to George Washington, was revived in the 1890s and touched tangentially on the Association's interests. The movement to create a capstone public university in the nation's capital was championed by John W. Hoyt from 1869 until his death in 1912. Early on, however, Hoyt had made the supreme tactical error of disparaging most of the existing American universities, thus antagonizing their presidents—Charles Eliot of Harvard in particular. The idea languished legislatively until a Senate bill was introduced in 1890. Hoyt arrived on the scene shortly thereafter, and over the next two decades mounted a huge letter-writing campaign to secure the support of prominent Americans, educational leaders in particular. By the mid-1890s, Hoyt had put together a Committee of 400 and claimed that the national university would now be financed by major philanthropic gifts rather than the public treasury. Despite Hoyt's persistence, support for the idea of the national university was nominal rather than substantive.[79]

Hoyt targeted Penn State's George Atherton, among hundreds of others, as a worthy patron of the movement and began writing to him to enlist his support. By 1896, however, it was apparent that a number of hindrances had arisen. Among them, Hoyt wrote to Atherton, were the depressed national economy, the lack of interest in Congress, and most important, the "open and active opposition" of the chancellor of the American University, a Methodist institution, and the reluctance of politicians to challenge his position.[80]

In 1898, Hoyt spoke to the Association and suggested that a national postgraduate university would be a logical outgrowth of the national university.[81] By 1899, however, the movement had stalled. Hoyt wrote Atherton that, aside from the opposition of the Methodist church, there were more formidable opponents in the field, "some in high places in Washington and some connected with or blindly attached to certain of the proud old universities of the East."[82] Two years later, Atherton told Hoyt that he had found some sentiment among Association members for a national university, "but with the undefined feeling that such an Institution must be a slow growth rather than a specific creation. . . . The truth is that we are all so absorbed with our own affairs that it seems impossible to turn aside for other matters, however important."[83]

The idea had outlived its usefulness. In the century following George Washington's suggestion of a national institution, America had given rise to a profusion of colleges. There was, simply put, no need for such an institution in turn-of-century America. And as Henry C. White had suggested to the Association in his president's address of 1898, the land-grant colleges already had reified Washington's national university ideal:

> Morrill has here wisely laid an appropriate foundation for the realization of the dream of Washington and prepared a proper way for the coming of the scholar of Emerson: that within these great national schools lies the germ of the national university. . . . Here we have not one institution but a great number of similar institutions with oneness of purpose.[84]

The Association and Military Instruction

Just as the Association had entered into closer relationships with the departments of Agriculture and the Interior (Education) in the 1890s, it found itself dealing more frequently with the Department of War. Every land-grant college took seriously the provision of the original Morrill Act to include the teaching of military tactics; indeed, the sixty-five colleges reported a total of 11,024 students enrolled in military classes in 1901. The specifics of the military programs varied considerably from campus to campus, however, as much was left to local interpretation. An act of 1866 provided for the detailing of army officers as instructors of military science at land-grant institutions, but the Army—reduced to a small standing force for peacetime—did not provide them consistently. Thus the colleges often appointed a faculty member who could do double duty: teach an academic discipline and provide military instruction. After the Civil War, such men were not hard to find. The Pennsylvania State College in 1865 employed General John Fraser as professor of mathematics and lecturer on military tactics. At Rutgers, George Atherton had been hired in dual capacities as well.[85]

A quarter-century after the Civil War, the situation began to change. The colleges began to agitate for the Department of War to provide supplies, particularly uniforms and arms, for student drill. At the same time, the War Department began to regard the land-grant colleges as an unwelcome expenditure as it sought to economize. The Navy entered the picture too. In 1890, Atherton had represented the Association in congressional hearings for a bill to increase the number of engineers in the Navy's engineering corps. The bill resurfaced in early 1896 as H.R. 3618 (S. 735) to "establish and maintain courses of instruction in naval engineering in the scientific and technological schools of the United States." The Association appointed Atherton to chair a committee to study the matter, and Atherton made an extensive report on the proposed legislation at the 1896 convention.

The intent of the so-called "Wilson–Squire bill" was to halt the decline in the number of engineering officers in the Navy. The engineering corps had been reduced from a high of 2,279 in 1865 to 173 in 1895—one fewer than the total before the war. At the same time, the Navy was building a modern fleet, in which steel and steam were replacing wood and wind. The demand for engineers who could operate the new vessels was acute. The bill, Atherton reported, would select mechanical engineering graduates and give them a year's appointment as engineer cadets. The best engineering cadets would be appointed to vacancies in the engineering corps. The benefit to the colleges would be to gain an engineering faculty member, detailed from the Corps of Naval Engineers at no cost to the colleges. The bill also provided for the establishment of an engineering experiment station that would relate to the Corps of Naval Engineers. The Association endorsed the bill and bade Atherton's committee pursue its passage, but the measure died in the next session of Congress.[86]

Reversing a tradition of ignoring the colleges, the Department of

War in 1890 issued general orders No. 91, which finally addressed the manner in which the land-grant institutions were to interpret the Morrill Act. The orders called for a course that was both theoretical and practical, recommending an hour a week for the former and two hours for the latter. By that time, however, most colleges were requiring an average of four hours per week, according to a study by Charles Dabney, president of the University of Tennessee. By the early 1890s, because of growing labor unrest, the colleges and government officials had begun to see the utility of land-grant military training in a different light. State militias were being used increasingly to quell labor riots, and as Dabney had noted, in a recent "miners' war" in Tennessee "nearly all of the commissioned officers in the state militia . . . were the graduates of our Tennessee University."[87]

If the value of land-grant military training had suddenly become apparent, the Association reasoned, then the time had come to press the Department of War for uniforms and other supplies that would make that training more effective. The Association authorized the executive committee to ask for legislation that would "enable the Secretary of War to supply the military departments of the . . . colleges with the necessary uniforms and garrison equipment." The Association figured the cost to be about $240,000 for equipping the land-grant "army" of 12,000 cadets, most of whom were still drilling with Civil War muzzle-loaders. Officers to provide military instruction were needed as well. Yet there was disturbing evidence that the Army and Navy had detailed more officers to "private educational institutions or voluntarily military schools" than to land-grant colleges. After the Association had exerted some pressure, Congress in 1893 approved an increase in the number of officers permitted to be detailed to educational institutions.[88]

In 1894, however, the situation was entirely different. It was as if the secretary of war, Stephen B. Elkins, had himself ordered a frontal attack on the land-grant colleges, but the actions were part of the general federal retrenchment ordered by the Cleveland administration in response to the economic downturn of 1893. The Army appropriations bill had proposed to cut off the housing allowance for officers detailed to the institutions and to ask the colleges to provide housing for free. In its wake came a report from adjutant general proposing to stop detailing officers to land-grant colleges with fewer than 150 students in their military contingent, and instead to assign these officers to large urban high schools. Under Alvord, the executive committee lobbied successfully in Congress to excise the offensive housing clause from the appropriations bill, but the other matter would not be so quickly resolved. In the following year, 1895, the executive committee managed to obtain a clause in the bill, still pending, that purported to detail officers to large high schools: the Army promised not to transfer these officers from land-grant colleges.[89]

In 1896, Atherton was appointed chairman of the Association's new Committee on Military Instruction, the need for which had become obvious. The charge was to adjust relations between the Department of War and the land-grant colleges, and especially to protest the department's refusal to detail officers to colleges that had only small military contingents.

Atherton and his colleagues found that the Spanish-American War of 1898 altered the relationship of the War Department with the colleges, and not necessarily for the better. The order of the U.S. President to appoint a certain number of second lieutenants from the ranking student cadets upset the colleges because they were not first consulted. Worse, the failure of a small number of these cadets to pass their physical examinations caused the Army to bypass the colleges in general and look elsewhere for recruits.

Nonetheless, the land-grant college contribution to the war effort was considerable, especially in terms of the number of graduates staffing the officer corps of the volunteer army. A study by Dabney showed that, although comparatively few students were accepted into the army outright, a total of 1,345 officers in the war had received their military training at land-grant colleges. These represented more than 10 percent of the total volunteer and regular army officer corps of 11,108.

Atherton's military instruction committee concluded that the time had come for the government to "recognize the military departments of these colleges as actual military colleges." The committee recommended that regular army commissions be awarded to honors graduates from the colleges and that the colleges be supplied with armories and be furnished with modern arms and equipment.[90]

The next year, Atherton and Goodell twice visited Washington, D.C., to present the case of the land-grant institutions to the War Department, but they were told that the detailing of officers to the colleges was not likely to increase for the time being. The officer ranks had been reduced by Spanish-American War casualties, and the ongoing hostilities in the Philippines made it unlikely that officers would be detailed soon for college instruction.[91]

In 1902, a new set of general orders (No. 94) inflamed the colleges. Secretary of War Elihu Root was now requiring a minimum of five hours a week of military instruction (up from three hours, with most colleges offering four). The order also required a daily guard mounting and, aside from many other irritants, reduced the traditional number of years for an officer's detail at the colleges from four to two.[92] Atherton's committee was willing, reluctantly, to accept the five-hour minimum, but it also presented three other recommendations to the secretary. These called for the required number of years for military instruction to be held at two, the modal figure at most colleges; that military instruction and discipline be confined to military exercises; and that instruction be weighted toward strategy and tactics rather than drill.

A series of unproductive meetings with the secretary of war caused the usually taciturn Atherton to vent his frustrations with the War Department at the Association's 1903 convention—in fact, he called for a disbanding of his Committee on Military Instruction. The reduction of the detail from four to two years, Atherton said, "may be just to the officers...[but] it is extremely hard on the institutions." He added that some of the officers, particularly the younger ones, "come to the college with an impression that they have been sent to take command of the institution. I have often wished in the course of these years that . . . the Secretary of War would consult us in advance."[93]

Yet Atherton's committee was kept intact, and though his health was rapidly deteriorating and his energy and interest were waning, some limited success was in the offing. Through another visit to the secretary of war, he was able to secure a revision in the colleges' favor regarding the detailing of officers. The tour of duty was revised upward from two to three years, thereby providing more stability for the institutions.

But Atherton had no success in securing a reduction of the five-hour minimum for military instruction, which was solidified by the issuance of new general orders No. 65. Atherton's report to that effect upset several of his colleagues, in particular Charles R. Van Hise, president of the University of Wisconsin. With Atherton absent from the 1904 convention, Van Hise rammed through a resolution calling for no more than two hours a week and authorizing the executive committee—not Atherton's military instruction committee—to present it to the secretary of war. The executive committee in 1905 reported that it had secured "very desirable modifications" of the regulations.[94]

Mining School Legislation

By 1900, the mining industries of the United States had surpassed the billion-dollar mark in total output for the year, representing a 90 percent increase since 1870. The growth of the mining industry brought new academic departments of mines and mining engineering into being at land-grant and some state colleges and universities. In addition, independent schools of mines were established in at least five states. At the Pennsylvania State College, instruction in mining engineering was provided for the first time in 1893, and a School of Mines was one of seven new schools created in the curriculum reorganization of 1895–96. By 1901, about 5 percent of the land-grant baccalaureate enrollment—806 of 15,814—were studying mining engineering, and the demand for such graduates was insatiable.[95]

In late 1899 and early 1900, several congressmen had introduced bills to establish federally endowed schools of mines in their localities. Sensing the threat, the Association moved to introduce legislation providing for such schools at land-grant colleges. The executive committee, chaired by Goodell, turned to its master craftsman—Atherton—to draft such a bill. By April 1900, the bill (S. 3982) had been introduced by Benjamin R. Tillman of the Senate Committee on Mines and Mining. The bill, proposed to benefit land-grant colleges by applying proceeds from the sale of the public lands "to the endowment, support and maintenance of schools or departments of mining and metallurgy." It called for an immediate grant of $10,000, to be increased by annual $1,000 increments until the ceiling of $20,000 a year had been reached. And the uses of the appropriation were quite liberal:

> for geological instruction, mining engineering, metallurgy, research in road-building material and its proper application, and the branches of learning pertaining thereto, including the various branches of physical, natural and economic science, and the facilities for such instruction, research and experiment in order to promote a liberal and practical education and secure the most intelligent use, conservation, and development of the mineral resources of this country.[96]

The bill passed the Senate, but failed to move in the House. After asking Representative John Dalzell of the House Ways and Means

Fig. 13.   **Atherton at His Desk, Circa 1900.**

Committee to place the bill on the docket, Atherton received a disappointing response. Dalzell said he saw no possibility that the bill would be passed during the current session: "It ultimately means a very large draft upon the federal treasury and serious doubts are entertained by many as to the propriety of the federal government going any further in the direction of higher education."[97] The executive committee adopted the bill as its most important priority, and Atherton, having been returned to the committee at the 1900 convention, played the key role in pressing for the bill's passage. He succeeded in having the bill reintroduced in both the House (H.R. 250, December 2, 1901, sponsored by Charles H. Grosvenor) and the Senate (S. 634, December 4, 1901, sponsored by Tillman).

Hearings by the House Committee on Mines and Mining in January and February 1902—at which Atherton testified for the Association—produced a compromise amendment. The independent schools of mines, in the process of forming their own national association, and the old state universities, having already formed their own national organization, wanted a share of the bounty. Atherton did not propose to fight on two fronts, but he suggested that including the state universities would be a breach of congressional policy. The acts of 1862 and 1890, he said, had clearly construed the land-grant colleges to be the federal government's instrument of national policy in higher education: "For Congress to change its policy now and divert any of these grants to the old universities ... will be to say, we will go back on the policy Congress has established and consistently followed in the last forty years."[98] Nonetheless, a compromise amendment was reached. In states with an independent school of mines or a state university with a department of mining of at least two years' standing, the funds would be split evenly with the land-grant college. Even with the amendment, however, the House Committee on Rules failed to rule on the bill's consideration.

In 1903, Atherton was approached by the new National Association of State Mining Schools. One of its leaders, noting that the motives for organizing included "the hope that we might work more effectively in the effort to get the right kind of a Mining School appropriations bill through Congress," invited Atherton to join the organization and attend their conference. This he did, writing to the president of Purdue that he "did not know how far the movers propose to try to ignore the land-grant colleges, but do know that we cannot afford to let them."[99]

Atherton had gone off the executive committee with Goodell after the 1902 convention, yet he maintained a strong interest in the mining bill. As the Association's champion of the measure, Atherton worked on its behalf with Henry C. White, president of the University of Georgia and the new executive committee chairman. In early 1904, they succeeded in having the compromise bill reintroduced through Representative Franklin W. Mondell as H.R. 10869, but the bill failed. According to the executive committee, the bill's demise was attributable to the brevity of the congressional session and to the political currents of a presidential election year. By 1905, five years after the original bill had been introduced, the executive committee withdrew its support for the bill. The Association always took pains to choose its legislative support campaigns carefully, and the Adams bill had taken precedence.[100]

A Vehicle for Institutional Development

For the second generation (post–Hatch Act) of land-grant college presidents, the overarching value of the Association during the period 1890–1905 was its usefulness as a vehicle for institutional development and reform—mainly along the broadening and liberalizing lines that Atherton had long envisioned and articulated. The Association played a crucial role in representing the interests of the colleges vis-à-vis Congress and the federal administrative agencies, but this role came as a means to a larger end: the development of the colleges toward broad university structure and function. Far from being a mere presidents' club wherein members could compare notes and vent frustrations, the Association became the mechanism for shaping the colleges, not merely fine-tuning them.

Through the Association, the colleges approached the central issue of the land-grant curriculum, ensuring that the bachelor of science degree would represent intellectual breadth as well as depth, at a time when engineering dominated the institutions. The Association also sought creative solutions for the provision of graduate education—solutions beyond merely allowing it to evolve according to the vagaries of sixty-five different institutions.

In areas more directly involving agencies of the federal government, the Association sought both to strengthen financial support and to maintain autonomy and independence. This delicate balancing act met with various results. In the case of military affairs, in which Atherton was deeply involved, the Association succeeded in preserving institutional autonomy in terms of military instruction but failed to secure financial support for equipment and supplies. Conversely, in the realm of agricultural research, the Association succeeded in winning additional financial support (through the Adams Act) but lost a great deal of institutional autonomy in the process.

The effort to secure mining school legislation, which Atherton directed, should be examined in a different light, however. Although it can be viewed superficially as an attempt to add another federally supported dimension of scientific teaching and research to the colleges, it was a preemptive move as much as anything else. Many land-grant colleges already were offering mining engineering courses, but the proliferation of bills to endow independent mining schools prompted the Association to try to clear the field for the land-grant colleges. And the legislation that did emerge under Atherton's direction was at first only nominally designed to endow mining engineering schools. In actuality, it was a veiled attempt to create *another* second Morrill Act to obtain funds that would benefit a broad range of academic programs.

Through all of this a pattern remained constant: the college presidents used the Association as a vehicle for institutional development according to a common vision. But their task was all the more difficult because of enduring tension with the experiment station directors, who maneuvered the agricultural research function away from college control and into the hands of the Department of Agriculture, and the unwillingness of the federal government to provide additional financial support for anything other than agriculture.

7

The Atherton Legacy

A MAJOR REASON FOR George Atherton's central position among the second generation of land-grant college presidents was his close relationship with Senator Justin Morrill. For more than a quarter-century, the two men conferred and collaborated on legislation, worked together on its behalf, and otherwise corresponded and visited on matters related to the land-grant colleges. The correspondence from Morrill to Atherton reveals a personal affection as well as a professional admiration. When Morrill died in late 1898, there was no question among leaders of the Association of American Colleges and Experiment Stations as to who should deliver the eulogy.

George Atherton's Justin Morrill

For his part, and notwithstanding his own respect and affection for Morrill, Atherton showed no reluctance about using the senator's prestige to advance a vision of the land-grant college as a liberal and comprehensive institution. Indeed, there was no reason not to do so. Morrill's and Atherton's interpretations were identical, although there is strong reason to suspect that Atherton had an influence on Morrill that was as strong as the influence the senator had on the Penn State president.

Fig. 14.　**Justin Smith Morrill.**

Few American politicians below the office of U.S. President have
attracted the effusive praise bestowed on Justin Morrill, Vermont
congressman (1854–66), then senator (1866–98), and for the thirty
years between Presidents Grant and McKinley one of the most distinguished leaders of the Republican party. Morrill's hand was in a
staggeringly high number of bills and acts over his forty-four-year
tenure in Congress, but nowhere was his imprimatur more widely felt
than in the land-grant colleges he "fathered" in his acts of 1862 and 1890.

And nowhere did he have more enthusiastic admirers than among
the land-grant college presidents. Andrew D. White ranked Morrill's
educational achievements alongside "those of Hamilton in advocating
the Constitution, of Jefferson in acquiring Louisiana, and of Clay in
giving us a truly American policy."[1] Speaking in 1899, six months
after Morrill's death on December 28, 1898, President James K. Patterson
of the University of Kentucky placed him on a higher pedestal. Among
those who would remain "conspicuous for all time" would be "George
Washington . . . the creator; Abraham Lincoln . . . the preserver; and
Justin S. Morrill . . . who has laid deep forever, upon an enduring
foundation, the prosperity and perpetuity of republican institutions."[2]
And, as historian Earle Ross said, Morrill "gave a version of land-
grant history in no way dissuasive to his admirers," claiming credit for
unilaterally devising the 1862 bill that bore his name. Ross claimed
that Atherton, "one of the more ardent of this group," in his eulogy of
1900 "asserted that the titular author was in truth the real deviser
and founder. The address, undocumented and resting largely upon
assumption, was to be cited thereafter along with the Senator's memoranda as a definitive statement."[3]

Atherton's eulogy of Morrill was really a veiled exegesis of the
land-grant movement from the origin of the 1862 act through Morrill's
last initiative, a bill in 1898 to ensure that the colleges would receive
their 1890 annuities directly from the U.S. treasury if the proceeds
from public-land sales ever proved deficient. Atherton asserted that
"Mr. Morrill once assured me, in answer to an inquiry, that the
language [of the 1862 act] was his own." Indeed, in an 1883 letter to
Atherton, Morrill confirmed, "I think that the whole of it was drafted
by me. I do not now remember that anything was added by any other
person."[4] Morrill repeated that answer in an 1894 letter to Atherton, in
which he said: "My first bill . . . was introduced, and passed both
houses, in 1858. I do not remember of any assistance prior to its
introduction."[5]

For Atherton, the legitimacy of Morrill's claim to authorship did not stem from blind faith in the senator's assertion, but rather rested with Morrill's ex post facto interpretation of the act. If Atherton had an enduring frustration in his life, it lay in the appallingly narrow and inaccurate interpretations of the original Morrill Act tendered by farmers, agricultural societies, state legislators and congressmen. To Atherton, a literal reading of the act denoted a broad mandate: agriculture and the mechanic arts, yes, but also "the branches of learning related thereto." And just as explicitly, science, classical studies, and military tactics were to be among the subject matter. The intent, also stated in black and white, was to promote not only the practical education of the industrial classes but their "liberal" education as well.

Atherton contended that no one could interpret the act more liberally and comprehensively than Morrill, who did so often and consistently over forty years. To Atherton, the liberality of Morrill's interpretation offered irrefutable proof of authorship. Atherton pointed out in the eulogy that Morrill "on repeated occasions, public and private, stated the true intent and object of the law in language that leaves no room for doubt or question." He then quoted Morrill as saying publicly:

> It is perhaps needless to say that these colleges were not established or endowed for the sole purpose of teaching agriculture.... It never was intended to force the boys of farmers going into these institutions so to study that they should all come out farmers.... Obviously, not manual but intellectual instruction was the paramount object.... Classical studies were not to be excluded, and therefore, must be included. The act of 1862 proposed a system of broad education by colleges, not limited to a superficial and dwarfed training such as might be had at an industrial school, nor a mere manual training such as might be supplied by a foreman.[6]

Atherton added that, in Morrill's bill introduced on December 15, 1873 (which Atherton had helped to craft), the senator had called the institutions "national colleges for the advancement of general scientific and industrial education." Such a descriptor implied a far broader mission for the colleges than the name that had already been popularly attached to them: agricultural colleges.

Atherton did strike an occasional sycophantic note in eulogizing

Morrill (for example, "His excellences were so uniformly diffused through the whole man that no one seemed especially to predominate"), but it is fair to say that Atherton's interpretation of history saw "great men" not so much as causative factors as "the embodiment and representative of the life of [their] era." In short, though Atherton conferred "fatherhood" of the particular legislative act on Morrill, he saw the senator as the epitome of the movement, not the progenitor of it.

Atherton's peroration drew its inspiration from the famous epitaph for London architect Christopher Wren: "If you seek his monument, look around you." By 1899, Atherton said, the land-grant colleges totaled sixty-four institutions enrolling 35,956 students, of whom 18,899 were baccalaureate and graduate students, the rest being preparatory or special students. The same colleges had 2,893 faculty members and an annual income totaling $5,543,108.91.

In terms of finances, the essential point for Atherton was that, of the $5.5 million income, $4.2 million of it came from sources other than the federal government—state government, local government, and other sources, such as private giving and tuition and fees. (Although *The Report of the Commissioner of Education* shows the federal contribution to be nearly $2.5 million, rather than the $1.3 million Atherton had suggested, state funding alone outpaced federal support by nearly half a million dollars.) "Instead of encouraging inaction or indifference on the part of the States," Atherton said, congressional policies had "stimulated them to a degree of activity far in advance of that of Congress." Atherton's critical point was that the land-grant colleges were both beneficiaries and instruments of national policy, but they were hardly wards of the federal government.[7]

Atherton's address, "The Legislative Career of Justin S. Morrill," was reprinted as a booklet and widely circulated, and may have been partly responsible for the "Turner-Morrill controversy" over ownership of the idea behind the 1862 act. The controversy began in 1907 when Dean Eugene Davenport of the College of Agriculture at the University of Illinois advanced the "historical query" of whether Jonathan B. Turner, father of the Illinois industrial movement, had not "provided the ideas for the basic act." The question gained momentum when President Edmund James of the same university ordered an investigation of the matter in connection with a semicentennial project. James published a bulletin propounding the thesis that Turner was the first to formulate a plan for a national grant of land to each state for the promotion of education in agriculture and the mechanic arts. Turner was also alleged to have agitated sufficiently to get a bill for his plan passed by the Illinois state legislature.

The Morrill and Turner families became embroiled in argument. Later studies, such as one conducted by the Carnegie Foundation in 1917, either found the Turner claim to be unsubstantiated or declined to resolve the matter. In his own analysis, Ross found an 1865 statement by Turner in which Turner had written that Morrill "first presented the bill to Congress, known as the 'Morrill bill,' and secured its passage through the House. We forwarded to him all our documents and papers, and gave him all the aid and encouragement that we could. He managed the case most admirably." Ross therefore concluded: "There is no suggestion here of Illinois initiative which would have been stressed if true, and all other evidence is to the same effect. Less than two months before Morrill introduced his bill the Illinois interests at home and in Washington had no legislative plan, and that was obviously too short a time to prepare the measure and coach the spokesman. Most conclusive is the nature of the bill which differed so radically from Turner's general plan and the specific requests of his league."[8]

Ross's analysis substantiated Atherton's contention that Morrill wrote the measure on his own accord, although the Vermont legislator could hardly have been unaware of the strong desire for such a measure. Nevertheless, the key phrase to Ross's conclusion is that too little time was available to "coach the spokesman" (Morrill). That was precisely Atherton's point. Morrill hardly needed coaching, because he knew what he intended the colleges to be: the liberal as well as practical institutions that he had described in his bill, not the vocationally oriented institutions Turner had suggested. Whatever the occasion—a public speech or a Senate debate—Morrill never rejected the opportunity to interpret the colleges in the most liberal fashion or to correct anyone so ill-informed as to suggest a narrow, strictly vocational function for his beloved land-grant colleges.

Atherton's Role in Seminal Legislation

There is little question that George Atherton played the pivotal role in drafting, promoting, and otherwise instigating the major legislation that benefited the land-grant college movement after the Civil War. As early as 1873, Atherton began working with Morrill to fashion and promote a succession of the senator's "educational fund" bills, designed to create a federal endowment from the sale of public lands to aid public education — in particular the common (or elementary) schools and the land-grant colleges. The 1890 Morrill Act, minus the common school provision, was descended from the long line of such bills. The "educational fund" bills were based on the arguments for federal funding of public education that had been broached in Atherton's 1873 address, "The Relation of the General Government to Education."

Atherton's dominant role in rewriting and promoting the legislation that became the Hatch Act of 1887, establishing federally funded agricultural experiment stations in each state, is supported by ample evidence. From 1884 on, the initiative for the legislation lay mainly in his hands. And Atherton played a prominent role in the Association's campaign for the 1890 Morrill Act, which provided annual federal annuities for a range of educational purposes at land-grant colleges. He may have engineered Morrill's introduction of the bill in March 1890, he worked closely with Alvord and others in Washington to devise the promotional strategy for the bill, and he helped fashion the compromise amendment with the Grange.

Although Atherton's involvement with the Adams Act of 1906 was slight, it was important. He pointed to an oversight in the original bill, which failed to make explicit mention of the connection between the land-grant colleges and the agricultural experiment stations, the federal annuities for which were to be doubled. The version of the bill that eventually succeeded carried the desired language.

Not every legislative initiative was successful. In 1900, Atherton was pressed by the Association into a campaign to establish federally endowed schools of mines at land-grant colleges. Atherton wrote, or assisted in writing, the Tillman bill (S. 3982), introduced in April 1900, and he later represented the Association in congressional hearings on the legislation in 1902 and again in 1904. But Congress was reluctant to pass such legislation, and the Association abandoned its effort in favor of concentrating on the Adams Act.

Atherton's promotion of federal legislation to help support land-grant colleges was born of considerations beyond pure expediency. His efforts grew out of his educational and political philosophy. In his 1873 address titled "The Relation of the General Government to Education," Atherton contended that the federal government, in creating the colleges, had incurred a continuing obligation for their successful operation. Moreover, he refuted the argument that the U.S. Constitution implicitly relegated the responsibility for education to the states rather than the federal government. To Atherton, the Hatch Act, the 1890 Morrill Act, and the Adams Act were a congressional acknowledgment of the continuing federal obligation to public education and particularly to land-grant colleges. Taken as a whole, these acts represented a realization of Atherton's basic argument, which he articulated in his 1873 address and at every opportunity thereafter: "The United States Government must take a more direct and active interest than it has hitherto done in the promotion of public education."[9] The extent of federal involvement with public education at all levels in the twentieth century, although declining somewhat in recent years, owes much to Atherton's persistent efforts in the nineteenth century.

Ascertaining individual responsibility for such legislation is critical to a balanced understanding of the land-grant movement. Land-grant historiography—principally the works of Ross, Eddy, Nevins, and Edmond—tends to be romantic, evolutionary, and deterministic. Edward Eddy, for example, concluded that "a unique system of American higher education evolved over the years from the times rather than from a sudden revelation of a new type of educational endeavor." He added: "One cannot expect to find in the thinking of one man or the legislation of one act historical evidence of an eventual result. Evolution marks the land-grant colleges—a gradual, slow but steady evolution reflecting the needs of the nation."[10]

The present study contends just the opposite: that the Hatch Act, the 1890 Morrill Act, and the Adams Act were produced by individuals for clear and compelling reasons. The acts were not the culmination of irrepressible evolutionary forces. Had the land-grant colleges been subjected to a Darwinian survival test without benefit of legislative intervention, their development would have been slowed considerably. Contrary to Eddy's assertion that legislation cannot produce "historical evidence of an eventual result," these acts left a telling legacy. The Hatch Act spawned a national network of agricultural experiment stations, the great majority under the aegis of the land-grant colleges. The 1890 Morrill Act created the sorely needed financial underpinning for educational programs, encouraged an increase in state funding, and led to the establishment of seventeen black land-grant colleges in the South. Therefore, these acts, and the land-grant college movement, are better understood if interpreted as the legislative contrivances of individuals dedicated to advancing special interests—worthy interests, in this case, but special interests nevertheless.

Despite the federalistic philosophy that guided Atherton's legislative initiatives, he was not averse to opportunistic thinking. For example, Atherton saw in the Hatch Act the potential for creating, through the agricultural experiment stations, a federally subsidized academic department of agriculture for each college. These departments would provide not only research but also instruction and service, and in the process they would help eradicate the source of greatest embarrassment to the "agricultural colleges": the constant accusations that they were doing little for agriculture. At the same time, Atherton was keenly aware that a federal subsidy to the agriculture "department" would free up limited college resources for other academic areas. Indeed, he had openly complained that the colleges' obligations to agriculture had drained resources from other educational programs. As much as Atherton sought the experiment station legislation for the explicit purpose of supporting agricultural instruction and research, his ulterior motive was to recoup resources that would permit the creation of comprehensive universities, "national schools of science."

In deference to the evolutionists, an experiment station act of some sort might have eventually made its way through Congress; there were fifteen stations extant at the time of Hatch Act's passage, although half bore no relationship to land-grant colleges. On the other hand, it is also easy to misinterpret the act as a response to eleventh-hour agitation by the agricultural press and the powerful agricultural societies, or, as Eddy mistakenly did, to the persuasive powers of Representative Hatch. But such interpretations ignore the persistent effort over five years on the part of land-grant college presidents, agricultural scientists, and sympathetic congressmen— Atherton salient among these individuals.

Despite the compromise with the Grange which was intended to permit the continuation of independent stations, the act did quite the opposite: almost every new station established was attached to a land-grant college. Indeed, as Atherton had imagined, such an attachment naturally made for the best use of available resources. In the process, the stations entered into a carefully crafted subordinate relationship to the college—a relationship that would cause problems from the scientists' perspective, perhaps, but a relationship that was in no way accidental.

The "eventual result" of this legislation was to produce sixty stations by 1906, fifty-five of which were operated by land-grant colleges.

The critical point, however, is that—Eddy's assumption notwith-standing—the "thinking of one man" had a palpable impact on this seminal bill. George Atherton's Hatch Act was substantially different from Seaman Knapp's. Because of that difference, which centered on the role of the Agriculture Department, agricultural experiment stations developed as predominantly local institutions during the 1890s, responsible mainly to their colleges and to their local agricultural constituencies.

Neither was the 1890 Morrill Act in any respect evolutionary or inevitable. There was no ground swell of support for the measure from any quarter, as occurred in the eleventh hour of the Hatch Act. Even the Association no longer considered such legislation immediately possible, and was caught off guard by the bill's introduction. When the House Education Committee refused to report the bill favorably because of the common school provision, Morrill himself lost heart. Had it not been for the effort of the Association's executive committee, with Atherton's involvement, Morrill might not have introduced an acceptable substitute bill. And without intense lobbying by the college presidents, the substitute bill might never have passed through Congress. Speculation of this sort is risky, to be sure, but it offers valuable counterpoise to the evolutionary assumption that the colleges would have developed apace without such legislation, or that a vague popular demand might have produced supportive legislation for the colleges.

Part of the reason for the success of the Hatch Act and the 1890 Morrill Act was, of course, their obvious connection to agricultural constituencies, which struck a sympathetic note with Congress. Nevertheless, the Morrill Act of 1890 was explicitly "sold" to the Congress as a general institutional aid bill, with the funds being distributed to a range of educational programs and purposes that included agriculture and the mechanic arts but went far beyond them as well.

The "eventual result" of the 1890 Morrill Act was to facilitate the transformation of the colleges into comprehensive institutions of higher education. In 1889–90, the thirty-six land-grant colleges enrolled 6,147 students in collegiate courses, with 3,078 enrolled in the preparatory curriculum. By 1899–1900, the sixty-five land-grant colleges were enrolling 39,505 students—19,238 of whom were of collegiate grade. In the larger context, the land-grant colleges in 1900 were enrolling about 20 percent of the nation's 98,923 undergraduate and resident graduate students in universities, colleges, and schools of technology.[11]

Atherton's Impact on the Association and the Land-Grant Colleges

The proposition that Atherton's formal and informal leadership in the Association was critical to the development of the land-grant colleges between 1885 and 1905 is more problematic than the question of his role in advancing key legislation. Between 1885 and 1890, for example, no single Association member exerted more influence than Atherton, and the evidence suggests that his views predominated. His leadership in securing the Hatch Act was recognized and appreciated by his colleagues, who elected him twice to the Association's presidency, in 1887 and in 1889. At his final convention as president, he was able to stave off the Armsby proposal to split the Association into mutually exclusive sections of college presidents and station directors. Instead, Atherton supported a change in the constitution that reconfigured the Association into six "technical" sections while preserving the "general session" format for the resolution of the larger questions by presidents and directors alike.

After stepping down from his two-term presidency in November 1889, Atherton continued to be vitally active in Association affairs. He and Henry Alvord were recognized as the leading lights behind the passage of the second Morrill Act, secured in August 1890, and they continued working into early 1891 to ensure that the colleges would receive the federal annuities in timely fashion. In addition to being reelected chairman of the Section on College Work in 1890, Atherton was named chairman of the Association's committee on the collective agricultural college exhibit at the World's Columbian Exposition, scheduled for 1893 in Chicago. Although he resigned his chairmanship of the exposition committee in the spring of 1892, citing poor health, his election to these and other important posts suggests that he continued to be viewed as the leading college spokesman within the Association during the several years that followed his presidency.

Even in these early years of the Association, however, it would be inaccurate to characterize Atherton as the grand old man of the organization. The Association attracted too many strong-willed members to permit any one individual to consistently command deference to his views. In addition, the Association was a dichotomous organization, with college and station interests often pulling in opposite directions. Atherton came to epitomize the college interests, arguing that the Association existed to resolve the broader issues of educational policy and government relations rather than the narrower technical questions of the scientific disciplines. As such, a certain dynamic emerged in the case of Atherton's leadership within the Association. In the first five years, 1885–90, his influence was predominant. During the 1890s, his influence and that of the other college presidents grew a bit weaker vis-à-vis the station directors, but it remained strong enough to hold the upper hand. In the last five years, 1900–1905, his influence—and that of the presidents—began to wane quickly vis-à-vis the station directors. Atherton was fighting what amounted to a holding action to prevent the Association from splitting into the two sections Armsby had desired in 1889. Elected to the executive committee in 1900 on the strength of his eulogy to Morrill, and reelected in 1901, Atherton was replaced in 1902 by the station director Whitman Jordan, an act symbolic of the rising power of the stations. The Adams Act of 1906 represented a tacit refutation of the Atherton station philosophy that the stations should provide instruction and service as well as research. Instead, the act took away the college presidents' voice in determining how the new funds for agricultural experiment stations would be spent (though they still had their say in the disposition of Hatch Act funds).

Notwithstanding the decline of Atherton's influence after twenty years, it would not be misleading to characterize the Pennsylvania State College president as the captain of the "old guard," meaning that second generation of land-grant college presidents instrumental in founding and guiding the Association. Willits had died in 1896; Alvord in 1904; Goodell in 1905. Atherton's death on July 24, 1906, from a chronic bronchial disorder, meant that the ranks of this second generation were nearly depleted. At the 1906 convention, Association Executive Committee Chairman Henry White memorialized Atherton as "foremost among those who organized this Association; ever chief among the wisest of its councilors." Armsby delivered the official eulogy, subsequently reprinted as a pamphlet by the Office of Experiment Stations. Armsby dwelled mainly on Atherton's accomplishments at the Pennsylvania State College and in public service, praising "his services in securing the passage of the Hatch Act and the second

Morrill Act, his part in the organization of this Association, his services for two years as its first president, and his varied activities in
other capacities." More substantive remarks regarding his contributions
to the Association were given by James K. Patterson, president of the
University of Kentucky and one of the Association's founding members:

> With two or three able cooperators and lifelong friends, he
> both stimulated and controlled the mighty onward impulse
> which found expression in the land-grant colleges and univer-
> sities of today. The Congressional legislation subsequent to
> 1862 in behalf of these institutions was greatly influenced and
> largely shaped by him. He was one of the pioneers who
> brought this Association into being. . . . The constitution, origi-
> nal and modified, under which it lives . . . is the product of his
> genius for organization. Whatever success this organization
> has achieved is due in large degree to the impetus of his
> intellect and will. Doctor Atherton wielded an uncommon
> influence with public men in the halls of legislation. Leaders
> in the Senate and leaders in the House gave him a willing
> audience, and were won by his quiet, dignified, persuasive
> presentation of his views. For years he was the chief repre-
> sentative of this body before the law-making power, and in
> this capacity his tact and wisdom and discretion never failed
> him.[12]

Atherton's influence, and that of fellow college presidents, remained
fairly strong during the 1890s, despite several efforts by the station
directors to dislodge it. Not until shortly after the turn of the century
did his influence begin to fade.

During his latter years, Atherton's most significant contribution
may have occurred at the 1896 Association convention. There, through
a deft political maneuver, he defeated a motion introduced a year
earlier to remove the stations from accountability to the college
presidents. The motion would have made the station director responsible only to the college's governing board, placing the director in
a position roughly equivalent to the college president. Sensing the
rebellious mood, Atherton instead suggested that a comprehensive
effort to amend the constitution was in order. The Association agreed.
The committee Atherton suggested also was approved: Alvord, Goodell,
and James Smart of Purdue.

The 1898 convention brought the schismatic tensions into the open. Alvord's committee had proposed to eliminate all sections and turn the Association into a general session of presidents and directors discussing questions of policy. Armsby argued against the proposal, maintaining that the resolution of technical questions—related to scientific work—was the true function of the Association. Atherton argued that the Association existed not for the discussion of particulars in the agricultural science disciplines, but to resolve questions involving educational policy and government relations. He saw two issues gathering on the horizon: the creation of a logically integrated system of public education for the nation, from elementary through higher education, and the attendant need for a strategy to erode the Eastern prejudice against public funding of education. He wanted an organizational scheme that would allow for the discussion of such issues, but it was not to be. The proposal for the abolition of sections was defeated overwhelmingly, 44 to 8.

At the 1900 Association convention, Atherton staved off another attempt to revise the constitution. The proposal, stemming from a committee appointed at the previous convention, was to streamline the Association into three sections: on college work, on agriculture, and on the mechanic arts. Atherton argued that the committee, in devising its plan privately, had flouted the procedure for introducing constitutional amendments, and his argument was upheld. The 1903 convention produced the schism, however, splitting the Association into a Section on College Work and Administration, and a Section on Station Work. The station directors—led by Jordan of New York, Henry of Wisconsin, and Armsby of Penn State—generated the legislation that eventually became the Adams Act, which provided funds only for original research.

To construe Atherton and his fellow presidents as reactionaries fighting the inevitable, however, is to miss an essential point. Atherton's animating vision was to transform struggling agricultural colleges into comprehensive universities in which agriculture was one among scores of academic departments. He was viscerally opposed to any alteration of this scheme.

During this same time, Atherton was also part of the effort to standardize and liberalize the land-grant college curriculum, as part of a five-man Committee on Entrance Requirements, Courses of Study, and Degrees (1894–96). In response to evidence that a number of colleges were offering college-grade work in only a nominal sense, the committee recommended, and the Association accepted, a standard and minimum series of entrance requirements. The committee also decreed that general and liberal studies should comprise about 40 percent of the coursework for the bachelor's degree, which for technical subjects should henceforth be offered as a bachelor of science degree.

Atherton served for eight years, 1896–1904, as chairman of the Association's Committee on Military Instruction, the need for which had become apparent after the election of President Grover Cleveland in 1892. Just as the colleges had begun agitating for increased federal financial support for their students' military contingents, the Department of War began to retrench. Despite a constant tug-and-pull with the War Department during the years that followed, Atherton was able to extract only one concession from the department, involving the length of an officer's tenure at the colleges. He lost the battle to reduce the number of hours mandated by the War Department for military instruction, but the executive committee was eventually able to secure a victory in this regard.

Finally, Atherton was the Association's chief strategist and spokesman in the effort to secure federally funded schools of mines and mining at land-grant colleges. Atherton drafted, or helped draft, the initial Tillman bill of 1900. He represented the Association in congressional hearings and fashioned a compromise amendment that allowed for independent schools of mines and department of mines at certain state universities to share in the legislation. Although unsuccessful, Atherton sought to create a bill that, in addition to establishing schools of mines, would provide an annuity for a broad range of academic programs, like that in the 1890 Morrill Act.

The Second Great Triumvirate

George Atherton's contributions to the Association of American Agricultural Colleges and Experiment Stations need to be assessed not only in terms of Atherton's individual activity but also in light of his interaction with colleagues. The people with whom he worked most consistently over the years were Alvord and Goodell. As noted in Chapter 1, Earle Ross made the case for a "great triumvirate" of land-grant educators: Gilman, of the Sheffield School, the University of California, and Johns Hopkins; White of Cornell; and Walker of the Massachusetts Institute of Technology. Despite their contributions, particularly as builders of what eventually became great land-grant universities, none of the three was active in land-grant affairs after 1885, when White retired from the Cornell presidency.

It was not until after 1890, however, that the land-grant colleges began to emerge as a viable class of educational institutions. The facilitators of this emergence were a second and more central triumvirate in the land-grant movement: George W. Atherton, Henry E. Alvord, and Henry H. Goodell. Without the Hatch Act (resulting largely from Atherton's efforts) and the 1890 Morrill Act, in which Alvord and Goodell played critical roles, and their management of the colleges' ensuing relationship with the federal government, it is probable that the development of most land-grant institutions would have been far more difficult during the 1890s.

With Atherton as the Association's founding president and chief legislative strategist, and Alvord and Goodell serving as chairmen of the executive committee from 1887 to 1894 and from 1895 to 1902, in addition to their own terms as Association president (Alvord in 1895, Goodell in 1891), this "great triumvirate" provided the de facto nucleus of leadership that guided the Association into the twentieth century. This triumvirate of second-generation presidents functioned effectively for a number of reasons. First, Atherton had a recognized skill in writing and promoting legislation, had been engaged in such activity since 1873, and, in or out of an Association office, was habitually consulted in matters of legislation. Atherton was conversant with numerous representatives and senators and was consistently chosen to lead the Association's delegations to visit Presidents and Presidents-elect, from Grover Cleveland's first term through Theodore Roosevelt's first term.

The triumvirate was also effective because they shared a problem peculiar to the eastern land-grant college: they faced a strong prejudice against using public dollars to fund higher education. Thus, despite the popular association of the land-grant movement with large midwestern universities, where the political climate for public higher education was much warmer, it was primarily the presidents of the eastern land-grant colleges who conducted the Association's business and guided its interests. They sought a strong association with the federal government, partly as a means of compensating for the bias against public higher education in their states. Toward the end of his life, Atherton summarized the problem:

> The idea of State support for Higher education was then [in the 1880s] practically, if not theoretically, dead in Pennsylvania, but the maintenance of the State College has now come to be accepted as one of the regular objects of the care of the Legislature. Only those who have labored in this field, in the older States east of the Allegheny Mountains, can have any conception of the amount of labor involved in bringing about such a change.[13]

The third reason for the triumvirate's effectiveness was proximity to each other and to the nation's capital, as well as an inclination to communicate with one another. One of the more fascinating aspects of this triumvirate is logistical — the manner in which Alvord and, later, Goodell used the mails, the telegraph, and the rails to work the Association's will. The linchpin of the triumvirate was Henry E. Alvord, who as president of the Maryland Agricultural College in College Park from 1887 to 1892 functioned as the eyes, ears, and message bearer of the Association. Alvord frequently made day visits to Washington, D.C., to talk with legislators and officials at the various agencies. He was a prolific letter-writer and, if the occasion demanded, would think little of writing two letters a day to several individuals. When important issues were at stake, Alvord would often ask Atherton to come to Washington to visit a legislator or official. The rail transportation was such that Atherton could be there the day after receiving the letter or wire.

Executive committee work was extremely demanding, particularly for the chairman. Goodell wrote in one of his reports that the committee had produced 383 letters and circulars during one year. The committee carried out assignments emanating from the previous convention, prepared business to be submitted at the next convention, made reports of what it had accomplished, and kept a sharp eye on national legislation. It also coordinated the Association's testimony before the various congressional committee hearings. Little of the executive committee's work was routine, often requiring the collection of data and much hard thinking. In 1896 alone, Goodell reported, the executive committee dealt with nine separate bills that had touched on the Association's interests, ranging from establishment of a naval engineering cadet program to the reorganization of the Bureau of Education to the regulation of the Department of Agriculture's seed distribution program.[14]

The fourth reason for the triumvirate's effectiveness was personal chemistry. Atherton, Alvord, and Goodell worked well together as colleagues and as friends, and each had an overriding commitment to the Association. Alvord and Goodell had known each other since 1868, when Alvord, then a major in the U.S. Army, became the first officer to be detailed for military instruction at a land-grant college—the Massachusetts Agricultural College, where Goodell had been hired in 1867 as one of four "founding" faculty members. Alvord later managed the private Houghton experimental farm in Orange County, New York; returned to Massachusetts Agricultural College as a professor of agriculture from 1885 to 1887; and then served in the Maryland presidency until his ouster in a political battle with a new governor and his board of trustees in the summer of 1892. In March 1893, Alvord was appointed as special assistant for the Department of Agriculture, managing the collective college-station exhibit for the World's Columbian Exposition. In 1894–95, he served as president of Oklahoma Agricultural College at Stillwater and was also elected president of the Association. On July 1, 1895, he was appointed chief of the new Dairy Division within the Department of Agriculture's Bureau of Animal Industry, which altered his status in the Association from delegate to convention visitor and marked an abrupt decline, though not a cessation, of his activity therein.

Alvord did not hold a college degree, but he was a scientist of national reputation, having written four books and twenty articles on dairy science. During the five years of Alvord's presidency of the Maryland Agricultural College, a five-fold increase in income occurred—from $10,000 to $50,000 a year. Although he eliminated tuition, reduced student living expenses, and doubled the number of faculty from six to twelve, the college failed miserably at attracting students. In an epitaph for Alvord at Maryland, written by a latter-day historian, he was described as "well-known but inept."[15] In view of Alvord's manifold contributions to the Association and to the land-grant movement generally, that characterization is puzzling.

Henry H. Goodell spent his entire professional life at the Massachusetts Agricultural College at Amherst. He was a faculty member in modern languages and English literature until his appointment as president in 1886, and his tenure lasted until his death in 1905.

Goodell shared Atherton's educational and political philosophy; indeed, they were replaced by station directors on the Association's executive committee in 1902, when the nomination process was liberalized. Aside from his work in the campaign for the 1890 Morrill Act, his association presidency in 1891, and his executive committee chairmanship from 1895 to 1902, Goodell was particularly active in working with Senator Morrill to secure legislation that would protect the colleges from a reduction in the 1890 Morrill Act annuities should proceeds from public-lands sales become insufficient to support payments. By 1905, Massachusetts Agricultural College was "small in size but solidly grounded." Goodell had strengthened both the faculty and the curriculum and further solidified the experiment station by attracting increased state support.[16] Goodell's efforts were, of course, handicapped by the split land-grant endowment in Massachusetts, with one-third of the annual income being directed to The Massachusetts Institute of Technology.

Neither Atherton, Alvord, nor Goodell built a leading institution of higher learning during his lifetime, as Gilman did at California and Johns Hopkins and as White quickly accomplished at Cornell and Walker at MIT. Rather, this second triumvirate focused on building an entire class or system of colleges—institutions that, whatever their history and local context, were beneficiaries of the 1862 and/or 1890 Morrill acts and instruments of federal policy in higher education. This "building" they accomplished by their continual efforts to influence the external environment—in this case the federal government— and to control the college's internal environment by keeping agricultural science strong scientifically but within its place as one of many academic departments.

Through their efforts, the land-grant colleges became the first group of higher education institutions to forge a shared identity through a formal association, the Association of American Agricultural Colleges and Experiment Stations. This triumvirate also secured the means for the colleges to nurture a range of academic programs, through the 1890 Morrill Act. Their less obvious but vitally important contributions were the generating, precluding, or reshaping of bills in Congress and of rulings of federal administrative agencies; the influencing of federal appointments; and otherwise negotiating relationships with the federal government, according to the Association's best interests and without precedent to guide them. Finally, they struggled to keep the Association intact and pointed toward the larger issues of the day, particularly those related to public higher education.

The volume of activity undertaken by these three men further belies the evolutionary thesis of land-grant college history. The evolutionary view implies a gradual process in which change occurs reactively, as the colleges respond to shifts in the external environment. But the state of affairs from 1885 onward might more accurately be interpreted as an interactive process involving reciprocal influences. The colleges seized the initiative in the mid-1880s, via the Hatch Act and the 1890 Morrill Act, requiring a response by the federal government (the establishment of the Office of Experiment Stations and a more accountable relationship with the Bureau of Education). The Association's executive committee, for fifteen years headed by Alvord and Goodell and strongly influenced by Atherton, functioned as the colleges' medium for responding to the subsequent initiatives of Congress and the federal agencies. The committee also generated its own fair number of initiatives that required a response by the government.

The Association, the Land-Grant Colleges, and Higher Education

Both Edward Eddy and Hugh Hawkins suggest that one of the Association's primary contributions was to create or strengthen the colleges' shared sense of identity. To Eddy, the Association was instrumental in elevating the stature of land-grant colleges "as a system of education recognized in its collective form."[17] The issue of whether the land-grant colleges constituted a distinct system of higher education is important to understand, because the answer provides additional insight into the behavior of the Association and its principals during the period in question.

To George Atherton and many of his colleagues, there was a sharp difference between the land-grant college and the "old-line" state university—the state universities that did not hold the land-grant designation in their respective states. Those differences have been blurred in recent decades, partly because of the merger of the Land-Grant College Association and the National Association of State Universities in 1963, and the tendency of historians (Nevins in particular) to fail to distinguish between the two. In his admittedly "impressionistic and incomplete" lectures of 1962, Nevins interpreted the value of the 1862 Morrill Act as being primarily the acceleration of the state university movement. In his view, land-grant colleges and state universities had no real theoretical or functional differences.

But such thinking is ahistorical, and the failure to find the distinction might have appalled Atherton. It is true that in thirty of the fifty states today the land-grant college and state university designations are merged within a single institution. But it is equally important to note that, in the years following the original Morrill Act, the land-grant designation was given to extant state universities in only seventeen cases, and that in three of those cases the land-grant status was later rescinded and given to new institutions (Mississippi, North Carolina, South Carolina). In thirty-three of the fifty states, however, the land-grant college was established as a separate institution, and not as a state university. In sixteen of those thirty-three states, the original land-grant college later took on the added designation of "state university."[18]

Atherton and his fellow college presidents maintained that the land-grant colleges were accountable not only to their states but also to the federal government that created them. Thus, land-grant colleges came to view themselves as the instruments of federal educational policy in the various states. In fact, the states had to accept certain conditions imposed by the federal government in order to receive the grants of land. The states were to agree to establish a college where the "leading objects" were to be, without excluding scientific and classical studies and military tactics, "to teach such branches of learning as are related to agriculture and the mechanic arts." Other conditions involved the investment of land-grant proceeds in bonds bearing not less than 5 percent interest, and the stipulation that no endowment income was to be spent to purchase or maintain buildings (such outlays were considered to be the responsibility of the states).

The distinction, and the tension, between the land-grant colleges and the old-line state universities became evident with the emergence of the National Association of State Universities in 1895 and the legislative campaign, spearheaded by Atherton and described in Chapter 6, to establish schools of mines and mining in conjunction with land-grant colleges. Inspired by the Association's success in the legislative arena, the National Association of State Universities came into being from discussions of about eight state university presidents at the

1895 National Education Association convention. The prime mover of the new association was Robert B. Fulton, president of the University of Mississippi (which lost its land-grant status in 1878 to the A&M college that became Mississippi State University). After a period of relative inactivity, the state university association, according to Hawkins, "was stirred to new liveliness in part by the appearance of the third association of institutions of higher education in 1900," the Association of American Universities.[19]

It was also stirred to action by the initiative of the Association of American Agricultural Colleges and Experiment Stations in generating the Tillman bill of April 1900 to establish and endow schools of mines at land-grant colleges. A handful of state universities had established their own departments of mines or mining engineering, and a few bills had been introduced in Congress to endow such departments. When the land-grant colleges produced their own preemptive bill, drafted by Atherton, University of Mississippi President Fulton sought to amend it such that state universities would share in the federal endowment.

The Association viewed Fulton's effort as a threat that would undermine the land-grant colleges' unique relationship with the federal government. As Enoch A. Bryant, president of the State College of Washington, wrote to Atherton in July 1901:

> I think this movement on the part of the State universities which are not federal institutions a grave menace to the success of any future legislation which would strengthen the federal colleges. It seems to me that not only the state colleges which are mere free Universities but the state University which embraces the colleges of agriculture and mechanic arts will find it to their interest to preserve the precedent of forty years relative to such legislation. You are more familiar than any one else with the whole history of the movement and will take in far more quickly perhaps the bearing of this new attempt.[20]

At the Association's 1901 convention, George Atherton was appointed to head a special committee to meet with its counterpart from the National Association of State Universities—which, convening at the same time in Washington, D.C., had approached the Association "with the object of forming some plan of cooperation." The Atherton committee reported that, as a result of that conference, the state university committee thought it expedient to withdraw the proposal. Atherton then recommended that "the proposal for formal cooperation between the two associations be deemed withdrawn." Atherton's report noted, however, that the two associations had "many common interests and constituencies largely identical" and should "cooperate in maintaining educational principles, fostering educational ideals, and developing the educational resources of the several states." He added, "The peculiar relation between the National Government and this Association and its constituent members should in no way hinder the freest intercourse of the most mutual fellowship."[21]

The veneer of that comity wore off several months later, in the hearings of the House Committee on Mines and Mining relative to the Grosvenor bill (H.R. 250). Both the independent schools of mines in the West and several old-line state universities sought an amendment that would divert part of the federal subsidy to them as well as to the land-grant colleges. Atherton reluctantly agreed to the compromise, but not before pointing out that it flouted the standing congressional policy of relying exclusively on the land-grant colleges to carry out federal educational policy.

Fulton, testifying on behalf of the state universities, attempted to construe those institutions as "land-grant" colleges after a fashion: "These State universities are certainly the children of the Federal government, founded as they are upon grants of land made by Congress for this purpose." Atherton begged to differ: "These grants were made directly to the State; and Congress retained no supervision over them in any way whatever," and continued, "It did not retain even in its own hands the power . . . of supervising the use and the administration of the land, or even to follow them with an inquiry whether they were used for the purposes for which they were granted."[22]

The argument was moot because the legislation failed in Congress, but it is nevertheless illustrative of the manner in which the Association inspired an imitative organization from the federally "neglected" sector of public higher education. Even though Executive Committee Chairman Henry White later told Atherton he was "convinced it will become necessary for us to join general forces with that organization in the near future" and that "they are anxious to unite with us," the union lay sixty years in the future.[23]

It is difficult to imagine how the land-grant movement might have fared in the late 1880s without the Association of American Agricultural Colleges and Experiment Stations. There was no aspect of the movement that was not reflected in the discussions of the conventions and in the activities of the Association's executive committee. If the Association had done nothing more than secure the passage of the 1890 Morrill Act its existence would have been forever justified. But it did much more. It served as a buffer between the college-stations and the federal government, reserving for them a degree of independence and autonomy that otherwise might have been compromised. In ways that the individual colleges, acting unilaterally, could not hope to do, the Association solved myriad problems with the agencies of the federal government. Just as important, the Association provided the means for institutional self-examination by providing bases of comparison with other colleges. All this contributed to the Association's less obvious but vitally important accomplishment: creating the climate in which colleges struggling to provide "practical" agriculture instruction could begin to develop as comprehensive universities. The remarkable aspect is that the Association accomplished this at a time when it was entering into a much more complex relationship with the Department of Agriculture. Notwithstanding the attention that necessarily had to be focused on agricultural affairs, the Association also managed to deal successfully with the issue of balance and breadth in the land-grant curriculum.

The Association's focus on agriculture, despite embarrassingly small agriculture enrollments at its constituent institutions, was necessitated by a number of factors. The first was the receptivity of Congress to legislation purporting to benefit agriculture—hence the Hatch Act in 1887 and the act elevating the Department of Agriculture to cabinet status in 1889. The attention Congress gave to agricultural affairs was fixed by grass-roots agitation from the Grange and the National Farmers' Alliance, culminating in the Populist party and the Bryan campaign of 1896. This agitation grew out of a psychological and economic malaise that had beset American agriculture since the early 1870s. In fact, the sense of malaise eventually reached such proportions that Theodore Roosevelt established a Commission on Country Life in 1908 to address the problem. Given these conditions, it would have been remiss for the so-called "agricultural colleges" not to have devoted their energies to the national crisis. More to the point, the problems of American agriculture provided the colleges with an opportunity to ask for the means to improve their effectiveness.

In addition, and in response to the problems of the American farmer, the Department of Agriculture quickly became the most heavily funded agency of the federal government. Beginning in the early 1880s, relatively substantial funding increases were given to the department, mainly for research, but the truly impressive increases occurred after 1897, under the administration of Agriculture Secretary James Wilson. These increases facilitated remarkable breakthroughs—at the experiment stations, but especially within the department's scientific bureaus. The period from 1880 to 1920 has in fact been termed "one of the golden ages of agricultural science." By the end of the Wilson era in 1913, the Department of Agriculture was the giant among the federal agencies, with a $24 million budget and nearly 15,000 employees.[24] Given these circumstances, and the reporting relationship mandated by the Hatch Act and the 1890 Morrill Act, the Association found itself inextricably intertwined with this growing department. Indeed, with the colleges' weak record in agricultural education, the Association's scientists—while feeling somewhat threatened by Secretary Wilson's maneuvers—realized that their professional future lay in a close relationship with the Department of Agriculture.

The Association itself, despite one scholar's assertion that the early institutional associations tended to be "presidents' clubs," drew half its membership from the ranks of agricultural scientists. Indeed, the large number of scientific "visitors"—station men who attended association conventions for the programs of the five scientific sections—caused the ranks of the agricultural science contingent to vastly outnumber the college presidents. Furthermore, a remarkably strong faction of station directors, led by Henry P. Armsby, William A. Henry, and Whitman Jordan, resisted the control the college presidents exercised over the experiment stations. Their secessionist tendencies were constantly flaring up during the 1890s, and their persistence paid off in 1903, when they reshaped the Association to their liking. Further compounding the Association's internal tensions was the ambivalence felt by the college presidents and station directors alike toward the growing power of the Department of Agriculture.

The goal of the Association's work was, of course, to facilitate the development of land-grant colleges and, within that context, the agricultural experiment stations. Despite their seemingly rapid progress after the 1890 Morrill Act, the colleges need to be put into perspective with the other developing sectors of American higher education—an exercise that constitutes a test of the Association's effectiveness.

Colin Burke's revisionist history of nineteenth-century higher education attendance patterns provides a counterbalance to the deterministic advocacy models of the land-grant movement advanced by Ross, Eddy, Nevins, and Edmond. Citing the "relatively weak record of the technical schools during the late nineteenth century," Burke argued that the democratization of higher education did not hinge on the land-grant and state university movements after the Civil War. Rather, he contended, the growth in college and professional school enrollments— from about 32,000 students in 1860 to 256,000 in 1900—came as a result of changes in two traditional professions, law and medicine; the emergence of a semiprofession, education; and the increased number of female students. For the most part, he implied, this increase was accommodated by institutions other than land-grant colleges.

Burke's statistics show that liberal arts colleges alone increased their aggregate enrollment from 16,600 to 82,000 over those forty years; law schools from 1,500 to 13,000; medical schools from 8,000 to 49,000; theological schools from 1,500 to 8,000; normal schools from 3,000 to 76,000; women's colleges from virtually nothing to 16,000; and technical schools (it is not clear whether Burke includes land-grant colleges in this category) from nothing to 12,000.[25]

If intended to represent land-grant colleges, Burke's statistics for technical schools may be slightly askew, according to statistics submitted by the land-grant colleges to the Department of Agriculture for the year 1900. At that time, the overall land-grant college enrollment (at sixty-five institutions) was reported as 39,505. Only half that number, exactly 20,000 students, were enrolled as regular baccalaureate degree students (19,268) or graduate students (732).[26] Thus, assuming Burke's statistics to be approximately correct, the land-grant colleges at the turn of the century were enrolling about 8 percent of the nation's total undergraduate, professional, and graduate student population.

The land-grant proportion rises considerably, however, when compared with the total enrollments of undergraduate and resident graduate students in universities and colleges for men and for both sexes, in colleges for women, in Division A, and in schools of technology, as reported to the commissioner of education for 1899–1900. The total enrollment for that year was 98,923, with 20 percent of that total deriving from land-grant colleges.

Even more telling is the increase in enrollments between the year 1889–90 and 1899–1900. For the same categories, according to the commissioner of education, enrollments grew from 55,687 to 98,923, a 78 percent increase. Land-grant college enrollments grew from 6,147 to 19,238, an increase of 213 percent. Part of the reason for this increase is institutional proliferation, from thirty-six land-grant colleges in 1889–90 to sixty-five in 1899–1900.[27]

If the land-grant colleges were not so instrumental in "democratizing" higher education as previously supposed, they could still lay claim to several important contributions in the context of American higher education by the turn of the century. Although agricultural enrollments had remained disappointing at the baccalaureate level—2,852 in 1899–1900, according to the commissioner of education—the land-grant colleges had made significant contributions to agricultural science through their experiment stations. Despite the demands of providing classroom instruction and service to farmers, the station scientists devised new experimental techniques, created an extensive literature, helped train a new generation of scientists, and left as their legacy considerable contributions, such as the Babcock test to determine the butterfat content of milk. Devised in 1890 by a station scientist at the University of Wisconsin, the procedure proved to be a great boon to the emerging dairy industry.

The other fork of technical education—engineering—developed apace in the context of the land-grant college. By the turn of the century, nearly 60 percent of the nation's land-grant college enrollment was pursuing engineering degrees, and land-grant colleges as a class were the primary providers of engineers to a nation increasingly driven by technology. Although engineering courses were offered at other colleges and universities, enrollments remained relatively low in the applied programs. Burke said that about 4 percent of the graduates of the major northern colleges during the 1880s and 1890s became professional engineers.

The emphasis on engineering and agriculture suggests that the land-grant colleges made a strong contribution to the inclusion of applied science in the undergraduate curriculum. Certainly, as Gilman had suggested, science would have found a home in the American university movement with or without the land-grant colleges. But the land-grant movement greatly accelerated the process. Although such revisionist historians as Stanley Guralnik and Colin Burke make a strong case for the inclusion of science in the curriculum of the antebellum colleges, the scientists tended to be clustered in the established eastern colleges. Burke, in fact, was forced to conclude that antebellum colleges would have offered more science coursework, "but the high costs of teaching the subject, the lack of student demand, and the scarcity of adequately trained instructors hindered many of the institutions."[28] Indeed, the leadership of the land-grant colleges in emphasizing applied-science curricula was a source of pride to the presidents. In 1889, Atherton said with some exaggeration, "The establishment and growth of these institutions has resulted in compelling the older colleges to modify their courses of study, their methods of instruction, and the whole spirit of their work."[29]

The enduring contribution of the land-grant colleges during the Atherton era, however, was that they forced the issue that the federal government had a legitimate and significant role to play in higher education and in due course in all of public education. After years of agitation for such measures, the Hatch Act and the 1890 Morrill Act broke the back of the conservative argument that the federal government was constitutionally barred from participating in education. Both acts, and the subsequent relationship with the federal administrative agencies that ensued, set important precedents, although substantial federal involvement in higher education was still more than a half-century away.

Nonetheless, one lesson learned was that federal funding for science, to decentralized research units scattered across the nation, produced impressive results. Another lesson was that federal initiative could play the leading role in educational policy. The 1890 Morrill Act showed that federal funding could breathe life into struggling educational institutions. Just as important, the example of the federal government encouraged the states to increase their support. When the federal government moved in 1887 and 1890 to use the land-grant colleges as instruments of federal policy, the ripple effect at the local level was significant. Presciently, perhaps, Atherton had suggested as much in 1873.

There is yet another legacy to the Atherton prospectus for land-grant education: the extent to which land-grant universities have become assimilated into the mainstream of American higher education, and the extent to which the tenets of the land-grant movement have suffused all of American higher education. Atherton had long disdained the vocational strain to land-grant education, and he resisted the overwhelming tendency of his day to characterize the institutions as agricultural or technical institutions. He worked to establish a system of broad, comprehensive institutions that offered liberal arts and scientific education and research of a caliber that would rank the land-grant universities as being among the nation's most vigorous institutions of higher education.

To a large extent, that prospectus has been realized, though this is not to imply a cause-and-effect relationship between Atherton's efforts and the status of land-grant institutions today. But of the 105 institutions judged to be "Research Universities I" by the Carnegie Council on Policy Studies in Higher Education, 37 were land-grant universities,[30] and of the top twenty universities for research and development expenditures (from all sources) in science and engineering in fiscal year 1986, nine were historically land-grant universities.[31]

As the land-grant colleges eventually became absorbed into the mainstream value structure of the American university movement, so has the American university system been shaped by the values associated with the land-grant movement. Egalitarianism and populism, "practical" or "useful" education, applied research, public service, and of course the idea that the federal government has a key role to play in educational policy—these tenets have become generalized throughout the whole of American higher education.

Appendix

"Memoranda as to George W. Atherton"

This appendix consists of the undated "Memoranda as to George W. Atherton," Atherton's own attempt to detail his most important professional contributions, written toward the end of his life in the 1905–6 academic year. The account is incomplete; the nine pages that survive are reproduced here photographically. Handwritten changes and additions are in Atherton's own hand. Two typewritten additions to the first surviving page (the "Ms. A" and "Ms. B" insertions) are the last two pages of the reproduction, headed "(A)" and "B." by Atherton.

The original, housed among the George W. Atherton Papers in The Pennsylvania State University Archives, is on brittle onionskin paper. Its delicate nature required excellent care and precise photographic technique to obtain even the less-than-ideal reproduction provided here. The document is reproduced courtesy of the Pennsylvania State University Archives.

6

Personal

Memoranda as to George W. Atherton

24. Member of the Board of Visitors to the United States Naval Academy, 1873-1891. *and*

Member of the Commission appointed by President Grant to investigate the affairs of the Red Cloud Indian Agency, 1875.

Chairman of the "Republican State Convention" (N. J.),1876.

Chairman of the "New Jersey Tax Commission", 1878.
In 1885, Chairman of the Commission of Five appointed (See Ms."A")
First President of "The American Association of Agricultural Colleges and Experiment Stations", (1888-   ), and reelected the second year for the expressed purpose of recognizing his services in securing the passage of the "Hatch Act".

25. While it is difficult for one to speak impartially of his own work, yet a frank statement from one's own point of view may furnish the necessary counterpoise to the views or the facts presented by others with reference to the same transactions. Bearing this fact in mind, I conceive myself to have performed at least two highly important and permanent public services:-

(a). In drafting and aiding to secure the passage of the so-called "Hatch Act". *(Insert Ms. B.)* Soon after coming to Pennsylvania, in 1882, I began to cast about for some means of allying the Agricultural interests of the State to the work of the State College, and, in the winter of 1882-03, I secured the passage of an act appropriating $10,000. a year to the College, for the purpose of carrying on "Agricultural Experiment Station Work", an interest which was then almost entirely new in the United States, there being not more than five or six "Stations" then established, or institutions in which that kind of work

2.

was being carried on. My attention had been called to it
while I was associated with Dr. George A. Cook, in Rutgers
College, New Jersey, and, although it was out of my immediate field of work, I had caught the conviction that the
development of Agriculture in the immediate future lay
along that line. The act was passed by the Pennsylvania
Legislature with only three dissenting votes in the Senate
and less than twenty-five in the House, but it was vetoed
by Governor Patterson, who was then serving his first term,
and who made his veto the occasion of a vindicative attack on
the College. I have no reason to believe that Governor Patterson
knew or cared anything about the Institution, but supposed
him to have been instigated to his attack by parties who were
then extremely hostile to leading influences in the Board of
Trustees of the College.

While my own mind was on the alert to find some means
to neutralize the antagonism of Governor Patterson and those
behind him, my eye caught a brief paragraph in a Washington
despatch, to the effect that a member from Iowa had introduced
a bill for the establishment of Agricultural Experiment Stations,
under the auspices and by the aid of the United States. I took
occasion of an early visit to Washington to introduce myself to the member, for the purpose of becoming more fully informed respecting his plan. He very frankly told me that he
had not introduced his bill with the idea of securing its passage at once, but rather as a means of directing public attention to the subject; that the thought was a wholly new one
to him, and had been suggested by some testimony before a
Committee of which he was a member, with reference to the
growing importance of scientific tests in every branch of
industry, and that the query had presented itself to his mind,
why the same method could not be successfully applied in Agri-

3

culture, he being evidently quite uninformed as to what was
already being done in Germany, France, and England.

He told me, however, that while he did not expect himself to secure the passage of any bill during that Congress,
and that he expected to close his term of service at the
expiration of the Congress, his successor had already been
indicated, though not nominated, and that he proposed to
undertake to enlist the interest of that successor in this
project.

Soon after the opening of the first session of the
following Congress, I visited Washington and sought out the
new member from Iowa, Mr. A. J. Holmes of the   District.
He furnished me a copy of a bill which he had already introduced in pursuance of the suggestion of his predecessor,
which, after a very thorough examination, I decided was
altogether ineffective and unworkable. At that time I had
received no suggestion as to the authorship of the bill, but
assumed that Mr. Holmes was the author, and felt, therefore,
a degree of hesitation about making suggestions of change.
Mr. Holmes, however, entered very cordially into the matter
and gave me the largest possible freedom in modifying the
bill to suit my own views. After I had done so, he secured
me a hearing before the Agricultural Committee, of which Mr.
Hatch of Missouri was then Chairman, and accompanied me at
the hearing. The Committee had before it the original "Holmes'
Bill", and I therefore addressed my remarks and criticisms to
that, in connection with a discussion of the general subject.
The Committee gave me a very attentive hearing, and, at the
close, asked if I would prepare and present to them a bill
embodying my suggestions. This was, of course, precisely

4

what was desired by both Mr. Holmes and myself. I subjected
the matter to further careful review, and shortly had a second
hearing before the Committee, when the modified bill was approved and referred to a sub-committee of which Mr. Cullen of
Illinois was Chairman.

Without going further into this detail, which is given
for the sake of showing my intimate identification with the
first stages of the preparation of the "Hatch Act", I may
say briefly that the bill was reported favorably to the whole
Committee by Mr. Cullen, and that Mr. Cullen died directly
after the close of that session of Congress, and I then cast
about as to the best method of starting anew. During all
this early process, I had worked without a confidant, and
without consultation with any one, except in the later stages
of it, when I took up the matter with Dr. Cook of New Jersey,
who, from that time on, was my one trusted counselor and confident, and who was identified with every stage of the movement
until its successful consummation.

With Dr. Cook's knowledge and full assent, I undertook
to secure the services of Mr. Hatch as sponsor for the bill.
I venture to say that neither he nor any other member of the
Committee, when the matter was first presented to him, had the
remotest notion of what was meant by an "Agricultural Experiment Station", but he soon showed an apt and appreciative
grasp of the main purpose of such Stations, and gave me his
personal assurance that he would undertake to secure the
passage of the bill. From that time forward and of set purpose,
we everywhere spoke of it as the "Hatch Act". As soon as the
movement was well under way, we sought the cooperation of all
Land Grant Colleges (I had changed the original crude form of
bill prepared by Mr. Holmes in such a way as to make the
Stations branches of those Colleges) and most efficient service

5.

was rendered by correspondence and, in a few cases, by personal
visits to Washington. Among the Presidents of Colleges who made
such visits I recall President Adams of Cornell, President
Goodell of Massachusetts, President Gates of New Jersey, President
Willets of Michigan, and, I think, President Patterson of Kentucky.

After the bill was passed by Congress, Mr. Hatch requested
those of us who were then in Washington to go with him to ask
the favorable action of President Cleveland. Mr. Hatch called
upon me to present the matter to the President, which I did. He
gave us a very attentive and careful hearing, and shortly after
(March 2, 1887) signed the bill.

The results of this measure have been far beyond the most
sanguine expectations of those who were interested in securing
its passage. In consequence of it, an Experiment Station is in
active and successful operation in every State and Territory in
the United States. In most cases these Stations have secured
the confidence of the great body of the Agricultural people on
the one side and of those who are engaged in scientific investigation on the other side. They have revolutionized the character
and scope of the Agricultural press throughout the United States.
They have greatly enlarged, if not revolutionized, the work and
shaped the methods of the United States Department of Agriculture,
and they have given an impulse to the action of European and other
foreign governments in the same direction to such an extent that
there is today no more promising field of research in any branch
of applied science than in those which relate directly to the
development of Agriculture.

These results would doubtless have come at some time, but
the manner and time of their coming I know to have been very
largely attributable to my own action, very briefly outlined
above, and, looking at the matter from the point of view of my
present experience, I am satisfied that I have, in this way,

6

rendered one of the greatest services that any man ever had the privilege of rendering to his fellowmen.

In *all this* I do not mean at all to disparage the services, or to under-estimate the influence, of others, and it is fair to say that Professor Knapp, then of Iowa, after the passage of the bill was secured claimed that he had personally done *substantially* all those things which I have above stated as done by myself. As to that, I have only to say that I never knew Professor Knapp in the the matter from the beginning to the end of the affair, except that after the "Hatch Act" was well under way I received copies of a printed circular from Professor Knapp, advocating the passage of the original "Holmes Bill".

I was able to render a public service of almost equal importance in aiding to secure the passage of the "Morrill Act" of 1890. I had been closely associated with Senator Morrill ever since 1873, when he accepted as his own a bill which I drafted and which, with modifications, was kept alive Congress after Congress until the final passage of the Act of 1890. In that case, however, Mr. Morrill is entitled to full credit for the conception of his measure, and my own service consisted in a protracted and exacting legislative campaign, together with a body of able and devoted associates after Mr. Morrill had given up all hope of securing the passage of his bill during that Congress.

(b). The other important and permanent public service that I count myself happy to have done is in connection with the rehabilitation of The Pennsylvania State College. When I came to the Institution in 1882 the total number of students in the four College classes was 34, and the Freshman Class, which entered in 1883, consisted of 9 members. Last year (1904-05)

7

The number of students in the four College classes was 626,
and the Freshman Class entered 236 strong, and it is now recognized as one of the leading Technical institutions in the United
States--being 4th or 5th in the number of its Engineering students.
The Legislature for twenty years following the acceptance of the
congressional Land Grant had not appropriated a dollar toward the
maintenance or enlargement of the work of the Institution. Since
that time, from 1887 to 1905, both inclusive, the Legislature
has appropriated for buildings, equipment, and maintenance the
total sum of

    The idea of State support for Higher education was then
practically, if not theoretically, dead in Pennsylvania, but the
maintenance of the State College has now come to be accepted
as one of the regular objects of the care of the Legislature.
Only those who have labored in this field, in the older States
east of the Allegheny Mountains, can have any conception of the
amount of labor involved in bringing about such a change, and
one of the greatest educational services that the College is now
doing is in stimulating the ambition of young men in all parts
of the State who could never hope to secure a College education
except by public aid, and in compelling Secondary schools, whether
public or private, to maintain such standards of instruction as
will enable their graduates to prepare at home for the State College

(A)

by the Governor of Pennsylvania to inquire into the subject
of "Industrial Education". In the course of this inquiry, I
was sent to Europe by the Commission, and the report presented
to the Legislature was recognized then as the most comprehensive
exhibit of the condition of "Industrial Education" that had
been anywhere published. The Legislature authorized the printing of an edition of 10,000. copies, and the work of the Commission gave impulse and direction to the introduction of
"Manual Training" in the Normal schools and other public schools
of the State, which has continued until the present time and is
still advancing.

B.

(To be inserted under "a"(in Ms. C)

My connection with the Scientific Department of Rutgers College, which was receiving from the Legislature of New Jersey the income from the United States Land Grant Act of 1862, had naturally led me to examine the provisions and the underlying principles of that Legislature. I had become convinced that it was not only a measure of far-reaching wisdom as a means of promoting Higher public education, but that it was peculiarly in keeping with the genius of our system of institutions. In 1873 I had read a paper before the "National Education Association" at its meeting in Elmira, New York, showing the extent to which the action of Congress was already in operation in the several States, and especially the extent to which the States and localities were doing their part in carrying out the Act of Congress. The inquiry that I made in the preparation of this paper was the beginning of my active association with Senator Morrill, and of my later identification with all congressional legislation in the same direction, and this was the key to my particular action with reference to the "Hatch Act".

Notes

Chapter 1. A New Interpretation

1. Quoted in George W. Atherton, *The Legislative Career of Justin S. Morrill*, An address delivered at New Haven, Connecticut, November 14, 1900 (Harrisburg, Pa.: J. Horace McFarland, 1900), 32.

2. See Bruce A. Kimball, "Writing the History of Universities: A New Approach," *Minerva* 24 (Summer–Autumn 1986), 375–389.

3. Some of the biographies in question are: Calvin Stebbins, *Henry Hill Goodell* (Cambridge, Mass.: Riverside Press, 1911); Mabel Hardy Pollitt, *A Biography of James Kennedy Patterson, President of the University of Kentucky, 1869 to 1910* (Louisville, Ky.: Westerfield-Bonte Co., 1925); Joseph C. Bailey, *Seaman A. Knapp: Schoolmaster of American Agriculture* (New York: Columbia University Press, 1945); Jean Wilson Sidar, *George Hammell Cook: A Life in Agriculture and Geology* (New Brunswick, N.J.: Rutgers University Press, 1976).

4. Stanley M. Guralnik, *Science and the Antebellum College* (Philadelphia: American Philosophical Society, 1975); Colin B. Burke, *American Collegiate Populations: A Test of the Traditional View* (New York: New York University Press, 1982); and David B. Potts, "Curriculum and Enrollments: Some Thoughts on Assessing the Popularity of Antebellum Colleges," *History of Higher Education Annual* 1 (1981), 88–109.

5. Land-grant history, such as it is, has been buttressed by some notable works on the history of agricultural science. Seminal among them are Alfred C. True's *History of Agricultural Education in the United States, 1785–1925,* U.S. Department of Agriculture, Misc. Pub. No. 36 (Washington, D.C.: Government Printing Office, 1929), and his *History of Agricultural Experimentation and Research in the United States, 1607–1925,* U.S. Department of Agriculture, Misc. Pub. No. 251 (Washington, D.C.: Government Printing Office, 1937). To those have been added such modern studies as H. C. Knoblauch, E. M. Law, and W. P. Meyer, *State Agricultural Experiment Stations: A History of Research Policy and Procedure,* U.S. Department of Agriculture, Misc. Pub. No. 904 (Washington, D.C.: Government Printing Office, 1962), as well as two recent books written in anticipation of the 1987 centennial of the Hatch Act: Alan I. Marcus, *Agricultural Science and the Quest for Legitimacy* (Ames: Iowa State University Press, 1985), and Norwood A. Kerr, *The Legacy: A Centennial History of the State Agricultural Experiment Stations, 1887–1987* (Columbia: University of Missouri at Columbia, 1987).

Although these works are valuable in revealing the tensions between land-grant college presidents and their agricultural scientists, they treat the emerging colleges only within an agricultural context. Because the colleges are analyzed for their involvement with agricultural research and instruction in general and for their relationship with the agricultural experiment stations in particular, these books tend to reinforce prevailing but erroneous "cow college" assumptions about the nature of the early land-grant institutions. For example, in terms of student interest and enrollments, engineering far outweighed agriculture on most land-grant college campuses.

6. Alfred C. True, *Statistics of the Land-Grant Colleges and Agricultural Experiment Stations of the United States, 1900,* U.S. Department of Agriculture, Office of Experiment Stations, Bulletin No. 97 (Washington, D.C.: Government Printing Office, 1901), 8.

7. See esp. Wayland F. Dunaway, *History of the Pennsylvania State College* (Lancaster, Pa.: Lancaster Press, 1946), 165–166.

8. True, *Agricultural Education,* 208.

9. Alexis Cope to George W. Atherton, August 20, 1890, Box 7, Folder C, Atherton Papers (MSG 6).

10. See Hugh Hawkins, "Problems in Categorization and Generalization in the History of American Higher Education: An Approach Through the Institutional Associations," in *History of Higher Education Annual* 5 (1985), 45.

11. See Earle D. Ross, "The Great Triumvirate of Land-Grant Educators," *Journal of Higher Education* 32, (December 1961), 480–488.

12. Quoted in Roger L. Geiger, *To Advance Knowledge: The Growth of American Research Universities, 1900–1940* (New York: Oxford University Press, 1986), 6.

Chapter 2. The Land-Grant Movement's First Fifty Years

1. "The Morrill Act, 1862," in *American Higher Education: A Documentary History,* ed. Richard Hofstadter and Wilson Smith, 2 vols. (Chicago: University of Chicago Press, 1961), 2:568–569.

2. Daniel C. Gilman, "Our National Schools of Science," *North American Review* 105, no. 217 (1867), 497.

3. George W. Atherton, "The Relation of the General Government to Education," in *Addresses and Journals of Proceedings of the National Education Association,* Session of the Year 1873, at Elmira, N.Y. (Peoria, Ill.: Nason, 1873), 68.

4. See Earle D. Ross, "On Writing the History of the Land-Grant Colleges and Universities," *Journal of Higher Education* 24 (November 1953), 411, and Edward D. Eddy, "The First Hundred Years, in Retrospect and Prospect," in *Development of the Land-Grant Colleges and Universities and Their Influence on the Economic and Social Life of the People*, Addresses given at a series of ten seminars sponsored by the College of Agriculture, Forestry, and Home Economics of West Virginia University during the year 1962 (Morgantown: West Virginia University, 1983), 5.

5. Kerr, *The Legacy*, 3.

6. See Lawrence A. Cremin, *American Education: The National Experience, 1783–1876* (New York: Harper & Row, 1980), 2–3, 103, 120, 483.

7. Edward H. Reisner, *Nationalism and Education Since 1789: A Social and Political History of Modern Education* (New York: Macmillan, 1922), 334.

8. Laurence R. Veysey, *The Emergence of the American University* (Chicago: University of Chicago Press, 1965), 2.

9. Frederick Rudolph, *The American College and University: A History* (New York: Knopf, 1962), 201–220.

10. Cremin, *American Education*, 122.

11. Richard M. Hofstadter, *Academic Freedom in the Age of the College* (New York: Columbia University Press, 1961), 209.

12. Ibid., 211.

13. Cremin, *American Education*, 400.

14. Earle D. Ross, *Democracy's College: The Land-Grant Movement in the Formative Stage* (Ames: Iowa State College Press, 1942), 15.

15. Colin B. Burke, *American Collegiate Populations: A Test of the Traditional View* (New York: New York University Press, 1982), 17, 54–55.

16. "Francis Wayland's Report to the Brown Corporation," in *American Higher Education* (ed. Hofstadter and Smith), 2:478–487.

17. See Burke, *American Collegiate Populations*, 92.

18. See Stanley M. Guralnik, *Science and the Antebellum College* (Philadelphia: American Philosophical Society, 1975), 139–140.

19. Potts, "Curriculum and Enrollments," 102.

20. See Geiger, *To Advance Knowledge*, 4.

21. True, *Agricultural Education*, 101.

22. A. Hunter Dupree, *Science in the Federal Government: A History of Policies and Activities to 1940* (Cambridge: Harvard University Press, 1957), 47.

23. Allan Nevins, *The State Universities and Democracy* (Urbana: University of Illinois Press, 1962), 16–17.

24. Quoted in William B. Parker, *The Life and Public Services of Justin Smith Morrill* (Boston: Houghton Mifflin, 1924), 263.

25. *Remarks of Senator Morrill Before the House Committee on Education Respecting the Land-Grant Colleges*, Circular, October 24, 1890, Box 7, Folder C, Atherton Papers (MSG 6).

26. *Proceedings of the Twelfth Annual Convention of the Association of American Agricultural Colleges and Experiment Stations, Held at Washington, D.C., November 15–17, 1898*, U.S. Department of Agriculture, Office of Experiment Stations, Misc. Bulletin No. 65, 90. (Washington, D.C.: Government Printing Office, 1899). NOTE: The proceedings of the Association conventions are hereafter referred to as *Association Proceedings*, followed by the appropriate year.

27. Quoted in Veysey, *Emergence*, 61.

28. Quoted in Ross, *Democracy's College*, 15.

29. Veysey, *Emergence*, 40.

30. E. A. Burtt, *The Metaphysical Foundations of Modern Science* (Garden City, N.Y.: Doubleday, 1954), 18.

31. Guralnik, *Science and the Antebellum College,* 154.

32. Dupree, *Science in the Federal Government,* 46.

33. See Alexandra Oleson, "Introduction: To Build a New Intellectual Order," in *The Pursuit of Knowledge in the Early American Republic,* ed. Alexandra Oleson and Sanborn Brown (Baltimore: Johns Hopkins University Press, 1976), xv–xvi.

34. Dupree, *Science in the Federal Government,* 8.

35. Nevins, *State Universities and Democracy,* 7.

36. See Guralnik, *Science and the Antebellum College,* vii, ix, 42, 46.

37. The studies are cited in ibid., 146, 138.

38. True, *Agricultural Education,* 34.

39. Quoted in Edward D. Eddy, Jr., *Colleges for Our Land and Time: The Land-Grant Idea in American Education* (New York: Harper, 1957), 6.

40. John S. Brubacher and Willis Rudy, *Higher Education in Transition: An American History, 1636-1956* (New York: Harper, 1958), 172.

41. Veysey, *Emergence,* 133.

42. See Eddy, *Colleges for Our Land and Time,* 9.

43. Oleson, "Introduction," xvii.

44. Dupree, *Science in the Federal Government,* 45–46.

45. *Association Proceedings 1903,* 36.

46. Gilman, "Our National Schools of Science," 500–501. Gilman does not mention all twenty schools by name. He does cite Rensselaer, Harvard, Yale, Dartmouth, Union, and Columbia and refers to "some other younger colleges." He also refers to the Massachusetts Institute of Technology and mentions the "vigorous efforts . . . to organize agricultural schools" in New York, Pennsylvania, Michigan, Illinois, "and other Western and Central States."

47. Dupree, *Science in the Federal Government,* 151.

48. Margaret A. Rossiter, "The Organization of the Agricultural Sciences," in *The Organization of Knowledge in Modern America, 1860–1920,* ed. Alexandra Oleson and John Voss (Baltimore: Johns Hopkins University Press, 1979), 213.

49. J. B. Edmond, *The Magnificent Charter: The Origin and Role of the Morrill Land-Grant Colleges and Universities* (Hicksville, N.Y.: Exposition Press, 1978), 30.

50. Margaret A. Rossiter, "The Organization of Agricultural Improvement in the United States, 1785-1865," in *Pursuit of Knowledge* (ed. Oleson and Brown), 281.

51. Edmond, *Magnificent Charter,* 29.

52. See Ross, *Democracy's College,* 29–30.

53. Kerr, *The Legacy,* 1.

54. Eddy, *Colleges for Our Land and Time,* 13.

55. Kerr, *The Legacy,* 2–3.

56. Rossiter, "The Organization of Agricultural Improvement," 281.

57. Edmond, *Magnificent Charter,* 30.

58. Rossiter, "The Organization of Agricultural Improvement," 279.

59. Ibid., 275.

60. True, *Agricultural Education,* 67.

61. Ross, *Democracy's College,* 22.

62. True, *Agricultural Education,* 60–62.

63. Michael Bezilla, *Penn State: An Illustrated History* (University Park, Pa.: The Pennsylvania State University Press, 1985), 4.

64. Ibid., 26.

65. Ross, *Democracy's College,* 106. Ross said: "In a period especially notable

for great college presidents, land-grant representatives like Evan Pugh, Daniel C. Gilman, Andrew D. White, Emerson E. White, Francis A. Walker, Paul A. Chadbourne, Adonijah S. Welch, John M. McBryde, John Bascom, William W. Folwell, and Cyrus Northrup were conspicuous."

66. Eddy, *Colleges for Our Land and Time*, 19.

67. Ross, *Democracy's College*, 55.

68. Ibid., 26.

69. Reisner, *Nationalism and Education Since 1789*, 339.

70. See Edmond, *Magnificent Charter*, 5–7.

71. E. D. Duryea, "The University and the State: A Historical Overview," in *Higher Education in American Society*, ed. Philip G. Altbach and Robert O. Berdahl (Buffalo, N.Y.: Prometheus Books, 1981), 27.

72. Ross, *Democracy's College*, 42.

73. Reisner, *Nationalism and Education Since 1789*, 368.

74. Ross, *Democracy's College*, 52–53.

75. Eddy, *Colleges for Our Land and Time*, 35.

76. Ross, *Democracy's College*, 62.

77. Eddy, *Colleges for Our Land and Time*, 28–29.

78. Quoted in Robert L. Kelly, *The American Colleges and the Social Order* (New York: Macmillan, 1940), 51.

79. Atherton, "The Relation of the General Government to Education," 66.

80. Eddy, *Colleges for Our Land and Time*, 58.

81. Ibid., 49.

82. Edmond, *Magnificent Charter*, 23.

83. Dunaway, *History of the Pennsylvania State College*, 42.

84. Bezilla, *Penn State*, 13.

85. Quoted in Ross, *Democracy's College*, 70.

86. See Harold W. Cary, *The University of Massachusetts: A History of One Hundred Years* (Amherst: University of Massachusetts Press, 1962), 7–35.

87. On the process in Illinois, see Winton U. Solberg, *The University of Illinois, 1867–1894: An Intellectual and Cultural History* (Urbana: University of Illinois Press, 1968), 1–99.

88. Merle Curti and Vernon Carstensen, "The University of Wisconsin: To 1925," in *The University of Wisconsin: One Hundred and Twenty-Five Years*, ed. Allan G. Bogue and Robert Taylor (Madison: University of Wisconsin Press, 1975), 11–12.

89. James E. Pollard, *History of the Ohio State University: The Story of Its First Seventy-Five Years, 1873–1948* (Columbus: Ohio State University Press, 1952), 3.

90. Eddy, *Colleges for Our Land and Time*, 36.

91. Edmond, *Magnificent Charter*, 15.

92. Nevins, *State Universities and Democracy*, 31.

93. Ibid., 29–30.

94. Quotation from Geiger, *To Advance Knowledge*, 6.

95. Andrew D. White, *Autobiography*, vol. 1 (N.p.: The Century Co., n.d.), 294–329.

96. Nevins, *State Universities and Democracy*, 31.

97. Fabian Franklin, *The Life of Daniel Coit Gilman* (New York: Dodd, Mead, 1910), 72–73.

98. Gilman, "Our National Schools of Science," 497–519.

99. Daniel C. Gilman's "Report on the National Schools of Science," in *Report of the Secretary of the Interior*, vol. 2 (Washington, D.C.: Government Printing Office, 1871), 434.

100. Ross, *Democracy's College*, 168.

101. See Clark Kerr, *The Uses of the University* (Cambridge: Harvard University Press, 1982), 18–19, 41.

Chapter 3. A New Advocate Emerges

1. Clipping from *The Farm Journal* (Philadelphia), December 1891, Box 13, Folder D, Atherton Papers (MSG 6), The Pennsylvania State University Archives Pattee Library, University Park, Pennsylvania.

2. Newspaper clipping from the *Arizona Daily Star,* January 10, 1906, Box 13, Folder D, Atherton Papers (MSG 6).

3. Gilman, "Our National Schools of Science," 518.

4. George W. Atherton, Inaugural Address, Commencement 1883, Box 5, Folder W, Atherton Papers (MSG 6).

5. Ibid., 17.

6. *Contemporary American Biography* (New York: Atlantic Publishing and Engraving Co., 1895), 218.

7. Journal of George Atherton for 1855, entry for December 3, 1855, Box 1, Folder A, Atherton Papers (MSG 6).

8. D. F. Wells, "George W. Atherton," *Bulletin of the Phillips Exeter Academy* 11 (September 1906), Box 1, Folder A, Atherton Papers (MSG 6).

9. Journal of George Atherton for 1860, Box 1, Folder B, Atherton Papers (MSG 6).

10. *Contemporary American Biography* (1895), 219.

11. Diary of George Atherton for 1864, summary entry for August 18, 1864, Box 1, Folder C, Atherton Papers (MSG 6).

12. *Contemporary American Biography* (1895), 219.

13. Solberg, *The University of Illinois,* 99, 109.

14. *Pennsylvania State College, Annual Report for 1896* (Harrisburg, Pa.: Clarence M. Busch, 1897), 4.

15. George W. Atherton to Edmund J. James, July 29, 1905, Box 5, Folder I, Atherton Papers (MSG 6).

16. William H. S. Demarest, *A History of Rutgers College, 1766–1924* (New Brunswick, N.J.: Rutgers College Press, 1924), 400.

17. Newspaper clipping from *New Brunswick Daily Times* (undated and untitled, but likely published in the spring of 1873), Box 13, Folder B, Atherton Papers (MSG 6). See also Demarest, *History of Rutgers,* 396, for a description of David Murray.

18. *Contemporary American Biography* (1895), 219.

19. Demarest, *History of Rutgers,* 419–420.

20. Clinton D. Fisk to George W. Atherton, July 27, 1875, Box 2, Folder D, Atherton Papers (MSG 6); Report of the Special Commission and letter of George W. Atherton to Ulysses S. Grant, October 16, 1875, Box 2, Folder D, Atherton Papers (MSG 6).

21. *Report of the Special Tax Commission of the State of New Jersey,* February 1880, Box 2, Folder C, Atherton Papers (MSG 6).

22. Newspaper clipping (early spring 1873?), *New Brunswick Daily Times* (see n. 17 above).

23. Edward P. Smith to George W. Atherton, December 15, 1874, Box 2, Folder H, Atherton Papers (MSG 6).

24. G. S. Richards to George W. Atherton, December 28, 1876, Box 2, Folder H, Atherton Papers (MSG 6).

25. Letter (author unknown and second page missing), to George Atherton, September 3, 1875, Box 2, Folder H, Atherton Papers (MSG 6).

26. Daniel C. Gilman to George Atherton, February 9, 1875, Box 2, Folder H, Atherton Papers (MSG 6).

27. Justin S. Morrill to George Atherton, January 28, 1878, Box 2, Folder G, Atherton Papers (MSG 6).

28. Erwin W. Runkle, "President Atherton and Pennsylvania State College," *Pennsylvania School Journal* 56 (January 1908), 297.

29. George W. Atherton, "Memoranda as to George W. Atherton" (undated, but written in 1905 or 1906), Box 1, Folder A, Atherton Papers (MSG 6). A facsimile of this memorandum is included in the Appendix to this book.

30. Bezilla, *Penn State*, 31.

31. Henry P. Armsby, *Memorial to President George W. Atherton* (Washington, D.C.: Government Printing Office, 1907). This pamphlet, authorized by the Department of Agriculture Office of Experiment Stations, is a reprint of Armsby's address at the Twentieth Annual Convention of the Association of American Agricultural Colleges and Experiment Stations, Baton Rouge, Louisiana, November 14–16, 1906. Originally published in *Association Proceedings 1906*.

32. True, *Agricultural Education*, 194.

33. Ibid., 195.

34. Ibid., 196.

35. Ibid., 197.

36. Circular, Rutgers College, January 13, 1873, Box 2, Folder A, Atherton Papers (MSG 6). The circular carries no individual names.

37. Quoted in Eddy, *Colleges for Our Land and Time*, 72.

38. The remarks of McCosh, Eliot, Reed, and White are contained in *The Addresses and Journal of the Proceedings of the National Education Association, 1873, at Elmira, N.Y.* (Peoria, Ill.: Nason, 1873), 32–47. The Atherton quotation is on p. 44.

39. Atherton's address, ibid., 61–73. Atherton's statistics for land-grant college and higher education enrollments would seem to be approximately correct, according to the *Report of the Commissioner of Education for the Year 1872* (Washington, D.C.: Government Printing Office, 1873), 764–809. The 298 universities, colleges, and collegiate departments reporting for 1872 enrolled a total of 18,597 students in college curriculums and slightly more (19,263) in their preparatory departments. The twenty-eight land-grant colleges reporting for the year 1871–72 enrolled a total of 2,674 students, of whom only 268 were listed as being in preparatory departments. This count was an underreporting, as forty-one land-grant colleges had been established, though not all were operational. Nevertheless, such sizeable land-grant colleges or departments as Cornell, Brown, Tennessee, and Missouri, to name only several, did not report enrollments.

40. See *Contemporary American Biography* (1895), 220; Bezilla, *Penn State*, 31.

41. Pollitt, *Biography of Patterson*, 116–118.

42. *Addresses and Proceedings of the NEA, 1873*, 75–76.

43. Questionnaire mailed to land-grant colleges by George Atherton, July 10, 1873, Box 2, Folder A, Atherton Papers (MSG 6).

44. Newspaper clipping, a reprint of Atherton's August 9, 1873, letter to the *New York Tribune*, where it was published on August 22 and reprinted in the August 23 edition of the *New Brunswick (N.J.) Fredonian*, Box 13, Folder B, Atherton Papers (MSG 6).

45. Newspaper clipping, "The National Educational Association," a reprint in the *New Brunswick Fredonian* of August 23, 1873, of an article published in the *New York Independent*, Box 13, Folder B, Atherton Papers (MSG 6).

46. *The Nation*, August 28, 1873, 141.

47. Newspaper clipping, preface written by George Atherton for the October 24, 1873, *New Brunswick (N.J.) Daily Times* publication of his letter to *The Nation*, Box 13, Folder B, Atherton Papers (MSG 6).

48. Andrew D. White to George Atherton, August 25, 1873, Box 2, Folder N, Atherton Papers (MSG 6).

49. Atherton, "Memoranda as to George W. Atherton."

50. S. 167, 43d Cong., 1st sess., December 15, 1873, Box 2, Folder F, Atherton Papers (MSG 6).

51. Atherton, "Memoranda as to George W. Atherton."

52. Justin S. Morrill to George Atherton, January 8, 1874, Box 2, Folder G, Atherton Papers (MSG 6).

53. Justin S. Morrill to George Atherton, February 13, 1874, Box 2, Folder G, Atherton Papers (MSG 6).

54. "Personal and Private Circular" from New Brunswick, New Jersey, February 25, 1874, Box 2, Folder A, Atherton Papers (MSG 6). Inscribed in Atherton's handwriting is this message: "These circulars were sent to every college, signed by Dr. George H. Cook and myself."

55. Andrew D. White to George Atherton, March 11, 1874, Box 2, Folder B, Atherton Papers (MSG 6).

56. B. L. Arnold to George Atherton, March 20, 1874, Box 2, Folder B, Atherton Papers (MSG 6).

57. Daniel C. Gilman to George Atherton, May 22, 1874, Box 2, Folder N, Atherton Papers (MSG 6).

58. House Report No. 57, *Agricultural Colleges,* 43d Cong., 2d sess., January 13, 1875 (Serial 1656), 2–10.

59. Andrew D. White to George Atherton, March 27, 1874, Box 2, Folder G, Atherton Papers (MSG 6).

60. John B. Bowman to George Atherton, December 21, 1874, Box 2, Folder G, Atherton Papers (MSG 6).

61. True, *Agricultural Education,* 198–199.

62. See "A Bill," Box 7, Folder C, Atherton Papers (MSG 6). This is a substantial revision of a printed bill, with the revisions in Atherton's handwriting, for a bill "to establish an educational fund and apply a portion of the proceeds of the public lands to public education, and to provide for the more complete endowment and support of national colleges for the advancement of scientific and industrial education." Although undated, the bill contains, in section 2, an effective date of June 30, 1875. This is most likely a revision to an earlier draft of S. 1187, which Morrill introduced on January 4, 1875.

63. John B. Bowman to George Atherton, January 29, 1875, Box 2, Folder G, Atherton Papers (MSG 6).

64. Justin S. Morrill to George Atherton, June 21, 1875, Box 2, Folder G, Atherton Papers (MSG 6).

65. George F. Hoar, *Autobiography of Seventy Years* (New York: Charles Scribner's Sons, 1903), 1:265.

66. See two letters: Justin S. Morrill and John B. Bowman to George Atherton, both of February 4, 1876, Box 2, Folder G, Atherton Papers (MSG 6).

67. Ross, *Democracy's College,* 169.

68. Circular under Atherton's signature, New Brunswick, New Jersey, March 20, 1878, Box 2, Folder G, Atherton Papers (MSG 6).

69. Bezilla, *Penn State,* 23.

70. True, *Agricultural Education,* 122–125.

71. Quoted in Nevins, *State Universities and Democracy,* 59.

72. Ibid., 65; Ross, *Democracy's Colleges,* 132, 135; Eddy, *Colleges for Our Land and Time,* 81.

73. John B. Bowman to George Atherton, February 25, 1876, Box 2, Folder G, Atherton Papers (MSG 6).

74. Pollitt, *Biography of Patterson,* 110.

75. James Y. McKee to George Atherton, May 15, 1882, Box 5, Folder W, Atherton Papers (MSG 6).

76. Dunaway, *History of the Pennsylvania State College,* 58.

77. George Atherton to James A. Beaver, July 17, 1882, Box 5, Folder W, Atherton Papers (MSG 6).

78. Bezilla, *Penn State,* 31.

79. Demarest, *History of Rutgers,* 455.

80. Atherton, "Memoranda as to George W. Atherton."

Chapter 4. The Hatch Act and "the Association"

1. Atherton, "Memoranda as to George W. Atherton" (see above, Chapter 3, n. 29).

2. *Congressional Record,* Senate, 49th Cong., 2d sess., 721.

3. Charles E. Rosenberg, *No Other Gods: On Science and American Social Thought* (Baltimore: Johns Hopkins University Press, 1961), 148.

4. See Marcus, *Agricultural Science,* 155–159.

5. Kerr, *The Legacy,* 11.

6. True, *Agricultural Experimentation,* 82–86. See also Marcus, *Agricultural Science,* 72.

7. True, *Agricultural Experimentation,* 87.

8. See Michael Bezilla, *The College of Agriculture at Penn State: A Tradition of Excellence* (University Park, Pa.: The Pennsylvania State University Press, 1987), 42–44; True, *Agricultural Experimentation,* 172. See also George H. Cook to George W. Atherton, June 21, 1883, Box 5, Folder D, Atherton Papers (MSG 6).

9. Ross, *Democracy's College,* 38.

10. Marcus, *Agricultural Science,* 4.

11. True, *Agricultural Experimentation,* 119.

12. Rossiter, "Organization of the Agricultural Sciences," 214–215.

13. Marcus, *Agricultural Science,* 38.

14. Ibid., 7.

15. Ibid., 22–31; Rosenberg, *No Other Gods,* 154.

16. See Marcus, *Agricultural Science,* 167–170; True, *Agricultural Experimentation,* 120.

17. H.R. 6610, May 8, 1882, 47th Cong., 1st sess. (Printer's No. 7120).

18. True, *Agricultural Experimentation,* 121. See also Marcus, *Agricultural Science,* 181.

19. H.R. 447, December 10, 1883, 48th Cong., 1st sess. (Printer's No. 447).

20. "Experiment Stations," an updated circular by Seaman A. Knapp (most likely published in the winter of 1884), Box 5, Folder D, Atherton Papers (MSG 6).

21. Marcus, *Agricultural Science,* 182.

22. Quoted in ibid., 184.

23. Ibid., 182–183.

24. Bailey, *Seaman A. Knapp,* xi.

25. True, *Agricultural Experimentation,* 122–123.

26. Atherton, "Memoranda as to George W. Atherton."

27. True, *Agricultural Experimentation,* 120; Marcus, *Agricultural Science,* 177–182; and Bailey, *Seaman A. Knapp,* 97.

28. According to *The Index of Unpublished Congressional Committee Hearings* (prior to January 3, 1935); *The U.S. Congressional Committee Hearings Index,* 23d–64th Congresses; and the *Congressional Record,* no published account of the committee hearings apparently exists.

29. *Proceedings of a Convention of Delegates from Agricultural Colleges and Experiment Stations Held at the Department of Agriculture, July 8 and 9, 1885,* U.S. Department of Agriculture, Misc. Special Report No. 9 (Washington, D.C.: Government Printing Office, 1885), 41–42.

30. Newspaper clipping from the *New England Homestead,* March 19, 1887, Box 13, Folder C, Atherton Papers (MSG 6).

31. *Proceedings of a Convention, 1885,* 160.

32. Clipping from *New England Homestead,* March 19, 1887 (see above, n. 30).

33. George W. Atherton to Whitman Jordan, October 1, 1900, Box 7, Folder A, Atherton Papers (MSG 6).

34. George W. Atherton to Charles Mills, October 23, 1903, Box 7, Folder A, Atherton Papers (MSG 6).

35. H.R. 7498, 48th Cong., 1st sess., July 2, 1884.

36. House Committee on Agriculture, Report to Accompany H.R. 7498, 48th Cong., 1st sess., H. Rept. 2034.

37. Circular urging passage of H.R. 7498 (the Cullen bill), by George W. Atherton and George H. Cook, July 1884, Box 7, Folder A, Atherton Papers (MSG 6).

38. Marcus, *Agricultural Science,* 185; True, *Agricultural Experimentation,* 123.

39. See *Proceedings of a Convention, 1885,* 3.

40. Ibid., 24, 54, 83.

41. Knoblauch et al., *State Agricultural Experiment Stations,* 59.

42. *Proceedings of a Convention,* 33.

43. Ibid., 67.

44. Knoblauch et al., *State Agricultural Experiment Stations,* 60.

45. *Proceedings of a Convention,* 102–103.

46. Ibid., 160.

47. George W. Atherton to the Delegates of the Washington convention, Circular, October 23, 1885, Box 7, Folder A, Atherton Papers (MSG 6).

48. *Congressional Record,* House, 49th Cong., 1st sess. The bills, in order of their appearance, are found on pp. 154, 386, 424, 430, 469, 473, 482, 530.

49. Atherton, "Memoranda as to George W. Atherton."

50. George W. Atherton to Herbert O. Myrick, March 5, 1887, Box 7, Folder B, Atherton Papers (MSG 6).

51. George W. Atherton to Charles Mills, October 23, 1903, Box 7, Folder A, Atherton Papers (MSG 6).

52. Henry A. Alvord to George W. Atherton, July 27, 1886, Box 7, Folder A, Atherton Papers (MSG 6).

53. House Committee on Agriculture, Report to accompany H.R. 2933, 49th Cong., 1st sess., H. Rept. 848.

54. Marcus, *Agricultural Science,* 199.

55. Charles K. Adams to George W. Atherton, March 25, 1886, Box 7, Folder A, Atherton Papers (MSG 6).

56. Henry A. Alvord to George W. Atherton, July 6, 1886, Box 7, Folder A, Atherton Papers (MSG 6).

57. *Congressional Record,* 49th Cong., 1st sess., 6650, 6677–6679.

58. George W. Atherton to Washington convention, Circular, December 1, 1886, Box 7, Folder A, Atherton Papers (MSG 6).

59. Marcus, *Agricultural Science,* 200.

60. Ibid., 201; True, *Agricultural Experimentation,* 127.

61. *Congressional Record,* Senate, 49th Cong., 2d sess., 721.

62. Ibid., 721–722. See also True, *Agricultural Experimentation,* 127; Marcus, *Agricultural Science,* 205.

63. *Congressional Record,* Senate, 49th Cong., 2d sess., 723–729; for Morrill's response, see p. 1042.

64. Ibid., 721.

65. Ibid., 1041. See also True, *Agricultural Experimentation,* 128–129; Marcus, *Agricultural Science,* 208.

66. *Congressional Record,* Senate, 49th Cong., 2d sess., 1043–1046.

67. Senate Committee on Agriculture, Report to accompany S. 372, 49th Cong., 2d sess., S. Rept. 3909. The report is one paragraph long, referring the reader to H. Rept. 848, which Atherton wrote to accompany the Hatch bill, H.R. 2933.

68. *Congressional Record,* House, 49th Cong., 2d sess., 2284.

69. Act of 1887 Establishing Agricultural Experiment Stations (Hatch Act), approved March 2, 1887 (24 Stat. 440), reprinted in Kerr, *The Legacy,* 208–211.

70. True, *Agricultural Experimentation,* 129.

71. George W. Atherton to Secretary of the Treasury, March 15, 1887, Box 5, Folder D, Atherton Papers (MSG 6).

72. Ibid.

73. See Marcus, *Agricultural Science,* 213.

74. Knoblauch et al., *State Agricultural Experiment Stations,* 63–64.

75. *Proceedings of the First Annual Convention of the Association of American Agricultural Colleges and Experiment Stations, Washington, D.C., October 18-20, 1887* (Washington, D.C.: Government Printing Office, 1941), 3. No original account of this convention was ever printed. The published proceedings, totaling four pages, were assembled mainly from manuscript notes supplied by the convention's secretary.

76. Marcus, *Agricultural Science,* 213.

77. *Association Proceedings 1889.*

78. Atherton, "Memoranda as to George W. Atherton."

79. Dupree, *Science and the Federal Government,* 170–172.

80. True, *Agricultural Experimentation,* 130–131.

81. Marcus, *Agricultural Science,* 217.

82. Ross, *Democracy's College,* 141–142.

83. Kerr, *The Legacy,* 25.

84. Burke, *American Collegiate Populations,* 220.

85. Rosenberg, *No Other Gods,* 158.

86. See *Association Proceedings 1890,* 4:15–18.

87. Atherton, "Memoranda as to George W. Atherton."

88. *Congressional Record,* Senate, 51st Cong., 1st sess., 6088.

Chapter 5. The Second Morrill Act

1. Marcus, *Agricultural Science,* 214–215.

2. Ibid., 214.

3. William H. Hatch to George W. Atherton, December 3, 1887, Box 7, Folder A, Atherton Papers (MSG 6).

4. *Association Proceedings 1889,* 24.

5. Ibid., 64.

6. W. O. Atwater, S. W. Johnson, and G. H. Cook, *Report of the Committee on Station Work,* Association of American Agricultural Colleges and Experiment Stations (Washington, D.C.: Government Printing Office, 1888), 32.

7. True, *Agricultural Experimentation,* 132, 176–177.

8. See Knoblauch et al., *State Agricultural Experiment Stations,* 71–72.

9. Atherton's address is in *Association Proceedings 1889,* 73–80.

10. Ibid., 48.

11. Ibid., 97.

12. Knoblauch et al., *State Agricultural Experiment Stations,* 67.

13. *Association Proceedings 1889,* 103–107.

14. *Association Proceedings 1902,* 52–53.

15. Henry P. Armsby to George W. Atherton, March 11, 1883, Box 5, Folder F, Atherton Papers (MSG 6).

16. George H. Cook to George W. Atherton, June 23, 1883, Box 5, Folder D, Atherton Papers (MSG 6).

17. Henry P. Armsby to George W. Atherton, March 4, 1887, Armsby ABVF, The Pennsylvania State University Archives.

18. Bezilla, *College of Agriculture at Penn State,* 48.

19. Ibid.

20. Henry P. Armsby to George W. Atherton, December 26, 1896, Board of Trustees Executive Committee file on Henry Armsby (1889–96); and Henry P. Armsby to the Pennsylvania State College Board of Trustees Executive Committee, July 3, 1897, Board of Trustees Executive Committee file on Henry P. Armsby (1896–97), The Pennsylvania State University Archives.

21. Circular, March 1884, Box 5, Folder B, Atherton Papers (MSG 6). The circular refers to a meeting held at the Department of Agriculture library on February 27, 1884, at which Atherton, Dabney, and Alvord offered their recommendations for founding the journal.

22. Quoted in *Cultivator and Country Gentleman,* March 10, 1887, p. 87.

23. James A. Beaver to Benjamin Harrison, February 21, 1889, Box 7, Folder A, Atherton Papers (MSG 6).

24. J. M. Rusk to George W. Atherton, March 17, 1890, Box 5, Folder F, Atherton Papers (MSG 6).

25. *Association Proceedings 1889,* 49.

26. Ibid., 50.

27. Ibid., 52–53.

28. Knoblauch et al., *State Agricultural Experiment Stations,* 72.

29. *Association Proceedings 1889,* 61.

30. Atherton's speech is in ibid., 66–76.

31. See ibid., 101–102, 113.

32. Ibid., 15.

33. Ibid., 86.

34. Ibid., 99, 94.

35. Ibid., 113.

36. See "A Bill," Box 7, Folder C, Atherton Papers (MSG 6). See above, Chapter 3, n. 62.

37. Ross, *Democracy's College,* 177.

38. Atherton, "Memoranda as to George W. Atherton" (see above Chapter 3, n. 29).

39. *Association Proceedings 1890,* 19–21.

40. *Congressional Record,* Senate, 51st Cong., 1st sess., 8836.

41. Justin S. Morrill to George W. Atherton, December 2, 1889, Box 7, Folder C, Atherton Papers (MSG 6).

42. Ross, *Democracy's College,* 176.

43. *Congressional Record,* Senate, 51st Cong., 1st sess., 771–772.

44. Ibid., 2435.

45. Henry E. Alvord to George W. Atherton, April 2, 1890, Box 7, Folder C, Atherton Papers (MSG 6). Also, Rutgers President Merrill Gates wrote to Atherton for advice on how to proceed. See Merrill Gates to George W. Atherton, March 27, 1890, Box 7, Folder C, Atherton Papers (MSG 6).

46. Henry F. Alvord to George W. Atherton, April 28, 1890, Box 7, Folder C, Atherton Papers (MSG 6).

47. Henry H. Goodell (April 28, 1890) and Merrill Gates (April 29, 1890) to George W. Atherton, Box 7, Folder C, Atherton Papers (MSG 6).

48. Letter from Alvord, Smart, Gates, Patterson, and Goodell on behalf of the Senate Committee on Education and Labor, April 26, 1890, reprinted in *Congressional Record,* Senate, 51st Cong., 1st sess., 6088.

49. *Congressional Record,* Senate, 51st Cong., 1st sess., 4003.

50. Ibid., 6337–6338.

51. Circular issued by the executive committee of the Association of American Agricultural Colleges and Experiment Stations, May 19, 1890, Box 7, Folder C, Atherton Papers (MSG 6).

52. Henry E. Alvord to George W. Atherton, May 16, 1890, Box 7, Folder C, Atherton Papers (MSG 6).

53. U.S. Senate, 51st Cong., 1st sess., Report to accompany S. 3714, S. Rept. No. 1028.

54. *Congressional Record,* Senate, 51st Cong., 1st sess., 6086–6087.

55. Ibid., 6333–6334.

56. Ibid., 6342.

57. Ibid., 6372.

58. Henry E. Alvord to George W. Atherton, July 2, 1890, Box 7, Folder C, Atherton Papers (MSG 6).

59. Henry E. Alvord to George W. Atherton, June 25, 1890, Box 7, Folder C, Atherton Papers (MSG 6).

60. Andrew D. White to George W. Atherton, June 30, 1890, Box 7, Folder C, Atherton Papers (MSG 6).

61. Andrew D. White to George W. Atherton, July 7, July 15, and July 29, 1890, Box 7, Folder C, Atherton Papers (MSG 6).

62. Henry E. Alvord to George W. Atherton, July 8 and July 26, 1890, Box 7, Folder C, Atherton Papers (MSG 6).

63. Circular by the executive committee of the Association of American Agricultural Colleges and Experiment Stations, August 6, 1890, Box 7, Folder D, Atherton Papers (MSG 6).

64. Alexis Cope to George W. Atherton, August 7, 1890, Box 7, Folder D, Atherton Papers (MSG 6).

65. Henry E. Alvord to George W. Atherton, August 12, 1890, Box 7, Folder D, Atherton Papers (MSG 6).

66. John Trimble to George W. Atherton, August 18, 1890, Box 7, Folder D, Atherton Papers (MSG 6).

67. *Congressional Record,* House, 51st Cong., 1st sess., 8834.

68. Ibid., 8839.

69. Alexis Cope to George W. Atherton, August 20, 1890, Box 7, Folder C, Atherton Papers (MSG 6).

70. George W. Atherton to the Association's executive committee, December 5, 1890, Box 5, Folder F. The missive asks for reimbursement of expenses for trips to Washington on behalf of the Association as follows: May 1–3, May 20–24, May 28–30, June 30–July 2, July 8–12, July 10–11, July 17–21, July 30–August 1, August 5–6, August 12–15, August 16–20,

plus a five-day trip in September to Richfield Springs, New York, where Atherton met with the secretary of the interior to ask his support in securing a quick release of the 1890 Morrill Act appropriations.

71. *Association Proceedings 1895,* 24.

72. Act of 1890 Providing for Further Endowment and Support of Colleges of Agriculture and Mechanic Arts (26 Stat. 417), in Kerr, *The Legacy,* 211–213.

73. Henry E. Alvord to George W. Atherton, September 8 and September 10, 1890, Box 7, Folder C, Atherton Papers (MSG 6).

74. See George W. Atherton to Henry E. Alvord, October 6, 1890, and Henry E. Alvord to George W. Atherton, October 4 and November 22, 1890, Box 7, Folder C, Atherton Papers (MSG 6).

75. "Brief of Points" prepared by George W. Atherton and Henry E. Alvord for George Chandler, assistant secretary of the interior, October 19, 1890, Box 7, Folder C, Atherton Papers (MSG 6).

76. Charles M. Gardner, *The Grange: Friend of the Farmer* (Washington, D.C.: National Grange Press, 1949), 128.

77. *Association Proceedings 1890,* 141–143.

78. "In the Senate of the U.S.: Letter from the secretary of the interior relative to action under the law to apply a portion of the proceeds of the public lands to the support of agricultural college," 52d Cong., 1st sess., Exec. Doc. No. 59, Box 7, Folder C, Atherton Papers (MSG 6).

79. Henry E. Alvord to George W. Atherton, January 4, 1891, Box 7, Folder D, Atherton Papers (MSG 6).

80. Ross, *Democracy's College,* 277.

81. *Report of the Pennsylvania State College for the Year 1890* (Harrisburg, Pa.: Edwin K. Meyers, 1891), 5, 6, 11.

82. Ibid., *1901,* 8; and Bezilla, *Penn State,* 36.

83. Bezilla, *Penn State,* 34–35.

84. Ross, *Democracy's College,* 180.

85. *Report of the Commissioner of Education for the Year 1889–1890* (Washington, D.C.: Government Printing Office, 1893), 2:1053–1055; *Report of the Commissioner of Education . . . 1894–1895* (Washington, D.C.: Government Printing Office, 1896), 2:1206–1209; *Report of the Commissioner of Education . . . 1899–1900* (Washington, D.C.: Government Printing Office, 1901), 2:2065.

86. Eddy, *Colleges for Our Land and Time,* 258, 103.

Chapter 6. The Association and the Emerging Federal Relationship

1. See Veysey, *Emergence of the American University,* 264.

2. Alfred C. True, *List of Publications of the Agricultural Experiment Stations (to June 30, 1906),* U.S. Department of Agriculture, Office of Experiment Stations, Bulletin No. 180 (Washington, D.C.: Government Printing Office, 1906), 5.

3. See Kerr, *The Legacy,* 43.

4. Alfred C. True, *Statistics of the Land-Grant Colleges and Agricultural Experiment Stations for the Year Ended June 30, 1901,* U.S. Department of Agriculture, Office of Experiment Stations, Bulletin No. 114 (Washington, D.C.: Government Printing Office, 1902), 8.

5. *Association Proceedings 1899,* 27–38.

6. *Association Proceedings 1892,* 72.

7. *Association Proceedings 1893,* 41–45.

8. See Knoblauch et al., *State Agricultural Experiment Stations,* 85.

9. See Kerr, *The Legacy,* 41.

10. See Gladys L. Baker, Wayne D. Rasmussen, Vivian Wiser, and Jane M. Porter, *Century of Service: The First 100 Years of the U.S. Department of Agriculture* (Washington, D.C.: Government Printing Office, 1963), 30.

11. Wilbur O. Atwater to George W. Atherton, February 9, 1891, Box 5, Folder G, Atherton Papers (MSG 6).

12. Edwin Willits to George W. Atherton, November 14, 1892, Box 5, Folder G, Atherton Papers (MSG 6).

13. Henry H. Goodell to George W. Atherton, December 30, 1892, and Henry E. Alvord to George W. Atherton, January 30, 1893, Box 5, Folder G, Atherton Papers (MSG 6).

14. Baker et al., *Century of Service,* 34.

15. See Henry H. Goodell to George W. Atherton, April 8, 1893, Box 5, Folder G; Henry E. Alvord to George W. Atherton, May 19, 1893, Box 5, Folder E; Henry E. Alvord to George W. Atherton, July 25, 1893, Box 5, Folder E, all in Atherton Papers (MSG 6).

16. Henry E. Alvord to George W. Atherton, January 12, 1894, Box 5, Folder H, Atherton Papers (MSG 6).

17. *Association Proceedings 1894,* 17.

18. Ibid., 47.

19. See Kerr, *The Legacy,* 42.

20. See *Association Proceedings 1893,* 31; Kerr, *The Legacy,* 42.

21. *Association Proceedings 1895,* 29–30.

22. Ibid., 59.

23. Circular from R. H. Jesse to Association presidents, October 26, 1896, Box 5, Folder H, Atherton Papers (MSG 6). Smart's note to Atherton was typed at the bottom of the circular.

24. Henry E. Alvord to George W. Atherton, June 15, 1897, Box 5, Folder H, Atherton Papers (MSG 6).

25. *Association Proceedings 1897,* 28–29.

26. Ibid., 22–25.

27. *Association Proceedings 1894,* 28.

28. *Association Proceedings 1896,* 45.

29. *Association Proceedings 1898,* 47–57.

30. Ibid., 46.

31. Wayne D. Rasmussen and Gladys L. Baker, *The Department of Agriculture* (New York: Praeger, 1972), 13–15.

32. *Association Proceedings 1896,* 44–45; ibid. *1897,* 41.

33. See Kerr, *The Legacy,* 43.

34. *Association Proceedings 1899,* 23–28.

35. *Association Proceedings 1900,* 44–50.

36. Ibid., 59.

37. Ibid., 76–84.

38. *Association Proceedings 1901,* 50, 28–33.

39. Henry C. White to George W. Atherton, October 22, 1903, Box 5, Folder O, Atherton Papers (MSG 6).

40. George W. Atherton to Henry C. White, October 26, 1903, Box 5, Folder O, Atherton Papers (MSG 6).

41. *Association Proceedings 1903,* 60, 193–194.

42. See True, *Agricultural Experimentation,* 165.

43. Kerr, *The Legacy,* 48–49.

44. *Association Proceedings 1902,* 55.

45. *Association Proceedings 1903,* 18.

46. *Association Proceedings 1906,* 37.

47. See Kerr, *The Legacy,* 50; Knoblauch et al., *State Agricultural Experiment Stations,* 98–99.

48. George W. Atherton to Henry C. Adams, February 15, 1904, Box 7, Folder F, Atherton Papers (MSG 6).

49. George W. Atherton to Henry H. Goodell, February 10, 1904, and February 18, 1904, Box 5, Folder H, Atherton Papers (MSG 6).

50. *Association Proceedings 1904,* 18.

51. True, *Agricultural Experimentation,* 187; *Association Proceedings 1905,* 15–16.

52. Knoblauch et al., *State Agricultural Experiment Stations,* 100–105.

53. James Wilson to Directors of Agricultural Experiment Stations, Circular, March 20, 1906, Box 7, Folder F, Atherton Papers (MSG 6).

54. True, *Agricultural Experimentation,* 171; Kerr, *The Legacy,* 52–53.

55. Rosenberg, *No Other Gods,* 176.

56. Kerr, *The Legacy,* 215–238.

57. See Michael Bezilla, *Engineering Education at Penn State* (University Park, Pa.: The Pennsylvania State University Press, 1981), 26, 41; Edwin E. Slosson, *The Great American Universities* (New York: Macmillan, 1910), 473, 209, 276.

58. True, *Statistics 1901,* 8.

59. Bezilla, *Engineering Education,* 37.

60. *Association Proceedings 1894,* 22.

61. *Association Proceedings 1895,* 18–19.

62. *Association Proceedings 1896,* 27–28.

63. *Association Proceedings 1898,* 33.

64. *Association Proceedings 1899,* 17.

65. Bezilla, *Engineering Education,* 64–65; Eddy, *Colleges for Our Land and Time,* 100, 128.

66. Quoted in Bezilla, *Engineering Education,* 23–24.

67. *Association Proceedings 1894,* 34.

68. *Association Proceedings 1896,* 19–20.

69. Ibid., 53–62.

70. *Association Proceedings 1897,* 29.

71. *Association Proceedings 1898,* 93.

72. *Association Proceedings 1900,* 33.

73. *Association Proceedings 1901,* 43.

74. *Association Proceedings 1903,* 39–41.

75. True, *Statistics 1901,* 8.

76. Geiger, *To Advance Knowledge,* 14–15.

77. *Association Proceedings 1897,* 48.

78. *Association Proceedings 1899,* 52.

79. See David Madsen, *The National University: Enduring Dream of the U.S.A.* (Detroit: Wayne State University Press, 1966).

80. John W. Hoyt to George W. Atherton, May 30, 1896, Box 6, Folder A, Atherton Papers (MSG 6).

81. *Association Proceedings 1898,* 63.

82. John W. Hoyt to George W. Atherton, April 27, 1899, Box 6, Folder A, Atherton Papers (MSG 6).

83. George W. Atherton to John W. Hoyt, November 18, 1901, Box 6, Folder A, Atherton Papers (MSG 6).

84. *Association Proceedings 1898,* 34.

85. Eddy, *Colleges for Our Land and Time,* 64–65.

86. *Association Proceedings 1896,* 33–41.

87. *Association Proceedings 1893,* 27.

88. Circular to Association members from Henry E. Alvord, March 24, 1894, Box 6, Folder F, Atherton Papers (MSG 6).

89. See *Association Proceedings 1894,* 16; ibid. *1895,* 6.

90. *Association Proceedings 1898,* 14, 64–68.

91. *Association Proceedings 1899,* 11–12.

92. Letter to land-grant college presidents from George W. Atherton, October 15, 1902, Box 5, Folder O, Atherton Papers (MSG 6).

93. *Association Proceedings 1903,* 54–55.

94. *Association Proceedings 1904,* 63, 98; ibid. *1905,* 17.

95. See True, *Statistics 1901,* 8; Bezilla, *Penn State,* 38.

96. See S. 3982 (April 7, 1900), 56th Cong., 1st sess., and the accompanying H. Rept. No. 1631, May 22, 1900, both in Box 7, Folder I, Atherton Papers (MSG 6). See also Atherton's printed draft of the bill, titled "A Bill" (undated). The Atherton draft was a bit less diffuse in appropriating the funds, but no less liberal. Atherton proposed to use it "only for instruction, research and experiment in mining and metallurgy and the branches of learning pertaining thereto, including English and other modern languages and the various branches of mathematical, physical, natural and economic science and the facilities for such instruction, research and experiment. . . . "

97. John Dalzell to George W. Atherton, November 24, 1900, Box 7, Folder I, Atherton Papers (MSG 6).

98. House Committee on Mines and Mining, *Hearings on the Proposition to Apply a Portion of the Proceeds of Sales of Public Lands to the Endowment of Schools or of Department of Mines and Mining, etc., in the Several States and Territories,* January 16, 1904, January 13, 1902, and February 4, 1902 (Washington, D.C.: Government Printing Office, 1904).

99. Alexander N. Winchell to George W. Atherton, July 28, 1903, and George W. Atherton to W. E. Stone, December 16, 1903, Box 5, Folder S, Atherton Papers (MSG 6).

100. *Association Proceedings 1904,* 16; ibid. *1905,* 18.

Chapter 7. The Atherton Legacy

1. Quoted in Parker, *Morrill,* 259.

2. *Association Proceedings 1899,* 36–37.

3. Earle D. Ross, "The 'Father' of the Land-Grant College," *Agricultural History* 12 (April 1938), 154.

4. Justin S. Morrill to George W. Atherton, April 27, 1883, Box 7, Folder C, Atherton Papers (MSG 6).

5. Justin S. Morrill to George W. Atherton, February 5, 1894, quoted in Parker, *Morrill,* 277.

6. *Association Proceedings 1900,* 67.

7. Atherton's eulogy, "The Legislative Career of Justin S. Morrill," is reproduced in ibid., 60–71.

8. Ross, "The 'Father' of the Land-Grant College," 164.

9. Atherton, "Relation of the General Government to Education," 66.

10. Eddy, *Colleges for Our Land and Time,* 267.

11. *Report of the Commissioner of Education 1889-1890,* 2:1053-1055; *Report of the Commissioner of Education 1899-1900,* 2:1874-1875, 2058-2065.

12. *Association Proceedings 1906:* White's words, 20; Armsby's words, 31-35; Patterson's words, 35-36.

13. Atherton, "Memoranda as to George W. Atherton" (see above, Chapter 3, n. 29).

14. Stebbins, *Goodell,* 108; *Association Proceedings 1896,* 12.

15. George H. Callcott, *A History of the University of Maryland* (Baltimore: Maryland Historical Society, 1966), 190-192, 238.

16. Stebbins, *Goodell,* 110-133; Cary, *University of Massachusetts,* 84.

17. Eddy, *Colleges for Our Land and Time,* 111; Hawkins, "Problems in Categorization," 5:44.

18. Edmond, *Magnificent Charter,* 23.

19. Hawkins, "Problems in Categorization," 5:45-46.

20. E. A. Bryant to George W. Atherton, July 3, 1901, Box 5, Folder S, Atherton Papers (MSG 6).

21. *Association Proceedings 1901,* 40-41.

22. House Committee on Mines and Mining, *Hearings,* 45, 25.

23. H. C. White to George W. Atherton, January 28, 1903, Box 7, Folder J, Atherton Papers (MSG 6).

24. See Rossiter, "Organization of the Agricultural Sciences," 213; Dupree, *Science in the Federal Government,* 182.

25. Burke, *American Collegiate Populations,* 212-262.

26. True, *Statistics 1900,* 8.

27. *Report of Commissioner of Education, 1889-1890,* 2:1053-1055; *Report of Commissioner of Education 1899-1900,* 2:1874-1875, 2058-2065.

28. Burke, *American Collegiate Populations,* 262.

29. *Association Proceedings 1889,* 76.

30. Carnegie Council on Policy Studies in Higher Education, *A Classification of Institutions of Higher Education,* rev. ed. (Berkeley, Calif.: Carnegie Council, 1976).

31. *Science Resources Studies Highlights,* April 29, 1988, NSF 88-314 (Washington, D.C.: National Science Foundation, 1988), 5.

Bibliography

Addresses and Journal of Proceedings of the National Education Association, Session of the Year 1873, at Elmira, New York. Peoria, Ill.: Nason, 1873.

Addresses and Journal of Proceedings of the National Educational Association, Session of the Year 1874, at Detroit, Michigan. Worcester, Mass.: Charles Hamilton, 1874.

Altbach, Philip G., and Berdahl, Robert O. (eds.). *Higher Education in American Society.* Buffalo, N.Y.: Prometheus Books, 1981.

Anderson, G. Lester (ed.). *Land-Grant Universities and Their Continuing Challenge.* East Lansing: Michigan State University Press, 1966.

Andrist, Ralph K. (ed.). *The American Heritage History of the Confident Years, 1865–1916.* New York: American Heritage/Bonanza Books, 1987.

Armsby, Henry Prentiss. *Memorial to President George W. Atherton.* Washington, D.C.: Government Printing Office, 1907.

Atherton, George W. *The Legislative Career of Justin S. Morrill: An Address Delivered at New Haven, Connecticut, November 14, 1900.* Harrisburg, Pa.: J. Horace McFarland, 1900.

———. Papers (MSG 6). University Archives/Penn State Room, The Pennsylvania State University, University Park, Pennsylvania.

———. "The Relation of the General Government to Education." In *Addresses* and Journals of Proceedings of the National Education Association, Session of the Year 1873, at Elmira, New York. Peoria, Ill.: Nason, 1873.

Bailey, Joseph C. *Seaman A. Knapp: Schoolmaster of American Agriculture.* New York: Columbia University Press, 1945.

Baker, Gladys L.; Rasmussen, Wayne D.; Wiser, Vivian; and Porter, Jane M. *Century of Service: The First 100 Years of the United States Department of Agriculture.* U.S. Department of Agriculture. Washington, D.C.: Government Printing Office, 1963.

Bezilla, Michael. *The College of Agriculture at Penn State: A Tradition of Excellence.* University Park, Pa.: The Pennsylvania State University Press, 1987.

——. *Engineering Education at Penn State: A Century in the Land-Grant Tradition.* University Park, Pa.: The Pennsylvania State University Press, 1981.

——. *Penn State: An Illustrated History.* University Park, Pa.: The Pennsylvania State University Press, 1985.

Bogue, Allan G., and Taylor, Robert. *The University of Wisconsin: One Hundred and Twenty-Five Years.* Madison: University of Wisconsin Press, 1975.

Brubacher, John S., and Rudy, Willis. *Higher Education in Transition: An American History, 1636–1956.* New York: Harper, 1958.

Burke, Colin B. *American Collegiate Populations: A Test of the Traditional View.* New York: New York University Press, 1982.

Burtt, E. A. *The Metaphysical Foundations of Modern Science.* Garden City, N.Y.: Doubleday, 1954.

Callcott, George H. *History of the University of Maryland.* Baltimore: Maryland Historical Society, 1966.

Carnegie Council on Policy Studies in Higher Education: *A Classification of Institutions of Higher Education.* Revised edition. Berkeley, Calif.: Carnegie Council, 1976.

Cary, Harold W. *The University of Massachusetts: A History of One Hundred Years.* Amherst: University of Massachusetts Press, 1962.

Conover, Milton. *The Office of Experiment Stations: Its History, Activities, and Organization.* Baltimore: Johns Hopkins University Press, 1924.

Contemporary American Biography. New York: Atlantic Publishing and Engraving Co., 1895.

Cremin, Lawrence A. *American Education: The National Experience, 1783–1876.* New York: Harper and Row, 1980.

Curti, Merle, and Carstensen, Vernon. "The University of Wisconsin: To 1925." In *The University of Wisconsin: One Hundred and Twenty-Five Years,* edited by Allan G. Bogue and Robert Taylor. Madison: University of Wisconsin Press, 1975.

Demarest, William H. S. *A History of Rutgers College, 1766–1924.* New Brunswick, N.J.: Rutgers College Press, 1924.

Development of the Land-Grant Colleges and Universities and Their Influence on the Economic and Social Life of the People. Addresses given at a series of ten seminars sponsored by the College of Agriculture, Forestry, and Home Economics of West Virginia University during the year 1962. Morgantown: West Virginia University Bulletin, 1983.

Dictionary of American Biography. 22 vols. New York: Charles Scribner's Sons, 1928.

Dunaway, Wayland F. *History of the Pennsylvania State College.* Lancaster, Pa.: Lancaster Press, 1946.

Dupre, J. Stefan, and Lakoff, Sanford A. *Science and the Nation: Policy and Politics.* Englewood Cliffs, N.J.: Prentice-Hall, 1962.

Dupree, A. Hunter. *Science in the Federal Government: A History of Policies and Activities to 1940.* Cambridge: Harvard University Press, 1957.

Duryea, E. D. "The University and the State: A Historical Overview." In *Higher Education in American Society,* edited by Philip G. Altbach and Robert O. Berdahl. Buffalo, N.Y.: Prometheus Books, 1981.

Dyer, Thomas G. *The University of Georgia: A Bicentennial History, 1785–1985.* Athens: University of Georgia Press, 1985.

Eddy, Edward D., Jr. *Colleges for Our Land and Time: The Land-Grant Idea in American Education.* New York: Harper, 1957.

———. "The First Hundred Years, in Retrospect and Prospect." In *Development of the Land-Grant Colleges and Universities and Their Influence on the Economic and Social Life of the People.* Addresses given at a series of ten seminars sponsored by the College of Agriculture, Forestry, and Home Economics of West Virginia University during the year 1962. Morgantown: West Virginia University, 1983.

Edmond, J. B. *The Magnificent Charter: The Origin and Role of the Morrill Land-Grant Colleges and Universities.* Hicksville, N.Y.: Exposition Press, 1978.

Flexner, Abraham. *Daniel Coit Gilman: Creator of the American Type of University.* New York: Harcourt, Brace, 1946.

Franklin, Fabian. *The Life of Daniel Coit Gilman.* New York: Dodd, Mead, 1910.

Gardner, Charles M. *The Grange: Friend of the Farmer.* Washington, D.C.: National Grange Press, 1949.

Geiger, Roger L. *To Advance Knowledge: The Growth of American Research Universities, 1900–1940.* New York: Oxford University Press, 1986.

Gill, Benjamin. "Moulded by an Idea: A Brief Memorial of President George W. Atherton." *Sermons and Addresses of Benjamin Gill,* 179–185. State College, Pa., 1913.

Gilman, Daniel Coit. *The Launching of a University.* New York: Dodd, Mead, 1906.

———. "Our National Schools of Science." *North American Review,* vol. 105, no. 217 (1867), 495–520.

———. "Report on the National Schools of Science." In *Report of the Secretary of the Interior,* vol. 2, pp. 427–441. Washington, D.C.: Government Printing Office, 1871.

———. *University Problems in the United States.* New York: The Century Company, 1898.

Goetzmann, William H. "Those Electrifying 1880s." *National Geographic,* January 1988, pp. 8–37.

Guralnik, Stanley M. *Science and the Antebellum College.* Philadelphia: American Philosophical Society, 1975.

Hawkins, Hugh. "Problems in Categorization and Generalization in the History of American Higher Education: An Approach Through the Institutional Associations." In *History of Higher Education Annual,* vol. 5. (Buffalo: SUNY/Buffalo, 1985).

Hoar, George F. *Autobiography of Seventy Years.* New York: Charles Scribner's Sons, 1903.

Hofstadter, Richard M. *Academic Freedom in the Age of the College.* New York: Columbia University Press, 1961.

Hofstadter, Richard M., and Smith, Wilson (eds.). *American Higher Education: A Documentary History.* 2 vols. Chicago: University of Chicago Press, 1961.

Isaacson, Walter. "History Without Letters." *Time.* August 31, 1987, pp. 65–66.

Kelly, Robert Lincoln. *The American Colleges and the Social Order.* New York: Macmillan, 1940. (Published in conjunction with the Association of American Colleges.)

Kerr, Clark. *The Uses of the University. 3rd edition.* Cambridge: Harvard University Press, 1982.

Kerr, Norwood Allen. *The Legacy: A Centennial History of the State Agricultural Experiment Stations, 1887–1987.* Columbia: Missouri Agricultural Experiment Station, University of Missouri at Columbia, 1987.

Kimball, Bruce A. "Writing the History of Universities: A New Approach." *Minerva* 24 (Summer–Autumn 1986).

Knoblauch, H. C.; Law, E. M.; and Meyer, W. P. *State Agricultural Experiment Stations: A History of Research Policy and Procedure.* U.S. Department of Agriculture, Misc. Pub. No. 904. Washington, D.C.: Government Printing Office, 1962.

Madsen, David. *The National University: Enduring Dream of the U.S.A.* Detroit: Wayne State University Press, 1966.

Marcus, Alan I. *Agricultural Science and the Quest for Legitimacy: Farmers, Agricultural Colleges, and Experiment Stations, 1870–1890.* Ames: Iowa State University Press, 1985.

Metzgar, Walter P. *Academic Freedom in the Age of the University.* New York: Columbia University Press, 1885.

Moos, Malcolm. *The Post Land-Grant University: The University of Maryland Report.* Adelphi: University of Maryland, 1981.

Murphy, Charlotte C. "Back to the Future: A Commitment Congress Made in 1887 Still Supports Long-Term Research." *Penn State Agriculture,* Spring 1987, pp. 3–7.

National Cyclopaedia of American Biography. 20 vols. New York: James T. White, 1929.

Nevins, Allan. *The State Universities and Democracy.* Urbana: University of Illinois Press, 1962.

Oleson, Alexandra. "Introduction: To Build a New Intellectual Order." In *The Pursuit of Knowledge in the Early American Republic,* edited by Alexandra Oleson and Sanborn C. Brown. Baltimore: Johns Hopkins University Press, 1976.

Oleson, Alexandra, and Brown, Sanborn C. *The Pursuit of Knowledge in the Early American Republic: American Scientific and Learned Societies from Colonial Times to the Civil War.* Baltimore: Johns Hopkins University Press, 1976.

Oleson, Alexandra, and Voss, John (eds.). *The Organization of Knowledge in Modern America, 1860–1920.* Baltimore: Johns Hopkins University Press, 1979.

Palmer, R. R., and Colton, Joel. *A History of the Modern World.* New York: Alfred A. Knopf, 1964.

Parker, William B. *The Life and Public Services of Justin Smith Morrill.* Boston: Houghton Mifflin, 1924.

Pennsylvania State College, Annual Report for 1896. Harrisburg, Pa.: Clarence M. Busch, 1897.

Pollard, James E. *History of the Ohio State University: The Story of Its First Seventy-Five Years, 1873–1948.* Columbus: Ohio State University Press, 1952.

Pollitt, Mabel Hardy. *A Biography of James Kennedy Patterson, President of the University of Kentucky from 1869 to 1910.* Louisville, Ky.: Westerfield-Bonte Co., 1925.

Potts, David B. "Curriculum and Enrollments: Some Thoughts on Assessing the Popularity of Antebellum Colleges." *History of Higher Education Annual* 1, no. 1 (1981), 88–109.

Proceedings of a Convention of Delegates from Agricultural Stations and Experiment Stations Held at the Department of Agriculture, July 8 and 9, 1885 (Preliminary Convention). U.S. Department of Agriculture, Special Report No. 9. Washington, D.C.: Government Printing Office, 1885.

Proceedings of the First Annual Convention of the Association of American Agricultural Colleges and Experiment Stations, Washington, D.C., October 18–20, 1887. (A prefacing note reads: "No account of this convention was ever printed. The following has been prepared mainly from manuscript notes supplied by Director C. E. Thorne, of Ohio, who was secretary for the convention.") This reconstruction was published by the executive committee of the Association of Land-Grant Colleges and Universities in 1941.

Proceedings of the Second Annual Convention of the Association of American Agricultural Colleges and Experiment Stations, held at Knoxville, Tennessee, January 1–3, 1889. U.S. Department of Agriculture, Office of Experiment Stations, Misc. Bulletin No. 1. Washington, D.C.: Government Printing Office, 1889.

Proceedings of the Third Annual Convention of the Association of American Agricultural Colleges and Experiment Stations, held at Washington, D.C., November 12–15, 1889. U.S. Department of Agriculture, Office of Experiment Stations, Misc. Bulletin No. 2. Washington, D.C.: Government Printing Office, 1890.

Proceedings of the Fourth Annual Convention of the Association of American Agricultural Colleges and Experiment Stations, held at Champaign, Illinois, November 11–13, 1890. U.S. Department of Agriculture, Office of Experiment Stations, Misc. Bulletin No. 3. Washington, D.C.: Government Printing Office, 1891.

(Note: With the exception of the reconstructed proceedings of the first annual convention (1887 founding convention), the foregoing Association convention proceedings are bound together as *AAACES Proceedings.* The following proceedings are bound in various volumes of "bulletins" published by the U.S. Department of Agriculture Office of Experiment Stations. Because the citations are uniform, with the exception of date, place, and bulletin number, the following format has been adopted for expediency: *Proceedings of the [successive] Annual Convention of the Association of American Agricultural Colleges and Experiment Stations, held at [variable place], [variable date].* U.S. Department of Agriculture, Office of Experiment Stations, [variable bulletin numbers]. Washington, D.C.: Government Printing Office, [variable date of publication].)

Fifth Annual Convention, held at Washington, D.C., August 12–18, 1891. Experiment Station Bulletin No. 7, 1892.

Sixth Annual Convention, held at New Orleans, Louisiana, November 15–19, 1892. Experiment Station Bulletin No. 16, 1893.

Seventh Annual Convention, held at Chicago, Illinois, October 17–19, 1893.
Experiment Station Bulletin No. 20, 1894.

Eighth Annual Convention, held at Washington, D.C., November 13–15, 1894.
Experiment Station Bulletin No. 24, 1895.

Ninth Annual Convention, held at Denver, Colorado, July 16–18, 1895. Experiment Station Bulletin No. 30, 1896.

Tenth Annual Convention, held at Washington, D.C., November 10–12, 1896.
Experiment Station Bulletin No. 41, 1897.

Eleventh Annual Convention, held at Minneapolis, Minnesota, July 13–15, 1897.
Experiment Station Bulletin No. 49, 1898.

Twelfth Annual Convention, held at Washington, D.C., November 15–17, 1898.
Experiment Station Bulletin No. 65, 1899.

Thirteenth Annual Convention, held at San Francisco, California, July 5–7, 1899.
Experiment Station Bulletin No. 76, 1900.

Fourteenth Annual Convention, held at Middletown and New Haven, Connecticut, November 13–15, 1900. Experiment Station Bulletin No. 93, 1901.

Fifteenth Annual Convention, held at Washington, D.C., November 12–14, 1901.
Experiment Station Bulletin No. 115, 1902.

Sixteenth Annual Convention, held at Atlanta, Georgia, October 7–9, 1902.
Experiment Station Bulletin No. 123, 1903.

Seventeenth Annual Convention, held at Washington, D.C., November 17–19, 1903. Experiment Station Bulletin No. 142, 1904.

Eighteenth Annual Convention, held at Des Moines, Iowa, November 1–3, 1904.
Experiment Station Bulletin No. 153, 1905.

Nineteenth Annual Convention, held at Washington, D.C., November 14–16, 1905. Experiment Station Bulletin No. 164, 1906.

Twentieth Annual Convention, held at Baton Rouge, Louisiana, November 14–16, 1906. Experiment Station Bulletin No. 184, 1907.

Rainsford, George N. *Congress and Higher Education in the Nineteenth Century.*
Knoxville: University of Tennessee Press, 1972.

Rasmussen, Wayne D., and Baker, Gladys L. *The Department of Agriculture.*
New York: Praeger, 1972.

Reisner, Edward H. *Nationalism and Education Since 1789: A Social and Political History of Modern Education.* New York: Macmillan, 1922.

Report of the Commissioner of Education for the Year 1872. Washington, D.C.:
Government Printing Office, 1873.

Report of the Commissioner of Education for the Year 1880. Washington, D.C.:
Government Printing Office, 1882.

Report of the Commissioner of Education for the Year 1889–90. Vols. 1 and 2.
Washington, D.C.: Government Printing Office, 1893.

Report of the Commissioner of Education for the Year 1894–95. Vols. 1 and 2.
Washington, D.C.: Government Printing Office, 1896.

Report of the Commissioner of Education for the Year 1899–1900. Vols. 1 and 2.
Washington, D.C.: Government Printing Office, 1901.

Robinson, W. L. *The Grange, 1867–1967: First Century of Service and Evolution.*
Washington, D.C.: National Grange Press, 1966.

Rosenberg, Charles E. *No Other Gods: On Science and American Social Thought.*
Baltimore: Johns Hopkins University Press, 1961.

Ross, Earle D. "Contributions of Land-Grant Education to History and the Social Sciences." *Agricultural History* 34, no. 2 (April 1960), 51–61.

——. *Democracy's College: The Land-Grant Movement in the Formative Stage.* Ames: Iowa State College Press, 1942.

——. "The 'Father' of the Land-Grant College." *Agricultural History* 12, no. 2 (April 1938), 151–186.

——. "The Great Triumvirate of Land-Grant Educators." *Journal of Higher Education* 32, no. 9 (December 1961), 480–488.

——. *The Land-Grant Idea at Iowa State College: A Centennial Trial Balance, 1858–1958.* Ames: Iowa State College Press, 1958.

——. "On Writing the History of the Land-Grant Colleges and Universities." *Journal of Higher Education* 24, no. 8 (November 1953), 411–414, 451–452.

Rossiter, Margaret A. "The Organization of Agricultural Improvement in the United States, 1785–1865." In *The Pursuit of Knowledge in the Early American Republic,* edited by Alexandra Oleson and Sanborn C. Brown. Baltimore: Johns Hopkins University Press, 1976.

——. "The Organization of the Agricultural Sciences." In *The Organization of Knowledge in Modern America, 1860–1920,* edited by Alexandra Oleson and John Voss. Baltimore: Johns Hopkins University Press, 1979.

Rudolph, Frederick. *The American College and University: A History.* New York: Knopf, 1962.

Runkle, Erwin W. "President Atherton and Pennsylvania State College." *Pennsylvania School Journal* 56, no. 7 (January 1908), 296–298.

Science Resources Studies Highlights. April 29, 1988, NSF 88-314. Washington, D.C.: National Science Foundation, 1988.

Sidar, Jean Wilson. *George Hammell Cook: A Life in Agriculture and Geology.* New Brunswick, N.J.: Rutgers University Press, 1976

Slosson, Edwin E. *The Great American Universities.* New York: Macmillan, 1910.

Solberg, Winton U. *The University of Illinois, 1867–1894: An Intellectual and Cultural History.* Urbana: University of Illinois Press, 1968.

Songe, Alice H. *The Land-Grant Idea in American Higher Education: A Guide to Information Sources.* New York: K. G. Saur, 1980.

Stebbins, Calvin. *Henry Hill Goodell.* Cambridge, Mass.: Riverside Press, 1911.

True, Alfred C. *A History of Agricultural Education in the United States, 1785–1925.* U.S. Department of Agriculture, Misc. Pub. No. 36. Washington, D.C.: Government Printing Office, 1929.

——. *A History of Agricultural Experimentation and Research in the United States, 1607–1925.* U.S. Department of Agriculture, Misc. Pub. No. 251. Washington, D.C.: Government Printing Office, 1937.

——. *A History of Agricultural Extension Work in the United States, 1787–1923.* U.S. Department of Agriculture, Misc. Pub. No. 15. Washington, D.C.: Government Printing Office, 1928.

——. *List of Publications of the Agricultural Experiment Stations (to June 30, 1906).* U.S. Department of Agriculture, Office of Experiment Stations, Bulletin No. 180. Washington, D.C.: Government Printing Office, 1906.

——. *Statistics of the Land-Grant Colleges and Agricultural Experiment Stations for the Year Ended June 30, 1901.* U.S. Department of Agriculture, Office of Experiment Stations, Bulletin No. 114. Washington, D.C.: Government Printing Office, 1902.

True, Alfred C. *Statistics of the Land-Grant Colleges and Agricultural Experiment Stations of the United States, 1900.* U.S. Department of Agriculture, Office of Experiment Stations, Bulletin No. 97. Washington, D.C.: Government Printing Office, 1901.

U.S. Congress. House. "Agricultural Colleges." In *Report of the House Committee on Education and Labor.* 43d Congress, 2d sess. H. Rept. 57.

——. *Hearings Before the Committee on Mines and Mining, on Proposition to Apply a Portion of the Proceeds of Sales of Public Lands to the Endowment of Schools or of Department of Mines and Mining, etc., in the Several States and Territories.* 57th Cong., 1st sess. (Washington, D.C.: Government Printing Office, 1904).

——. *Report of the House Committee on Agriculture to Accompany H.R. 7498.* 48th Cong., 1st sess. H. Rept. 2034.

——. *Report of the House Committee on Agriculture to Accompany H.R. 2933.* 49th Cong., 1st sess. H. Rept. 848.

U.S. Congress. Senate. *Hearing Before the Committee on Naval Affairs, December 10, 1890, in relation to the Bill (S. 2779) to Regulate the Number of Officers in the Engineer Corps of the Navy.* 51st Cong., 2d sess.

Veysey, Laurence R. *The Emergence of the American University.* Chicago: University of Chicago Press, 1965.

La Vie, Class of 1908 (Yearbook produced by Penn State undergraduates). Volume 19, pp. 12–18. State College, Pa., 1907. (Contains numerous quotations about George W. Atherton.)

White, Andrew D. *Autobiography.* Vol. 1. N.p.: The Century Company, n.d.

Works, George A., and Morgan, Barton. *The Land-Grant Colleges.* Prepared for the Advisory Committee on Education. Washington, D.C.: Government Printing Office, 1939.

Index